D1462125

This history is the story of two men, and of the stories they and others told in order that it might be known who they were. It is a history of identity, 'the self' and social identity, and also the realm of 'the social' itself in which identity is located. It explores critically the nature of class identity by looking at the formation and influence of two men who might be taken as representative of what 'working class' and 'middle class' meant in England in the nineteenth century. Class is seen to have been less significant than the various shapes of demos, and the two studies of individuals are complemented by a further study on narrative in pointing to the great importance of the collective subjects upon which democracy rested.

The book indicates the way forward to a new history of democracy as an imagined entity. It represents a deepening of Patrick Joyce's engagement with 'post-modernist' theory, seeking the relevance of this theory for the writing of history, and in the process offering a critique of the conservatism of much academic history, particularly in Britain.

Democratic subjects

Democratic subjects

The self and the social in nineteenth-century England

Patrick Joyce

University of Manchester

CAMBRIDGE
UNIVERSITY PRESS

Published by the Press Syndicate of the University of Cambridge
The Pitt Building, Trumpington Street, Cambridge CB2 1RP
40 West 20th Street, New York, NY 10011–4211, USA
10 Stamford Road, Oakleigh, Melbourne 3166, Australia

First published 1994

A catalogue record for this book is available from the British Library

Library of Congress cataloguing in publication data

Joyce, Patrick.
Democratic subjects: studies in the history of the self and the social in nineteenth-century England / Patrick Joyce.
    p. cm.
ISBN 0 521 44334 2
1. England – Social life and customs – 19th century. 2. Social classes – England – History – 19th century. 3. Democracy – England – History – 19th century. 4. Poets, English – 19th century – Biography. 5. Statesmen – Great Britain – Biography. 6. National characteristics, English. 7. Waugh, Edwin, 1817–1890. 8. Bright, John, 1811–1889. 9. Identity (Psychology) 10. Narration (Rhetoric) 11. Self. I. Title.
DA533.J68   1994
942.081 – dc20   93–37741
CIP

ISBN 0 521 443342 hardback
ISBN 0 521 448026 paperback

Transferred to digital printing 2004

CE

For Roisin and Sean, their own book, and for their uncle, who loved them, Frank Malone, 1953–1993

Contents

x   Contents

Plates

Acknowledgements

I am grateful to the following, who commented on parts of this book: Simon Gunn, Raphael Samuel, Carolyn Steedman, James Vernon, and David Vincent. Papers drawn from the book were presented in Britain, Australia, and the USA, and I should like to thank the participants and organisers of these seminars. I owe much to conversation with Antony Easthope, Rudra Mukherjee and Raphael Samuel, and the participants in the Historiography Study Group meeting in London. James Vernon and I travelled the same road during the period of this book's writing, and the debt I owe him is very considerable. I should also like to thank the following for differing kinds of help along the way: Joan W. Scott, Alf Lüdtke, Michael Mann, Jim Epstein, Peter Bailey, Tom Laqueur, Ross McKibbin, Peter Clarke, and my colleagues at Manchester University, John Breuilly, Iori Prothero, and Steve Rigby. As ever, my greatest debt of all has been to my wife Rosaleen, and to my children, Roisin and Sean. Margaret Riley of Broadbottom helped me produce the typescript with her usual unerring eye. I acknowledge permission to consult and use the Bright family papers given by C. and J. Clark of Street, Somerset. Some of the research for this book was made possible by funding from the Leverhulme Trust, the British Academy, and the Nuffield Foundation (the latter in the form of a Social Science Research Fellowship). Time for its writing was provided by study leave given by Manchester University. The photograph of Edwin Waugh was supplied by the John Rylands Library, University of Manchester, and those of the Waugh diary and the *Clock Almanack* by Manchester Central Reference Library. The Bright photograph is from the Radio Times Hulton Picture Library.

Introduction

This history is the story of two men, and of the stories they and others told in order that it might be known who they were. It is a history of identity, about 'the self' and about 'the social', the latter in the sense of collective identities, and the contexts in which these were set. The quotation marks signal that these terms have significance in so far as their meanings are made by us, and not found by us in a world beyond this assignation of meaning. In thinking about identities in the past, whether of the 'self' or of the collective, class has, until recently, occupied a very considerable role among social historians, especially those of the nineteenth century. The sorrows of Edwin Waugh, and the measured certainties of John Bright, serve to question this dominance, as do the democratic romances that gave shape to the social and political imagination of millions of their contemporaries. Other forms of the self and of collective identity emerge, long obscured by the concentration on class. And class itself, like any other collective 'social' subject, is seen to be an imagined form, not something given in a 'real' world beyond this form.

All three accounts involve looking at subjectivities, at the subject as a self and as an imagined collectivity. The two are seen to be inextricably connected. The 'social' or collective selves, that arguably had more significance than class at the time, were represented by terms like 'the people', 'humanity', 'mankind', 'the Million', and so on, selves that went to make up the sense of what it meant to live in a democratic polity, but also in a society and a culture that were also felt to be 'democratic' (or felt *not* to be democratic). The pun in my title points therefore to these linked subjectivities, to a subject as a person and as a subject of democracy.

The social subjects I describe, and the narratives that gave them meaning, are seen to be the means by which contemporaries named, and hence lived, the 'social relations' of their day. The inclusions and exclusions these subjects and narratives enforced are understood to have often been more important than class, though in their turn these distinctions were classifications of another kind. Many of them have been hidden from view because they have been naturalised, or reified, taken in a

1

'common-sense' way to exist beyond our naming of them: 'man' and 'woman' are good examples, as well as 'humanity' and the others. The aim of this book is to subvert perhaps the central distinction which enacts this naturalisation of the social and its categories, that between representation and the real. The studies have been chosen with this end in view, that of Edwin Waugh concerning the 'reality' of poverty, that of John Bright concerning the processes by which personal and public selves were made, and that of narrative as a means of analysis that can itself be said to blur the distinction between representation and the real.

The three studies, while linked by these concerns, are comprehensible in themselves, and designed to be so. They are 'studies', in deed as well as name, sustained and close observations of particular subjects which each has its own distinctiveness, meriting thereby a response on something like its own terms. The studies can be approached singly, but are best read in succession, as one builds on the other in order to achieve its full effect. Whichever way they are read, my aim is to make them accessible to readers not necessarily versed in the questions raised in this introduction. None the less, these questions comprise a context in which the book as a whole can usefully be situated.

The subject of class has become a matter for disputation among historians. The opening statement of the position taken here may itself seem disputatious to some of these. I had originally called this book *The Fall of Class*, hardly a neutral title. There is a powerful sense in which class may be said to have 'fallen'. Instead of being a master category of historical explanation, it has become one term among many, sharing a rough equality with these others (which is what I meant by the 'fall' of class). The reasons for this are not hard to find. In Britain, economic decline and restructuring have led to the disintegration of the old manual sector of employment, and of what was, mistakenly, seen to be a 'traditional' working class.[1] The rise of the right from the 1970s, and the decline of the left, together with that of the trade unions, pointed in a similar direction to that of economic change, towards a loosening of the hold class and work-based categories had, not only on the academic mind, but also on a wider public. Changes going on in Britain were mirrored elsewhere, but the greatest change of all was the disintegration of world communism, and with it the retreat of intellectual Marxism.

Feminism represented another current of change, one also combining social and intellectual elements: it presented a new object of analysis,

---

[1] On another level, a new gradualist reading of the 'Industrial Revolution' in Britain has removed a good deal of the ground from under the feet of the class idea. For an account see Patrick Joyce, 'Work', in F. M. L. Thompson (ed.), *The Cambridge Social History of Britain 1750–1950*, (Cambridge 1990), 3 vols., II.

gender, and problematised our understanding of identity itself. Allied to feminism, though of enormous significance in itself, post-structuralist thought led in a similar direction: an understanding of identity as radically de-centred and unstable could hardly be without consequences for the concept of class. The term 'post-structuralism' does not do justice to the range of what has been a fundamental rethinking of Western traditions: the term 'post-modernism' has often, and somewhat confusingly, been used to describe this range. Behind this rethinking, and behind all the other transformations so far described, may be said to emerge a new condition of society itself, the condition of post-modernity. Partly in the form of the so-called 'new cultural history' these currents have coalesced for historians in what has come to be known as the 'linguistic turn'. It is within this 'turn' that I would situate my own work.

Whether class has fallen quite so far as some think is another matter: the hold of older categories is still strong in labour and social history, both in Britain and the US, for liberal as well as for left historians. Among the former, if the accent on conflict is not so marked, then whole histories are narrativised around the collective subjects of classes: classes become the actors around which explanations of social change take place, and whole swathes of human behaviour are cast in the roles of these actors (such as 'working-class culture', or the 'pastimes of the working class').[2] This applies even when these same historians imagine they are not writing under the sign of class. In its historical origins, as will be evident in these studies, class was as much a product of the liberal, as of the Marxist, mind. One manifestation of the latter, in the form of the influence of E. P. Thompson, is still immense (and beyond historians too, a recent sociology textbook on 'current debates' on class seeing fit to cite Thompson as the only historical work worthy of note).[3] So, there are still arguments to be had, though as will become apparent class is more the occasion than the cause of such arguments.

By way of providing, first of all, a theoretical and historiographical context for the three studies that follow, and then a historical context, I will identify the position from which this book is written by means of a couple of quotations, the first from E. P. Thompson. Thompson's famous words from the opening of *The Making of the English Working Class* go as follows,

And class happens when some men, as a result of common experiences (inherited or shared), feel and articulate the identity of their interests as between themselves, and as against other men whose interests are different from (and usually opposed

---

[2] For a typical example, see F. M. L. Thompson, *The Rise of Respectable Society: A Social History of Victorian Britain, 1830–1900* (1988).

[3] Rosemary Crompton, *Class and Stratification: An Introduction to Current Debates* (Cambridge 1993).

to) theirs. The class experience is largely determined by the productive relations into which men are born – or enter voluntarily. Class consciousness is the way in which these experiences are handled in cultural terms: embodied in traditions, value systems, ideas and institutional forms. If the experience appears as determined, class consciousness does not.[4]

The familiar formula is apparent, one that has charmed a generation. Productive relations, themselves beyond discourse, are primary, despite the qualification. These then give rise to an 'experience' which itself seemingly floats free of 'culture'. 'Experience' is then acted upon by values, traditions, and so on. Despite the emphasis on culture it quite clearly comes at the end of things, not the beginning. What vast assumptions are made about people and knowledge in this contraption of causes and stages! Once this machine is set in motion it turns out a 'class consciousness' which then becomes both a class made and a class self-making as it progresses through history. Class has become the – unacknowledged – leading player around which the drama of history is then written.

A different understanding is possible when we begin to put 'culture' at the beginning of our thinking, not at the end, when we become aware that 'experience' and 'productive relations' cannot be understood outside discourse and the 'imaginary' to which it gives rise. This is Cornelius Castoriadis writing about the 'imaginary institution of society',[5]

Those who speak of 'imaginary', understanding by this the 'specular', the reflection of the 'fictive', do no more than repeat, usually without realising it, the affirmation that has for all time chained them to the underground of the famous cave: it is necessary that this world be an image *of* something. The imaginary of which I am speaking is not an image *of*. It is the unceasing and essentially *undetermined* (social, historical and physical) creation of figures/forms/images, on the basis of which alone there can ever be a question *of* 'something'. What we call 'reality' and 'rationality' are its works.

In this book I am concerned with an imaginary that is not the image *of* something else, but without which there cannot be something else. In the understanding of Castoriadis, and of myself, society and 'the social' are the outcome of this 'imaginary'.

I frequently employ the terms 'social imaginary' and 'democratic imaginary' in what follows. By using the former I point to the countless,

[4] E. P. Thompson, *The Making of the English Working Class* (1968), pp. 9–10. This is not at variance with Thompson's later formulation, E. P. Thompson, 'Eighteenth-Century English Society: Class Struggle Without Class?', *Social History*, 3:2 (May 1978), esp. 146–50.

[5] Cornelius Castoriadis, *The Imaginary Institution of the Social* (1975; translated by Kathleen Blaney, 1987), p. 3. See also 'The Imaginary: Creation in the Social Historical Domain', in L. Appignanesi (ed.), *The Real Me: Post-Modernism and the Question of Identity*, (1987).

and relatively uncharted forms in which 'society' has been understood. As well as the forms of its understanding I also include the ways in which these forms are produced. 'Society' is therefore itself an historical construct, one we might best approach through an etymology of the term.[6] The idea that 'society' comprised a *system*, was one particular manifestation of this much larger history of 'society', a manifestation taking clearer form in the eighteenth century. It was, however, a manifestation the people I write about in this book were not usually in tune with, though it has since grown to be a major part of our thinking.

I employ the term 'democratic imaginary' as one manifestation of this protean social imaginary, in the Victorian period a new and overwhelmingly important one. I might more correctly have used the term 'demotic imaginary', for, in order that a democracy could be imagined at all (and hence realised in practice), it was first necessary that a subject, and hence a cause and justification of this democracy, be imagined in the shape of demos. So that a democratic polity might be thought about, demos had first to be born, and in these studies it is the shapes of demos that are traced ('the people', 'mankind', and so on). They were indispensable to the feeling of living in a democratic culture and society, as well as a polity; the stability of the polity itself resting on these broader foundations of what was felt to be democratic. None the less, I have stuck with the term 'democratic imaginary' because so much of my attention is given to politics, and because I want to indicate how these different aspects were always in practice linked together (a 'demotic' reading 'public' say, with a democratic polity). These demotic identities, often formed outside and prior to politics, as it were, I consider to circulate within the 'political unconscious', a term I use in the study of narratives below. My use of this term is metaphoric not analytic, designed as it is not to denote an unconscious, but to signpost the significance of the proto-political, imagined forms of power and the social order which were articulated by formal politics.

In thinking about the shapes of demos I am interested in the 'soft, sticky, lumpenanalytical' notions Baudrillard describes:[7]

The term 'mass' is not a concept. It is a leitmotif of political demagogy, a soft, sticky lumpenanalytical notion. A good sociology would attempt to surpass it with 'more subtle' categories: socio-professional ones, categories of class, cultural status etc. Wrong: it is by prowling around these soft and acritical notions . . . that one can go further than intelligent critical sociology.

I, too, want to prowl around these soft and acritical notions, this time those of demos in the nineteenth century.

[6] Raymond Williams, 'Society', in *Keywords: a Vocabulary of Culture and Society* (1976).
[7] Jean Baudrillard, *In the Shadow of the Silent Majorities, or, The End of the Social and Other Essays* (New York 1983), p. 3.

When we look closer, as Baudrillard also says, the seeming hardness of 'more subtle' categories dissolves (categories like 'class', 'status'). It is necessary to pursue something of this history of the softness and hardness of concepts. The notion that some knowledge is 'hard' is inseparable from the idea that there is somewhere a basis or origin for it which sanctions this hardness, this certitude. Such modes of thought have been called 'essentialist' or 'foundationalist'. It is the immensely liberating, but immensely troubling, message of post-modernist thought that this is not so, that there is no 'centre' which will serve as a fixed point for knowledge and action. This is the burden of post-structuralism also of course, but I prefer the broader term, which speaks about the dissolution of centres in a post-modern condition of society as well as a post-modern condition of knowledge.[8]

This 'essentialist' mode of thinking, this idea that there is a 'bottom line' which serves as an epistemological foundation, has been attacked from many quarters, and not least by historians. Here the work of feminist historians has been inspirational, drawing heavily as it has upon post-structuralism. There is no more important figure than Joan W. Scott. Most recently the foundation she has challenged has been 'experience', a category central to earlier thinking about the social order, especially, as we have seen, that of E. P. Thompson.[9] Scott's one-time collaborator, Denise Riley, has been equally innovative in releasing us from the naturalised, 'essentialised' categories of 'man' and 'woman'.[10] A now enormous history of medicine and the body has similarly shaken the idea that the body itself is a foundation for knowledge and truth.[11] In historicising 'science' this new history has also undermined what was once a pillar of 'the real'. The category of 'the social' is similarly shaken, as will already be apparent, not least the idea of class itself, which has been a founding concept for 'social history' in Britain and the US. A history of class has emerged which has questioned the earlier ontological certitudes surrounding the concept,[12] and

---

[8] Zygmunt Bauman has been a crucially important figure in the field of sociology, looking at once for a sociology of the post-modern condition and a post-modern sociology, Zygmunt Bauman, *Intimations of Postmodernity* (1992), chaps. 4, 9.

[9] Joan W. Scott, 'The evidence of "experience"', *Critical Inquiry*, 17 (Summer 1991).

[10] Denise Riley, *'Am I That Name': Feminism and the Category of 'Women' in History* (1988).

[11] On the body and foundationalist thinking see the remarks of Judith Butler, 'Contingent Foundations: Feminism and the Question of "Postmodernism"', in Judith Butler and Joan W. Scott (eds.), *Feminists Theorise the Political* (1992).

[12] See for example Gareth Stedman Jones, *Languages of Class: Studies in English Working-Class History 1832–1982* (Cambridge 1983); Joan W. Scott, *Gender and the Politics of History* (1988); Patrick Joyce, *Visions of the People: Industrial England and the Question of Class, 1840–1914* (Cambridge 1991). See also Patrick Joyce, *Class: A Reader* (Oxford, forthcoming).

as a consequence of this a new questioning of social history has begun to emerge.[13]

Most of the forms of this philosophical foundationalism are related to ideas about 'the real'. The 'real' is the hard, the imaginary the soft. Concepts and procedures gain hardness, and hence credence, as they approach it. 'The real' is the ultimate guarantee that there is a centre or foundation to knowledge. 'Representation' rests upon its firm foundations, reflecting it in the secondary domain of the imaginary. It is the aim of these studies to question these distinctions, distinctions that are as firmly entrenched in history as elsewhere, perhaps more entrenched, as history has been particularly impervious to the intellectual ferment of the last quarter of a century, at least in Britain. The impact of what has come to be called 'post-modernism' has been registered as an attack on history itself, 'history' here becoming privileged as the beleaguered guardian of the real.

This sensitivity has been evident in several places in Britain and elsewhere,[14] also in the Anglo-American pages of *Past and Present*, still perhaps the most prestigious historical journal in the English-speaking world, and a noted keeper of the historian's conscience.[15] An exchange emerged following Lawrence Stone's *ex cathedra* denunciation of the post-modernist menace. Both Stone and Gabrielle M. Spiegel were willing to go so far but no further ('the right side of breakpoint' for Stone): the acceptable face of 'post-modernism' could be allowed, but in the end it was these historians' invocation of the certainties of the real that was most apparent (for which in Spiegel's case 'the social' interestingly

[13] David Mayfield and Susan Thorne, 'Social History and its Discontents: Gareth Stedman Jones and the Politics of Language', *Social History*, 17:2 (May 1992); Jon Lawrence and Miles Taylor, 'The Poverty of Protest: Gareth Stedman Jones and the Politics of Language – a Reply', *Social History*, 18:1 (January 1993); Patrick Joyce, 'The Imaginary Discontents of Social History: a Note of Response . . .', *ibid.*; D. Mayfield and S. Thorne, 'Reply', *Social History*, 18:2 (May 1993); James Vernon, 'Who's Afraid of the Linguistic Turn? The Politics of Social History and its Discontents', *Social History*, 19:1 (January 1994).

[14] Bryan D. Palmer, *Descent Into Discourse: The Reification of Language and the Writing of Social History* (Philadelphia 1990); Gertrude Himmelfarb 'Telling It as you Like It: Post-Modernist History and the Flight from Fact', *Times Literary Supplement*, 16 October 1992; Geoffrey Elton, *Return to Essentials: some Reflections on the Present State of Historical Study* (Cambridge 1992). For a welcome antidote to this negative understanding of 'post-modernism' see Raphael Samuel, 'Reading the Signs: Part I', *History Workshop*, 32 (Autumn 1991) and, 'Part II', *History Workshop*, 33 (Spring 1992). See also the citations of J. Vernon, 'Whose Afraid of the Linguistic Turn?'.

[15] Lawrence Stone, 'History and Post-Modernism', *Past and Present*, 131 (May 1991); Patrick Joyce, 'History and Post-Modernism I', and Catriona Kelly, 'History and Post-Modernism II', *Past and Present*, 133 (November 1991); Lawrence Stone, 'History and Post-Modernism III', and Gabrielle M. Spiegel, 'History and Post-Modernism IV', in *Past and Present*, 135 (May 1992). See also Gabrielle M. Spiegel, 'History, Historicism and the Social Logic of the Text in the Middle Ages', *Speculum*, 65 (1990).

enough stood proxy),[16] and their recourse to history as its defender.[17] For historians, there is the danger that 'the real' and 'history' themselves become a new foundation upon which to base a defence of truth against the perils of what is taken to be the chaos of relativism evident in post-modernism.[18] This outlook tends to rest on a view of language in which there is still a direct correspondence between it and the world.[19] Whereas it is the burden of the view of language that underlies the advent of 'post-modernism', however broadly it is defined, that this is not so. Rather, what has been called the 'semiotic challenge' questions our assumption that 'the difference between the signified and the signifier is the categorical difference between a phenomenal entity and its epiphenomenal *representation*'. I quote from a recent, and very useful, reformulation of this position to which I shall later return,[20]

the referential gap between sign and signified is integral to language itself, informing its very structure; all speech acts are structured metaphorically as the identification of one thing in terms of something different. The very act of 'understanding' merely indicates a specifically human capacity 'to express something new in the language of something old and familiar'. No knowledge of the world, no recognition of attributes pre-given in the concrete, material quality of the signified could therefore produce a perfect correspondence between the sign and the signified. The link between sign and signified is only established historically through the 'extraneous' power of social convention.

Some historians are in danger of defending history by assuming that a discourse is either a matter of fact or fiction, either a form of reference or 'merely' a discursive construction, which is to imagine that some texts can perfectly reflect the real. I paraphrase Antony Easthope's recent

---

16   Historians must cleave to 'an examination of the play of power, human agency and social experience as historians have traditionally understood them' (*ibid.*, p. 85), and – on texts – this history must be seen as involving 'the determinate social locations of texts', their 'social logics', the social sites that 'disclose the political, economic and social pressures that condition a culture's discourse at any given moment' (*ibid.*, pp. 77, 85).

17   As Spiegel puts it, historians must insist on 'the importance of history itself as an active constituent of the elements which themselves constitute the text' (*ibid.*, p. 84).

18   For an illuminating discussion of the reification of 'history' as a ground of appeal beyond, and superior to, the other human sciences, a 'certain test of knowledge' because of its immersion in the real, see M. Cousins, 'The practice of historical investigation' in D. Attridge, G. Bennington and R. Young (eds.), *Post-structuralism and the Question of History* (Cambridge 1987).

19   Even for a sophisticated historian like Spiegel a correspondence notion of language seems to come into play in her defence of what she terms the 'classical' view of language as mediating the world. This notion depends upon an equivalence obtaining between the different 'phenomenological categories' of language and the world, an equivalence secured by language. This seems to me to contradict the inherently *metaphorical* working of language as presented here. See G. M. Spiegel, 'History and Post-Modernism IV', pp. 197–202, esp. p. 198.

20   D. Mayfield and S. Thorne, 'Social History and its Discontents', pp. 180 and 181.

account of the unacknowledged rhetoric of history writing here, fittingly enough of a text of Stone's.[21] His particular point is that 'truth cannot escape participation in both fact and fiction, both a form of reference and a discursive construct, both logic and reference'. His overall argument, as to realism and anti-realism, is that the epistemological question is (a) insoluble and (b) not very interesting, and with this I am in considerable sympathy. The gist is: human beings are thrown into 'the middle of Being contingent on a world we have not and could never choose'. There is therefore 'no position available from which to inspect and assess the possible validity of the correspondence or non-correspondence between our discourse and the real. God could do it, but we cannot because we are inside it, always already part of it'.[22] As Easthope further observes, it does not follow that we are therefore thrown into some relativistic chaos in which anything goes, as some historians seem to fear. For a fact to be accurate or not there does not have to be a relation of correspondence or adequacy between discourse and the real. If the epistemological debate is not resolvable, then there is no problem about discriminating accurate from inaccurate data, and tenable from untenable arguments. We do this all the time, widely different protocols obtaining in different areas. None the less, these protocols are themselves the product of history, logic turning out on inspection to depend on 'consensus and social construction (rhetoric)'.[23]

These kinds of argument are not going to please everyone. However, my concern here is less with the status of epistemological arguments as with their effects: the ideology or rhetoric of 'the real' erected in part on the foundations of an unreflecting understanding of the real itself.[24] To this is due that 'hardness' of supposedly objective knowledge already described. The ideology of 'the real' has many sources, as does the element of conservatism and complacency that marks some historical writing in Britain (where the response to the currents of thought described here has more often been indifference than outright hostility). This conservatism is in part due to the institutionalisation of 'the real' in the discipline as it itself became institutionalised in the later nineteenth century.[25] Also, 'discipline' has often tended to be precisely that, a training in

[21] Antony Easthope, 'Romancing the Stone: History-Writing and Rhetoric', *Social History*, 18:2 (May 1993), 238. See also Dominick La Capra, 'Rhetoric and History', in *History and Criticism* (1985).
[22] Antony Easthope, 'Romancing the Stone', p. 237.   [23] *Ibid.*, p. 239.
[24] On the rhetoric of 'the real' see Roland Barthes, 'The Discourse of History' and 'The Reality Effect' in *The Rustle of Language* (1986).
[25] James Vernon, 'Narrating the Constitution: Macaulay, Stubbs, Maitland and the Inventions of Nineteenth-Century Constitutional History', in James Vernon (ed.), *Re-reading the Constitution: New Narratives in the History of English Politics* (Cambridge, forthcoming).

certain intellectual and moral procedures, rather than an encouragement to speculative thinking (and of course a training in the disciplines of rule as well as 'the real'). The weight of this past is considerable, and, despite the sound and the fury that is from time to time made, a conservative prognosis may not be inappropriate. Here it is apposite to quote Zygmunt Bauman on the way in which 'the advent of postmodernity' may turn out to have little effect on the academy:

There is nothing to stop one from doing just that (pursuing 'objective' knowledge and declaring 'post-modernity' to be a sham). In the vast realm of the academy there is ample room for all sorts of specialized pursuits, and the way such pursuits have been historically institutionalized renders them virtually immune to pressures untranslatable into the variables of their own inner systems; such pursuits have their own momentum; their dynamics subject to internal logic only, they produce what they are capable of producing, rather than what is required or asked of them; showing their own, internally administered measures of success as their legitimation, they may go on reproducing themselves indefinitely.[26]

However, one enters here an area far beyond the scope of the present account, so I will turn to much more specific matters. The studies that follow grow out of my previous book on class and 'populism' in nineteenth-century England, and this work, and its reception, provides me with a convenient way of relating some of the matters already broached to the studies in this book. *Visions of the People* drew upon itself a wide range of critical responses, ranging from the constructive, to straightforward denunciation for defying the sacred tenets of historical materialism.[27] The more measured strictures of the old New Left *Weltanschauung* betray a number of the usual confusions about 'identity' and 'experience'.[28] The most constructive responses suggested that I had not gone far enough down the 'post-modernist' road I had taken, and with this I agree, this book in many senses being a complement and completion of the previous one. One particular criticism was that I replaced one overarching category, 'class', with another, 'populism', so working against post-structuralism's understanding of texts as involving in their reading a constant

[26] Z. Bauman, *Intimations of Postmodernity*, pp. 103–4.
[27] Palmer's denunciation of myself, but especially Stedman Jones, has all the usual, and hateful, vocabulary of 'betrayal' and 'treachery' typical of the old New Left at its worst. See Bryan Palmer, 'The Poverty of Theory Revisited; or, Critical Theory, Historical Materialism, and the Ostensible End of Marxism', *International Review of Social History* (forthcoming at the time of writing).
[28] Also a little of that Left's sanctimoniousness. See Theodore Koditschek's review, *American Historical Review* (October 1992), 1217–18. This tells me that 'the pioneers of social history knew something I have forgotten, namely that language is a product of "social conflict", and that if we wish to understand the visions of the people we must study their experiences and identities first', as if the two could ever be separated. As usual there is the familiar shunting of some areas into 'the real' (experience and identity) and some into the imaginary ('visions').

subversion of stable meaning and structure. No doubt so, but two things might be said: first, I was at pains to say I employed these categories heuristically,[29] and second, that it is the very protean nature of categories like 'the people' and 'people' that make them interesting, as Baudrillard suggests.

One of the most interesting suggestions was that, like Stedman Jones, I took language as 'prefigurative', dealing in a 'linguistic determinism' that is the supposed mirror image of an older 'sociological determinism'.[30] I am held to believe that 'the definitive human relationship is a cognitive one between the perceiving human subject and objective things',[31] instead of (the *correct* 'definitive human relationship' presumably) 'a social one existing between and among people of different power and authority'. In the words cited already: 'The link between sign and signified is established historically through the "extraneous" power of social convention', itself 'a balance of conflicting social forces'.

However, rather than a new 'linguistic determinism', this earlier work was marked by a nostalgia for collective social subjects and bedrock 'experiences', upon which values and culture could be based. Collective subjects like 'the people' and 'the working class' still haunt the book, subjects that are taken as pre-constituted and which then function as the source of discourse, so that 'populism' is too easily given coherence by virtue of its origin in a supposedly coherent collective subject. Subjects are seen as constructing meanings, whereas meanings construct subjects. Therefore it was at the end of the book that I could come to understand 'the people', chiefly in the form of the Lancashire industrial labouring poor, as the collective author of the various 'traditions' and 'populisms' I described. Rather than language prefiguring the subject, the subject prefigured language (I am here using 'language', and 'discourse', as shorthand for all kinds of sign systems that inevitably extend to material life and practices. This sense is apparent in my previous work as well.). The problem there was that I made language too little, not too much, 'prefigurative'. I did this because I wanted still to write a grand, traditional narrative, and sought, uneasily, to find the subject of that narrative in 'the people' (just as 'the working class' was the subject of an earlier, grand, historical narrative). With the methodology and perspective I had begun to adopt I knew I could not do this.

In these studies I have put the creation of subjectivities at the centre of my concern, taking nothing for granted about how these were achieved, both at the level of the self and the social. A scepticism about subjectivities is extended to those subjects where scepticism has often been least

[29] P. Joyce, *Visions of the People*, pp. 11–16.   [30] D. Mayfield and S. Thorne, 'Reply'.
[31] *Ibid.*, p. 224.

evident, those of 'the working class' and 'the middle class'. I have chosen two figures who either have been, or could be regarded as being, very significant for the creation of such class identities, whether for themselves or for others. I question the central place often given these identities and explore the nature of other possibilities. I am concerned with the forms of these other subjectivities and the means by which they were brought about. All this extends to the study of narrative, where I go beyond individual subjects to collective ones.

An example of a conventional use of 'experience' in *Visions of the People* is the attempt to base an understanding of culture on some foundational 'experience of poverty', one marked by an immanent, existential uncertainty and insecurity. At places in that book I worked with the notion of a 'need for order' which was governed by the 'experience' of poverty, endemic economic insecurity and the demands of ordered industrial production.[32] The cultural activity expressing this need for order was seen to be dictated by a pre-existing experience. People's experience was seen to dictate a consuming need for order, boundary, and control. Not surprisingly, it is the prioritising of experience that has been applauded by those who would seek to defend 'the real'. In so doing, experience and culture are separated, the latter always acting on the former.[33] In the study of Edwin Waugh I have tried not to do this, arguing that meanings cannot be derived from an originary 'experience' of poverty and insecurity, and that what matters is the way in which people put this experience together in the first place. 'Poverty' and 'insecurity' are a part of culture then, not 'experience' so conceived. Their meanings are made and not found. In handling the real they inevitably construct it.

Therefore, rather than being shy about the 'prefigurative' role of discourse, I would want actively to advance this role in thinking about social, or any history. Here I am taking seriously the very words of those who inform me I am a linguistic determinist, words that so rightly inform us of the metaphoric nature of human discourse, how one thing is always identified in terms of something else inevitably different. If this means anything, it means that language is always a creative act. Language is intersubjective and communicative, and hence 'social', so that this is not a creation *ex nihilo*. But to identify one thing in terms of another is always to

---

[32] P. Joyce, *Visions of the People*, p. 151, pp. 151–8, and chap. 6.

[33] G. M. Spiegel, 'History and Post-Modernism IV', p. 202, n. 22. Spiegel is quite right to remark that the argument of my *Past and Present* intervention ran counter to the book, but the argument of the latter now seems unsatisfactory to me. It is satisfactory to Spiegel because she applauds subscription to 'the idea of a social reality which conditions the specific inflections of [the] working-class culture' with which I dealt. For her, it is still the familiar story of 'experience' and 'culture' being 'two distinct orders of phenomena', the latter always operating upon the foundation of the former.

reinterpret and remake, to being anew, indeed to 'constitute' or 'prefigure' the world. The interpretive act should not be subordinated to the régime of 'the social' (itself a régime created by interpretive acts). I draw this lesson from the 'linguistic turn' therefore: if language is the proper model for culture – which is the gist of the linguistic turn and the 'language revolution' of the twentieth century – then it follows that language describes a human condition itself always marked by the making of meaning, a making always occurring in symbolic, more loosely 'metaphoric', terms. Post-structuralism and the other currents of thought considered here turn centrally upon the problematic of meaning: they denote the elusive, de-centred nature of meaning, and the ways that it is secured, but they also can be understood as returning us to the making of meaning as a central human activity. It is this perspective that might help to revitalise 'social history', recalling it to the 'always already' constituted nature of 'the social' itself. What has been called the 'linguistic turn' might for these purposes better be termed the hermeneutic turn, or just simply interpretive history, which may be to create a new 'foundationalism', but if so it is a strange one, where the only true foundation is that there is no true foundation, only the making of meaning.

In the present book this making is approached in terms of identity, of 'the self' and 'the social', and it is to post-structuralist conceptions of identity that I now turn. Many readers will be aware of these understandings of identity as mobile, fractured, contradictory.[34] An indeterminate and unstable subject, without a centre, is 'positioned' by the play of the symbolic order. Meanings make subjects and not subjects meanings. The attack is upon what are taken to be Western concepts of the person, an attack begun long previously by anthropologists, above all Marcel Mauss.[35] Under scrutiny is the assumed universality of the category of the person as 'a bounded sphere of thought, will and emotion; the site of consciousness and judgement; the author of its acts and the bearer of a personal responsibility; an individual with a unique biography assembled over the course of a life'.[36] The 'I' of Western thought is simply not an integrated centre of awareness in this understanding, nor a subject of universal applicability. That it is 'positioned' by discourse need not, however, raise problems about agency, which is a fear often expressed when these arguments are confronted. The view of language as meta-

---

[34] For a useful introduction to these ideas, and one accompanied by social-psychological applications, see Edward E. Sampson, 'The Deconstruction of the Self', in J. Schotter and K. J. Green (eds.), *Texts of Identity* (1989), and other essays.

[35] Mauss' essay of 1938 is translated as 'A Category of the Human Mind: the Notion of the Person; the Notion of the Self', in M. Carrithers, S. Collini and S. Lukes (eds.), *The Category of the Person* (Cambridge 1985).

[36] Nikolas Rose, *Governing the Soul: the Shaping of the Private Self* (1990), p. 217.

phoric expressed earlier, that something new is always addressed in terms
of something old, means that 'agency' is built into the nature of language:
the ever-present gap between the signifier and signified means that rather
than being 'positioned' in the sense of immobile, the subject is inex-
tinguishably mobile and active because s/he is always *forced* to know, in
the sense of forever having to pursue a forever elusive past meaning with a
present one. In this sense there is no alternative but to be an active agent, if
knowing is to occur at all.

Contemporary ideas of the subject have considerable implications for
the history of 'the social' in turn. Following Derrida, a logic of the
'supplement' maintains that entities are not either/or but both/and. Seemingly opposed entities in fact constitute each other, absence is always
contained in presence and presence in absence. The 'other' is implicated
in the self, and in what follows it will be apparent how revealing I have
found this logic in thinking about conceptions of the self and the social.
The point here, however, is that traditionally in Western thought the self is
most often defined as an 'I' set against the social, either to maintain the
autonomy of the self or to express a desire for integration in this social.
But if we follow a post-structuralist, or anthropological, understanding of
the self it will be apparent that the self and the social always constitute one
another. This recognition invites a history of these categories, one charting the shifting relationship of the two, as they move apart, then together,
always joined by their mutual dependence.

The social has a history, no less than the self, though the great apparatus
of the 'sociological' disciplines has so often gone about its labours without
being aware of how it, too, is positioned by this history of the social.[37]
Where do we commence such a history then, one that is also a history of
the self? It is possible to draw on an emerging history of the self, and a
much less developed history of 'the social',[38] which help provide a frame-

[37] A history that also requires understanding of the psychological and philosophical bases of
the social. For an illuminating new study see Serge Moscovici, *The Invention of Society:
Psychological Explanations for Social Phenomena* (1993).
[38] In the history of the self the enormous literature on biography and autobiography has
been one very important avenue of approach. See, among so much, J. D. Lyons, *The
Invention of the Self* (1978); P. M. Spacks, *Imagining a Self* (Cambridge, Mass., 1976);
Felicity A. Nussbaum, *The Autobiographical Subject: Gender and Ideology in Eighteenth
Century England* (1989); R. Elbaz, *The Changing Nature of the Self: A Study of the
Autobiographic Discourse* (1988); P. Dodd, *Modern Selves: Essays on Modern British and
American Autobiography* (1986); J. Olney, *Metaphors of Self* (Princeton 1972). More
generally, but disappointingly wooden in its late Marxism, see the none the less useful
Regenia Gagnier, *Subjectivities: A History of Self-Representation in Britain 1832–1920*
(Oxford 1991); also Linda M. Shires, *Rewriting the Victorians: Theory, History and the
Politics of Gender* (1992). The magisterial Charles Taylor, *Sources of the Self: The Making
of Modern Identity* (Cambridge 1989) is indispensable. Peter Burke and Roy Porter (eds.),
Language, Self and Society: A Social History of Language (Cambridge 1991) is valuable.

work for these studies. In turn, the studies will suggest the possibility of new directions and amendments to existing views, but it is not my intention in the present work to bring out all these possibilities. I have already said how from the late eighteenth century we can think of views of 'society' as a system taking on new force. And I have said that Victorian contemporaries were often not in tune with this way of thinking. The Victorian period is, as it were, a period between two condensations of 'the social', when the social continued to be governed by a self uneasy about a social progressively becoming not just a system, but a kingdom of its own, with its own rules in which the responsibility once exercised by the self was becoming subordinated. The autonomous social began to have the deepest effect only from the late nineteenth century, and the Victorian period was in many respects an age before 'the social'. This periodisation, like all periodisations, leaves out the powerful continuities evident, just as it can distort the picture by presenting change as a linear process of stages. None the less, this very rough sketch has its uses.

One might consider the process whereby 'the social' eventually attains its autonomy by looking back to the eighteenth century and the idea of political economy as a 'science' of the economy and society, say, or to the elaboration of the notion of a 'civil society' separate from government. These developments were accompanied by the cognate idea of a 'public sphere' separate from the 'private sphere', the self increasingly becoming relocated in this area of privacy. But, if the social begins to emerge as autonomous, its power is kept at arm's length: 'civil society' and the 'public sphere' only really begin to be fully commandeered by the social much later. Until then they continue to exist to make the self free, to create the autonomy of the self rather than the social, allowing the self the room within which to govern itself. The limitations to the emergence of a clearly delineated public sphere have recently been emphasised by historians of the eighteenth century.[39] Instead of a clear demarcation of values and roles between the public and the private there is a constant interaction of the two, and a blurring of distinctions. Manners seen to be appropriate to

---

This has useful things to say about medicine, the body, pain, and the self, but not a great deal about 'the social', which is more generally the case. The Foucauldian perspective of Nikolas Rose, in his *Governing the Soul* and other work, is something I have found of great interest. See also Jacques Donzelot, *The Policing of Families* (1978); Graham Burchell, *et al.* (eds.), *The Foucault Effect: Studies in Governmentality* (1991), esp. Giovanna Procacci, 'Social Economy and the Government of Poverty'; S. Moscovici, *The Invention of Society*, and D. Riley *'Am I That Name'* (both cited above).

[39] See, for instance, Joanna Innes, 'Politics and Morals: the Reformation of Manners Movement in Late Eighteenth-Century England' in Eckhart Helmuth (ed.), *The Transformation of Polite Culture: England and Germany in the Late Eighteenth Century* (Oxford 1990); Paul Langford, *A Polite and Commercial People. England 1727–1783* (Oxford 1989).

one sphere constantly find expression in the other too. This understanding certainly fits the picture presented for much of the nineteenth century in this book. In the English language, Williams describes something of this very slow emergence of 'society' and 'social' from the meanings of sociability and company into the idea of 'a system of common life' (seen in the particulars of 'association' as well as in the general) and thence, much later, to society as the sum of human relationships construed now as an *object*, with its own laws of motion, a life of its own.[40]

Baudrillard describes the relationship of 'the social' to the political thus:

It is since the eighteenth century, and particularly since the Revolution, that the political has taken a decisive turn. It took upon itself a social reference, the social invested it. At the same time it entered into representation, its performance became dominated by representative mechanisms ... The political scene became that of the evocation of a fundamental signified: the people, the will of the people, etc. For a long time, nevertheless, a balance came into play between the proper sphere of the political and the forces reflected in it: the social, the historical, the economic. Undoubtedly this balance corresponds to the golden age of bourgeois representative systems (constitutionality: eighteenth-century England, the United States of America, the France of bourgeois revolutions, the Europe of 1848).[41]

A 'balance' did come into play, and this book is about this time of balance, when 'the social' continued to be carefully policed. The polity had to speak in the name of 'the social', but the social had not yet engrossed it, just as it had not yet engrossed the self. One example is evident in the 'romance of improvement' considered in the study of narratives. 'Improvement' was underpinned by a grandiose idea of 'science', which took its grandeur from its relation to the laws of nature. Functionalist sociology, the very embodiment of the autonomy of the social, was one of the heirs of this view of science as a product of the lawed domain of nature. But, as will be evident, the 'improvement' narrative was compatible with what was still much the more dominant understanding of the social as the condition enabling moral, religious and political conceptions of self and the social order to operate. The 'romance of science' in the end only enabled the self to exercise responsibility and be moral, to frame 'the social' as a moral creation. The political served the same ends.

The sway of the moral lasted long, later than Baudrillard's depiction of the 'second phase' of the social (and was obviously much wider than his, polemical, identification of Marxism with it):

It is with Marxist thought, in its successive developments that the end of the political and its particular energy was inaugurated. Here began the absolute hegemony of the social, and the economic, and the compulsion on the part of the

---

[40] R. Williams, *Keywords*.
[41] J. Baudrillard, *In the Shadow of the Silent Majorities*, pp.17–18.

political, to become the legislative, institutional, executive mirror of the social. The autonomy of the political was inversely proportional to the growing hegemony of the social.[42]

This hegemony can be understood in terms of the transition from an inner- to an outer-directed self. In the nineteenth-century dispensation responsibilities were seen as a matter of an inner-directed self, one marked for example by the exercise of 'self-help'. The vast importance of the idea of 'independence' in the Victorian period, seen at some length in these studies, bears greatly on this: independence secured the conditions in which responsibility could be exercised, and therefore the situation of freedom to which all should aspire. In the late nineteenth-century use of 'the social' responsibility became dispersed in a realm external to the self. Rights and obligations were seen in terms of collective solidarities and responsibilities, and articulated in a language of 'external', extra-personal, social responsibilities.[43] Individual needs were now seen as 'social' needs.

These changes were closely related to the increasing scope of state power, expressed in social welfare provision for instance, and a generally more interventionist kind of government. The state assumed increasing responsibility and with it 'society'. The state also took on greater than ever powers of surveillance. Responsibility was directed outwards, to the environment and to 'social forces', for instance to a class *system*, which echoed the idea of the social as a *system* (a system now that in its exemplification of 'laws' and regularities of all sorts was rapidly taking on a life of its own). Such an understanding of class illustrates a major point: that historians, and many others, have inherited the view of class as system-like, so missing the point that when nineteenth-century con-temporaries used the language of class they did not usually have such views in mind. They, 'workers' and 'middle class' alike, have anachron-istically been understood to have viewed class as the outcome of new 'systems', social and industrial, whereas their usages were moral and political, not 'sociological' in these senses.

Sociology was itself one of the outcomes of these changes. So was a psychology that situated responsibility not outside the self, but buried so far within it as to be almost beyond either control or recognition. The idea of the unconscious mind, and all these other changes outlined, under-mined the 'language of character' felt to be so important for most of the nineteenth century. In this study it is apparent that the shift from the moral framework of the language of character was also facilitated by new aesthetic understandings of the self and the social world, ones in which

[42] *Ibid.*, p. 18.
[43] N. Rose, *Governing the Soul*, pp. 214–28 for a very interesting discussion of historical change from the early twentieth century.

realism played a new and important part. Realist discourse in general can be said to have marked the consolidation of 'the social' far beyond the aesthetic field. The world of realist discourse was itself marked by the operation of laws. And, of course, with the loosened hold of religion in the twentieth century the foundations of the old order were fatally weakened. The moralism that had marked it owed an immeasurable amount to religion.

As Denise Riley has so acutely observed, this new 'social' was feminised from its beginnings:

This shining projection of 'women' alights on a newly conceived space which is deeply caught up in allied peculiarities. The nineteenth-century 'social' is the reiterated sum of progressive philanthropies, theories of class, of poverty, of degeneration; studies of the domestic lives of workers … [of] their need for protection as this bore on their family lives too. It is a blurred ground of the old public and private, voiced as a field for intervention, love and reform by socialists, conservatives, radicals, liberals, and feminists in their different and conjoined ways.[44]

'Women' became the object of concern, but the whole field of the social was itself feminised, irradiated with the special qualities of 'woman', in the process taking up a relation to the political, which was now seen as a masculine preserve. In the eighteenth century and much of the nineteenth woman had been seen in terms of nature: 'she was seen as thoroughly sexed through all the regions of her being, so that it became possible to *be* a sex'. It was in women's 'nature' to be like this. This 'nature' now became encompassed by a pervasive social. As with the domains of the political, the moral and the religious, so here, 'the social' became swollen to new proportions, engrossing nature as well as these other domains from the late nineteenth century.[45]

To indicate the history of the self before these manifestations of the social became apparent necessitates an even briefer presentation than that adopted so far. Certain key factors are invariably, though not incorrectly, invoked: the place of Christianity was obviously central, 'conscience' long before Protestantism becoming a means of governing the soul. Yet Protestantism was greatly important in further placing the burden of selfhood on the individual, a burden some of which was earlier taken by the bureaucracy, hierarchy, and doctrines of the Catholic Church, not least the doctrines and practice of the Eucharist.[46] The role of Enlightenment thinking, and of romantic individualism, have traditionally been given pride of place after Protestantism in this narrative of the self. Nikolas Rose has recently woven the work of Norbert Elias into a Foucauldian narrative

---

[44] D. Riley, 'Am I That Name', p. 49.   [45] Ibid., chap. 3, esp. 47–51.
[46] Miri Rubin, Corpus Christi: The Eucharist in Late Medieval Culture (Cambridge 1991).

of the self's history. The centralisation of state power is here understood as going hand in hand with 'the civilising process', the inner-directed, personal control of instinct serving the ends of social co-operation. The role of the state in this was to encourage the techniques and practice of 'self-control' as an instrument of governmentality.[47]

The Foucauldian perspective offers a productive approach to the history of the self. As Rose puts it,

'The self' does not pre-exist the form of its social recognition; it is a heterogeneous and shifting resultant of the social expectations targeted upon it, the social duties accorded it, the norms according to which it is judged, the pleasures and pains that entice and coerce it, the forms of self-inspection inculcated in it, the languages according to which it is spoken about and about which it learns to account for itself in thought and speech ... The history of the self should be written at this 'technological' level, in terms of the techniques for ... managing the self.[48]

This is a matter, too, of the technologies of communication, of the rise of print culture and literacy, of private reading, of diary keeping, but also the age-old technology of speaking itself.

Technologies of the self in the nineteenth century involved 'making the self visible to the self', so that the good life would be shown to be about the exercise of 'character' and the exertion of 'independence'. These were to be found within, in a realm where moral choice and religious duty had to be exercised in order to bring the good, and the good life, into being. But choice and duty were directed outwards in turn to shape contemporary understandings of the social and the political, above all the senses of the demotic and the democratic. Here 'democracy' itself emerges as curiously volatile and elusive, and immensely powerful. This is how it begins to appear in the study of Bright, and of the narratives through which social and political identities were conferred in the nineteenth century. In such narratives everyone speaks in the name of 'the people', yet the people are nowhere to be found outside the imagining of the people. This imagined people takes on a colossal force as the source of all sorts of claims for authority and legitimacy. One could say that it takes on a life of its own, something upon which everyone makes a claim, but which exerts an equally strong claim on everyone in turn. One can understand this autonomy of democracy in terms of the autonomy of a new 'social' from the late nineteenth century: the idea of 'social democracy' for instance relocated what had earlier been moral and political understandings into a new social realm. But the roots of democracy's autonomy go back far beyond this to the 'democracy' described in this book. The 'democratic romances' I describe later produced a democracy that was not, as often

[47] N. Rose, *Governing the Soul*, pp. 217–24.   [48] *Ibid.*, p. 218.

thought, so much about either religion or politics, as about the religion of politics, the religion of democracy, with demos as its god. This god was an imagined one, yet it had enormous power over its followers, a power of subjection which brings another meaning to 'democratic subjects'.

We, too, can be understood as followers of this god. Our democracy, just as theirs, depends on this imagined people: as Benedict Anderson showed, there is no nation without the nation imagined,[49] and so we may say that there is no democracy without democracy imagined. If the imaginary is real then it has its own weight, its own laws of motion. If democracy imagined is real in this way, then we can no longer understand its operation solely as we have traditionally done, in terms of sources of power lying 'behind' it and controlling it (classes, interests, parties and so on). The sum of so many imaginative projections, it itself has no centre. Yet this de-centred democracy is eminently real and eminently powerful, and we need to understand the power it has over us, which can be said to have begun in earnest in the period I discuss. It is then democracy begins its real sovereignty over our lives, in all the solidity of its imagined forms ruling us ever since as much as we have ruled it. There are many histories to be written about these imagined forms, many other ones than the Foucauldian history. The studies in this book are instances around which these future histories may be written, including future histories of the self.

[49] Benedict Anderson, *Imagined Communities: Reflections on the Origin and Spread of Nationalism* (revised edition 1991).

I   The sorrows of Edwin Waugh: a study in
     'working-class' identity

1 Edwin Waugh, after the period of the diary

I   The sorrows of Edwin Waugh: a study in 'working-class' identity

The miseries of servitude, and the double-distilled misery of ignorance ... the wretched retributions that hang over men's faults! I am a most miserable sorrowful soul – no not a soul. It is the want of soul within me that makes me grieve. But I am in very earnest both a continual and a secret sorrower and the only thing I have truly to rejoice at is this fast-abiding grief that I am what I am, and what I ought not to be – O God, this holy sorrow if it be not weak I beseech thee fortify it according to thy will. This sorrow for the depravity of my mental and moral condition is a divine treasure which I pray thee to preserve to me, and increase in me – Every hour convinces me of the insufficiency of man of himself to preserve and uplift himself ... O God, my life is fleeting and I am lingering helplessly in misery and slavery of mind and spirit ...
(Edwin Waugh, Diary, 6 November 1847)[1]

What a pitiful thing is man, or rather the curious animal that bears the name – unless he be a continual conqueror over the wrong within him and without. He is right heir to the majestic ... if he has the character to march into his own territory and take possession ... I am sometimes as wise as fifty Solomons for a few minutes in speech and writing but in hard active life there are few greater fools between me and Pendle Hill.
(Edwin Waugh, Diary, 20 March 1850)

On hearing a poor man in a Manchester street singing a Scots ballad, March 1850:

The whole street felt this simple song, and followed the slow steps of the singer, with intense heed. Rich and poor, all felt this universal appeal from the heart of a man, to all hearts that might beat after him.
(Diary, 10 March 1850)

In 1847 Edwin Waugh was aged thirty years, having returned to his native Rochdale after eight years travelling throughout the country as a journeyman. He had just married, and was working for a master printer in the

[1] The diary is kept in the Archives Department, Manchester Central Library.

23

town. By 1850 he had moved to Manchester, and his time was divided between secretarial work for the Manchester public education lobby and a budding literary career. This work was 'servitude' to him, literature emancipation. Waugh went on to become the major influence in a regional dialect literature which was of great social import far into the twentieth century.[2] His diary, kept between 1847 and 1850, is a record of how one 'working man' faced the world. But Waugh was a working man for whom manual work was of secondary account in how he saw himself, was most often drudgery in the same way as the servitude of the clerk. What mattered for Waugh was his soul, which if only God could save was also made by man himself, if he would but march into his own territory and take possession of it. The condition of this young man's soul as he confronted his situation was most often one of sorrow, over this period an unrelenting sorrow, real in the suffering it brought, yet also a condition in which he luxuriated, the medium of his emerging selfhood.

This is surely a strange working man, one whose preoccupation is the spiritual and the moral life, the conquering of wrong within as much as without? To be a working man is to be a man like all other men, to partake in the same struggle for the moral life. It is not to be a member of a class. To be a man is to be like all men, to feel 'this universal appeal from the heart of a man, to all hearts that might beat after him'. What light can this man throw on 'working-class history', a man who has deserted the world of the workers for the 'finer' life of literature, one who has exchanged physical for mental labour among the clerks and young 'gentlemen' of Manchester?

Contrary to prevailing ideas of class, a very great deal. For some understanding of why this is so, the recently translated work of Jacques Rancière can be considered.[3] The Nights of Labour is a remarkable synthesis of Marxist and post-structuralist concerns, strong in its desire 'that archives be discourses, that "ideas" be events'. Its rejection of the philosophical 'essentialism' that has marked so much thinking about the 'working class' is greatly liberating, as is the implementation of its injunction to consider the agency of representation, of texts. However, it is not the example of this implementation that concerns us here – the texts of ultra-radical, autodidact French workers as exemplified in the revolutionary movements of 1830 and 1848. Nor is it the theoretical stance taken after the 1970s rethinking of Marxism in France. Rather it is the threefold structure of the book, each stage of which represents a conceptualisation

---

[2] For an account of this literature see P. Joyce, *Visions of the People: Industrial England and the Question of Class, 1840–1914* (Cambridge 1991), chaps. 12, 13.

[3] J. Rancière, *The Nights of Labour: the Workers' Dream in Nineteenth-Century France* (Philadelphia 1989), translated by John Drury, edited by Donald Reid.

of the 'working class'. I shall employ this framework, but not its attendant class interpretation. There is, first, the relationship of work and the worker, then that of the worker intellectual, leader or activist to the workers more generally, and finally the relationship of 'class consciousness' to the worker. In all three areas, the life of Edwin Waugh, particularly as reflected, and constituted, in the diary, offers us important insights: Rancière's work can serve heuristically as a point of departure, the instance of Waugh in turn inviting comment on many elements outside Rancière's concerns.

First, the relationship between work and the worker. Here Rancière starts from the premise that 'those loudest in singing the glory of work are those who have most intensely experienced the degradation of that ideal'.[4] Notions of the 'artisan' and 'artisan work', for instance, do not reflect real social entities (which 'artisan' is so often taken to be), but are myths designed to handle economic or political situations, such as the nature of work in the mid-nineteenth century, or the later elaboration of the myth of a genuine artisanal socialism built as a defence by labour spokesmen against new currents of political socialism.[5] As Rancière puts it:

What defines the personages of my book as proletarians is not their identification with a job, nor their popular roots; it is the aleatory character of a situation daily put into question, the illusory or transitory character of apparently prestigious qualifications and trades. The condition described today as that of unstable worker is perhaps the fundamental reality of the proletariat.[6]

A number of objections may be made to this,[7] the first being that the economic instability Rancière describes may be the condition of many who were not 'workers'. Therefore, this condition cannot be the defining mark of 'the proletarian', unless we wish to stretch that term hopelessly wide. Further, the 'experience' of insecurity Rancière points to is only one response to economic instability. There may be many quite conflicting responses, in which 'insecurity' does not figure. Nor, as was said in the introduction, can we think of poverty itself as present in an 'experience'

---

[4] *Ibid.*, p. xxv.
[5] J. Rancière, 'The Myth of the Artisan: Critical Reflections', in S. L. Kaplan and C. J. Koepp (eds.), *Work in France: Representations, Meaning, Organization and Practice* (1986); also the English language extracts from Rancière's work in A. Rifkin and R. Thomas (eds.), *Voices of the People: the Social Life of 'La Sociale' at the end of the Second Empire* (1988), 'Good Times or Pleasure at the Barriers', and with P. Vaudray, 'Going to the Expo: the worker, his wife and machines'. See also 'Le Social. The Lost Tradition in French Labour History', in R. Samuel (ed.), *People's History and Socialist Theory* (1981).
[6] J. Rancière, *The Nights of Labour*, p. xxxiii.
[7] See the remarks of William Sewell Jr. and Christopher Johnson cited in J. Rancière, *The Nights of Labour*, p. xxv.

prior to and acted upon by 'culture'.[8] How 'poverty' is defined and responded to is something formed in culture.

This is not to say that poverty is 'invented', only that the real can only ever be known by terms that are culturally and historically formed, terms like 'poverty' and 'insecurity', ones which do not therefore give us direct knowledge of the real. This also applies to the economic instability Rancière points to as the defining mark of the 'proletarian': the instability and stability of livelihoods we may judge to be part of a real influencing people's options, but this judgement is itself culturally, which is to say historically, formed (the identification of 'economic instability' as crucial implies a model or narrative from which this identification is inseparable, and upon which it depends; what is 'instability' and 'insecurity' is always relative; and so on). No *necessary* consequences at all flow from economic instability, or from some supposed 'experience' of poverty and insecurity. For these reasons it would be unwise to reproduce a new 'foundationalism' by identifying either patterns of economic activity, or their assumed effects in poverty and insecurity, as sources for understanding how conceptions of the social order are formed.

Which is not to maintain that a shift in emphasis from work to poverty may not be very revealing: quite the opposite in fact, as it is the great merit of Rancière's work to do this, and to draw attention to situations of economic vulnerability. In the development of capitalist industry in the nineteenth century many workers were exposed to this vulnerability.[9] It is the meanings contemporaries put upon 'poverty' and 'insecurity' that matters here. I use the terms 'the poor' and 'the labouring poor' from time to time, but not as subjects which are the collective authors of the representations of poverty I describe. They are used because they were terms of identity current at the time. Poverty was a major source of people's understandings of who they were, and Edwin Waugh was a major force in creating its meanings for himself and for other of his contemporaries who chose to be addressed in these terms. Which is not to say that historians may not use collective nouns like 'the poor', or the 'working class', only that these terms tell us more about our own preoccupations than those of people in the past, unless we begin with people's understandings of these collectivities.

It is in calling attention to the ways in which economic situations are

---

[8] See above, pp. 11–12.

[9] However, the development of the labour process did not operate uniformly to produce a de-skilled, vulnerable, dependant workforce. Rather, situations of the 'independence' of labour, as well as the inter – dependence of labour and capital, were as much in evidence as those of the dependence of labour. See P. Joyce , 'Work', in F. M. L. Thompson (ed.), *The Cambridge Social History of Great Britain 1750–1950*, 3 vols., II (Cambridge 1990).

handled, seen in terms of the second of our relationships, that of the worker intellectual to the worker at large, that Rancière has most to offer. The true resolution of what Rancière calls the proletarian situation is the assertion of the humanity this situation denies, the 'universal appeal from the heart of a man, to all hearts that might beat after him'. As Rancière puts it:

[Workers seek] to appropriate for themselves the night of those who can stay awake, the language of those who do not have to beg, and the image of those who do not need to be flattered.[10]

These nights of labour are the nights of the worker intellectual, and it may be objected that such figures are unrepresentative. Of course, they are, but in the most essential way of all they are not. In a fine inversion of commonsense Rancière suggests how metaphysical concerns for working men were as much a necessity as a luxury. The worker intellectual could feel in a heightened sense only what all workers felt,

That is why those metaphysical problems, said to be good for bishops who find their supper ready and waiting for them, are even more essential for those who set out every morning to find the work on which their evening meal will depend. Who is better suited than those who hire out their bodies day after day to give meaning to dissertations on the distinction between body and soul, time and eternity, or on the origin of humanity and its destiny? ... Like the sham passions of poetry, the hinterworlds of metaphysics are simultaneously the supreme luxury and the supreme necessity for the common labourers.[11]

It is those who most keenly know uncertainty who are most keenly concerned with determinism and fate. For such men, therefore, what is memorable is not the quotidian world, whether of work or the life outside work. Rather, 'it is in the moments when the real world wavers and seems to reel into mere appearance, more than in the slow accumulation of day-to-day experiences, that it becomes possible to form a judgement about the world'.[12] And it is, of course, a matter of men, and not women.

The drive to transcend egotism and materialism drew upon, and reinforced, distinctions between men and women. Some of these distinctions will be viewed later, in terms of the ties that bound, and sundered, a newly married Edwin Waugh and his young wife. The autodidact, 'worker intellectual', was indissolubly related to the bulk of workers through the processes of gendering going on here. Though sundered from his fellows in some ways, he and they for the most part spoke the same language of gender, the presuppositions of which were one of the chief means by which communication between the two took place. The 'intellectual' and his fellows were, in Waugh's case, above all linked by his

[10] J. Rancière, *The Nights of Labour*, p. xxxiv.   [11] *Ibid.*, p. 19.   [12] *Ibid.*, p. 19.

literature: as we shall see, this turned on the connections between one man's and every man's humanity. This literature can be said to have been rooted in Waugh's life, and in that of his fellows, but it was far more than a simple working-up of this life. Waugh's writing had a central role in creating his reader's identity, their 'consciousness'. Thus a study of Waugh is especially pertinent to the third of our 'relationships', that of 'class consciousness' to the worker, which was always made in language, as much in the language of the dialect poet as that of the labour or political leader. And it was not about work, but about the getting of dignity through the realisation of a common humanity.

The situation of economic instability was handled not by rejecting but by embracing the 'bourgeois world', the world of those who can stay awake, who do not need to beg, and who do not need to flatter or be flattered. This world was an ideal world; as Ranciere puts it,

The workers' dream (was) a bourgeois civilization without exploiters, a chivalry without lords, a mastery without masters and servants. In short, the emancipation of the workers.[13]

Embracing this world, enacting this dream, meant both affirming and denying the reality of social distinctions. On the one hand, '... a class ideal of becoming completely like bourgeois people in order to better point up the difference and affirm the refusal entitling workers to be recognised as their equals'. The perfected bourgeois world of the workers' dream might issue in the elaboration and acceptance of class distinctions when such distinctions defended the worker against the denial of his humanity. Class was the expression of human dignity when these were denied, and class might eventuate when the possibility of partnership in the bourgeois world was refused. When, for instance, mastership was no longer possible in the trades, the impossibility of escaping their position was transformed by tradesmen into 'a positive refusal, a renunciation of servitudes from above'.[14]

The religion of humanity might be professed in the accents of class. None the less, it was still the religion of humanity, and it needs emphasis beyond that given by Rancière, that being a worker was at bottom an expression, a means, a passport to being human. On the one hand, 'a class ideology of becoming completely like bourgeois people in order to point up the differences', but on the other, 'In order to acquire citizenship in bourgeois civilization they [the workers] must wipe out the signs of worker specificity hearkening back to the naturalness of castes and the rule of force ... they must denounce the bourgeois blemishes of egotism and exploitation in their own behaviour.'[15] Class distinctions of all sorts, of

---

[13] *Ibid.*, p. 47.   [14] *Ibid.*, pp. 46–7.   [15] *Ibid.*, p. 47.

workers as much as any others, could be a selfish denial of humanity, the practice of a life-denying exclusion. Consideration of Edwin Waugh helps us chart something of this workers' dream, this dialectic of the rejection and acceptance of social distinction so fruitfully evident in Rancière's work.

What I have called the 'religion of humanity' was far more than the rhetorical expression of some underlying class identity, 'bourgeois' or 'worker' (though this is sometimes how Rancière phrases it). Social relations were at once conducted and constituted through it, and one may say that the discursive subject of 'humanity', and talk about this humanity, were perhaps the chief means by which the contemporary social was lived. Its heightened form in the 'religion of humanity', like its other forms, enforced all kinds of 'social' closure, unity and difference, of which class in the sense of 'work' and 'the worker' was only one variant. 'Class' in a much looser, non-Marxist, sense might also be the outcome, for instance in the vision of the poor, not the rich, as the truly human. But just as often a vision of social reconciliation and unity was involved. In the revolutionary France Rancière describes, this was less the case than in the comparative calm of mid-Victorian England. There, for many men like Waugh the dignity of being a man was not felt to be so violently denied, and so the script of the human spoke more of concord than of conflict. This will become evident as we approach Edwin Waugh more closely, first the young Edwin, and then his diary.

1 Young Edwin

Waugh's great-grandfather was one of the condition of men known as 'statesmen', farmers working their own smallholdings in the far northern uplands of England. Long after his great-grandfather's day these economic 'independents' retained a reputation for mental independence and cultural distinctiveness: as late as the 1860s, after the period of Waugh's diary, parliamentary education commissioners noted their long-established traditions of literacy and book ownership and their retention of a strong local dialect.[16] The Waughs farmed near Haltwhistle, just inside the Northumberland border. Waugh's grandfather was apprenticed as a shoemaker and leather dealer. He married into the Grindrod family of Rochdale, and set up as a leather dealer. How he came to Rochdale is unknown. But he was clearly a man of some substance, building several houses. He had ten children, seven sons and three daughters. The youngest of the seven sons was Edward, Edwin's father.[17]

Edward was a shoemaker in Rochdale. Little is known of him, but that he was extremely poor and that he received a charity education in the local grammar school. This 'poor man' married into the Howarths, a family that came from the area between Bury and Rochdale, in Lancashire. Edwin Waugh's family on his mother's side were both Methodist and musical: one relative was a preacher for Wesley, and his mother told of the visit of Wesley to their home when she was young. Another relative wrote a Wesleyan psalmody which enjoyed much popularity in the region.[18] When Waugh was nine his father died and his mother continued to run the shoe-shop in Rochdale, with the aid of her son from a marriage previous to that with Edward Waugh. This young man, still in his teens at the time, is said to have died early, worn out by the exertions of keeping his adopted family together. The Waughs spent three years in a cellar dwelling at this time, as Edwin later recalled, eating nettles and 'passion dock' and making 'poor man's cabbage'.[19]

What are we to make of this inheritance? This was undoubtedly a background in which manual labour and poverty figured prominently. Waugh surely deserves admission into the ranks of the workers? Certainly, if we conceive the proletarian condition as one of extreme insecurity, then Edwin's family history and his own early experience testify to the catastrophic effects of changing fortune. Yet the reality of independence is there

---

[16] P. Joyce, *Visions of the People*, pp. 198–9.

[17] Information on Waugh's family is taken from the 'Introduction' to G. Milner (ed.), *Lancashire Sketches*, I (1892–3).

[18] For further information on the family see G. Milner, 'Edwin Waugh, An Estimate and a Biographical Sketch', *Manchester Quarterly*, 12, 1893.

[19] E. Waugh, 'An Old Man's Memories', in G. Milner (ed.), *Lancashire Sketches*, I.

too, as is the aspiration to independence; in his forebears' solid circumstances, and in the family shop, where, if independence was mocked by circumstance, one called no man master but oneself. This is, however, a somewhat exceptional working man, one who was reared in a climate of education, whether the grammar-school education of his father's, the tradition of 'statesman' learning, or the self-education that complemented all these efforts, and marked his own early formation so deeply. In many ways this autodidact inheritance was unusual, but not so unusual perhaps when we remember that levels of literacy and standards of popular education were often higher before than during the Industrial Revolution (early industrialism in Lancashire seems to have *reduced* levels of attainment).[20]

Nor so unusual is the background of 'independency', whether on the Northumberland holding or in leather trading and the shoemaker's shop. Many working people looked back to some condition of 'a comfortable sufficiency', not least in the handloom weaving villages of industrial Lancashire. That this condition was often as much mythical as real matters little, for what counted in mid-nineteenth century contemporaries' perceptions of their immediate world was very often the standard of former days, however loosely this may have been based on fact. Waugh was no exception, constantly invoking in his life and his literary work the condition of independence he found exemplified in his own family circumstances and mythology. By so doing he in turn corroborated, and re-defined, the fantasies of independence so evident in his audiences. Again, Waugh's religious background was more marked than most. But, in an age when all categories of thought and feeling were suffused in the terms of religion, Waugh's formation was not unusual. Evident enough so far, as in so many other aspects of Waugh, is his exceptionalism, and also the great representativeness behind this. Above all, in looking from the gutter to the stars, in envisioning independence in the midst of poverty, something very similar to the 'workers' dream' is apparent.

Waugh's mother was an exceptional woman. After her husband's death, she ran a shoe-stall in Rochdale market as well as the shop. Her son had to help out at the stall, in all weathers and for long hours on Fridays and Saturdays. After this time, with the aid of a daughter, she seems to have opened up an infants dame-school in the town. Edwin Waugh's schooling seems to have been rudimentary, and the influence of his mother correspondingly enormous. He seems to have had some schooling

---

[20] D. Vincent, *Literacy and Popular Culture: England 1750–1914* (Cambridge 1989), also R. S. Schofield, 'Dimensions of Illiteracy in England 1750– 1850' in H. J. Graff (ed.), *Literacy and Social Development in the West: A Reader* (Cambridge 1981).

up to the age of seven, though frequently playing truant.[21] Sunday school made up some of the ground, but his mother's encouragement and his father's small library were crucial. His mother taught him to read when he was very young. What he read is revealing: the Bible, the *Book of Common Prayer*, Wesley's *Hymns*, Baxter's *Saints' Rest*, Bunyan's *Pilgrim's Progress*, Barclay's *Dictionary*, Culpepper's *Herbal*, a *Compendium of the History of England*, and Foxe's *Book of the Martyrs*, over which he 'pored so long and earnestly' that he thought he lived in the age of Queen Mary.

A little later, to his great delight at the time, he was introduced to literature through *Enfield's Speaker*, a collection of orations and recitations of a sort common at the time, and still commoner later on in the century as the publishing trade grew.[22] This was an introduction to history, to literature, to medicine (of an autodidact sort), to the world of standard English words. But, if this was a, characteristically eclectic, discovery of the world of 'high' culture, it was a view with a distinctive stamp, that of the Protestant outlook; a view of the past, but also very much a view of the present, bearing in mind Waugh's religious upbringing. It was a Protestant past that enshrined English liberties and traditions. It was a Protestant past that was often radical, with implications for the present particularly in its 'plebeian' appropriations, where Foxe and Bunyan in particular were taken by many autodidact working men as projections of their own and their nation's struggle for bread, freedom and knowledge.[23] Nor was this diet of knowledge solely the preserve of autodidacts, unless we expand that term to cover all who persevered in reading with little formal education. In an age when access to print was severely limited, at least up to the popular radical agitations of the 1780s and 90s, Foxe, Bunyan, and the Bible were often the only items read or owned by the poor, whose imaginations were powerfully formed by this forced seclusion with the classics of Protestant England.[24]

As Waugh developed his horizons expanded, but this early legacy was critical, as it was for probably most autodidact working men intellectuals and activists far into the nineteenth century and beyond. Waugh also took his inspiration from his immediate world. In his youth he is said to have delighted in rambling. He had a particular love for the river Roche, but his greatest passion was for the moors that surrounded the town. This was a world undergoing the transformation of industrialisation, yet still sufficiently in its pre-industrial form in the 1820s to offer the child and youth almost immediate access to the natural world from his town-centre home.

---

[21] G. Milner, *Lancashire Sketches*, p. xxiv.   [22] E. Waugh, 'An Old Man's Memories'.
[23] D. Vincent, *Bread, Knowledge and Freedom: A Study of Nineteenth-Century Working Class Autobiography* (1981), chaps. 2, 9.
[24] O. Smith, *The Politics of Language 1791–1819* (Oxford 1984), pp. 171, 180–3.

Waugh also lived in immediate contact with the pre-factory human world too, in particular with the culture of the handloom weaving communities that surrounded him. He numbered his relatives among the workers of domestic industry, just as later they were to become factory operatives. As he was to say, 'I never knew better or happier people than the poor, hard-working folk among whom I lived.'[25]

These worlds were not given to him simply through his direct apprehension of them. They were mediated through the imagination of a young man increasingly exposed to the world of high learning. He seems first to have become an errand boy for a local Wesleyan preacher who was also a printer. Then, around the age of twelve, he became an apprentice to one Holden, a printer and the owner of what seems to have been the town's only bookshop. His trade brought him into the world of high culture, and this was compounded by the experience of life in Holden's shop (where he worked from seven in the morning to nine at night). Holden was an Anglican and an ardent Tory, also the Tory printer for the town. As well as the world of political conflict, Waugh was introduced to the new interest in local history, customs, and language, the antiquarianism of the time that was later to develop into the study of 'folklore'.[26] The shop seems to have been something of a haven for devotees of this antiquarianism, particularly the Anglican clerics who gave so much of their ample spare time to it.

Holden's was visited by Canon F. R. Raines and Henry Roby. Roby, the son of a Wigan schoolmaster, appears to have been involved in Rochdale banking at this time. His work, *Lancashire Traditions*, was to leave a big impression on Waugh.[27] From both men he took a life-long interest in local and regional history, and accounts of him at the time speak of the influence of other works of local history too.[28] Roby's work, enjoying much public notice at the time, depicted the 'legends' of the county, such as those concerning the 'Abbot of Whalley' (in north Lancashire) and the 'Lancashire Witches', or the 'Goblin Builders' and 'The Fairies' Chapel'. Roby intermixed scholarship in local history, a desire to show something of the, supposed, beliefs of the common people of the present, and straightforward fiction, in which the fairy tale and romance were blended. These stories of old days, old knights, and old families and their halls, together with the interest in popular beliefs, seem to have had a powerful influence on the young Waugh, confirming him in his county and urban patriotism, but above all indicating to him that the common people out of which he came had their place in tradition.

---

[25] G. Milner, *Lancashire Sketches*, p. xxiv.
[26] For an account of this somewhat later on see P. Joyce, *Visions of the People*, pp. 180–2.
[27] H. Roby, *Traditions of Lancashire* (first edn. 1829, Manchester and London), 2 vols.
[28] Among which was J. Whittaker, *A History of Craven and Whalley* (Blackburn 1843).

Roby's account was an invented tradition, at one remove from the customary culture of the time, and in many ways pandering to the taste for the picturesque and quaint in its better-off readers. But this mattered little to Waugh. He set out to walk to every place mentioned in Roby's book. So, the rambles of this young man in his native countryside were quite literally guided by these 'high-cultural' representations of the local and the 'popular'. The same was so in his mental travels, Waugh interpreting the culture he knew at first hand through this medium. In his writing he adapted these representations for his own ends, though Roby's version of the days of yore before the factory seem to have coloured his view from the earliest days. What resulted was neither 'high culture' nor 'popular culture', but the constant influence of one upon the other, so that it is difficult and perhaps unnecessary to seek a point of origin in either.

Waugh also drew on other local traditions, most of all the mid-eighteenth century dialect writing of John Collier, 'Tim Bobbin', the Rochdale schoolmaster.[29] His own dialect writing was inspired by Collier, whose comic doggerel and dialogues, if often grotesque, were based on close observations of real popular life and language. Waugh was to retain the realism, supplanting the grotesque with the homely and the domestic. Collier's representation of the popular was distinctly more urgent, direct, and earthy than Roby's, and his tone and attitude satirical and subversive. Waugh's debt to both suggests the increasing complexity of the interplay of different forms of literary representation in his own formation, as he grew from childhood to manhood.

His early days were marked by more tumultuous events – he witnessed the shooting of eight men in a handloom weavers' riot in the town; heard Robert Owen speak, and observed the impassioned campaign against Church Rates seen in the town, an agitation led by John Bright. Waugh helped set up a working-men's educational institute in Rochdale, acting as editor for the journal it established.[30] As will be seen, John Bright was closely involved, as a patron, with this institute, and Waugh would have crossed his path fairly often. He was encouraged in his literary ambitions by Charles Howarth, a weaver and one of the founders of the Co-operative movement, a movement begun in Rochdale (a place that bids fair to have been the most socially creative town in nineteenth-century

[29] There are many editions of Collier's work, e.g. *The Works of Tim Bobbin Esq., in Prose and Verse with a Memorial of the Writer by John Corry* (Manchester and London 1862). This includes his best-known comic, dialect duologue, 'Tummus and Meary'. On Collier see Brian Maidment and Diana Donald, *Tim Bobbin's Humours, or Passion Delineated* (Rochdale 1990).

[30] The Manchester Central Library Local History Library cuttings files have much information on Waugh, most of it from the full obituaries that came out on his death in all the city newspapers; see the press for 1 May 1890.

England). Howarth himself seems to have talked politics long and earnestly with the young John Bright, even if they did not always agree. The influences at work on the young Waugh were socially as well as culturally varied.

By 1839 Waugh had become a journeyman printer, leaving Holden's employ and travelling throughout the country, including a stay in London. Little is known of this period in his life. Sometime in the mid 1840s he returned to Rochdale and the employ of Holden, choosing to live three miles outside the town, close by the Western edge of Hollingworth Lake, under Blackstone Edge, and in the company of nature and the 'country folk'. Blackstone Edge, it should be noted, was also one of the great meeting-places of the Lancashire radicals in their momentous political and industrial agitations of the 1830s and 40s. By the time the diary begins in 1847 he has a young wife of some two months' standing, and a child is to arrive soon after. The diary enables us to explore the inner world of this man, before he acquires a public life in the 1850s. With the coming of that public, literary life the private man falls silent. In the diary he talks, but others are silent.

During the time of the diary Waugh went through a long period of unrelenting suffering of mind. In this period he also changed jobs. In 1847, after a quarrel with Holden, he first secured work as a clerk, with the post of assistant secretary to the Lancashire Public Schools Association, based in Manchester. This organisation was set up by the rump of the Anti-Corn Law League in the city, and aimed at securing an unsectarian, public school system, outside the control of the state and the Established Church.[31] Waugh was responsible for writing reports and accounts, organising meetings, and canvassing subscriptions (out of which, in true market morality, his own wages were to come). None the less, the autodidact found a cause close to his heart. The artisan also encountered a 'middle-class' world, for it was in the company of clerks that Waugh was to find some solace in a city he always detested, especially the friendship of other young men working for the Association, who were not of labouring background. Despite its, to him, noble purpose, he seems to have found the work irksome, rarely beginning on time and disliking having to publicly canvas for his wages. Its putatively higher status notwithstanding, the living to be had from his work was precarious in the extreme, as well as being a poor one. We ought not to confuse Edwin's clerkship with membership of some putative 'petit-bourgeoisie'. The opportunities of such jobs at the beginning of the century were scarcely there at all. At the end of the century they were beginning to have real substance, and to

[31] S. E. Maltby, *Manchester and the Movement for National Elementary Education* (Manchester 1918); see also D. Vincent, *Bread, Knowledge and Freedom*, chap. 7.

carry much more social standing. This example of self-improvement creating 'white-collar' job opportunities, which turn out to be as insecure and ill-paid as the abandoned manual sector, is completely typical of Waugh's generation of autodidacts. Here, as so often, the young Edwin was like the workers, but not completely of them, a classically liminal figure who is forever half leaving what he came from in order to discover and to demonstrate that he wholly belongs to it. In this we see the point of studying Edwin Waugh: his liminality dramatises, and so reveals, the values and social relations of the time. He enables what may otherwise be silent to be said. Of course, he mediates the social in another important sense, connecting 'high culture' and the life of the poor as an autodidact and a writer.

What anguished Waugh during 1847–50 was therefore in part living in the smoke-blackened tumult of perhaps the greatest industrial city of the age, away from the natural world in which he had grown up. Partly it was the practice of his occupation. The new setting in which he moved also contributed, though in his Rochdale life he undoubtedly would have mixed with those of a higher social level: from the evidence of the diary, he seems to have slipped quite happily into the company of clerks, but moving in higher social circles seems to have been a cause of concern to him. More than these, perhaps, it was the indebtedness that his occupation got him into that troubled him: the fear of debt seems to have been almost an obsession with him.

His indebtedness was, however, also of his own making: all his life he had a reputation for being impulsive and reckless. More than any other single source, it seems to have been the marriage he entered into in 1847 that was the cause of his suffering. Perhaps that union was also a consequence of his impulsiveness. If the greatest source of his troubled mind came from within rather than from without – from the spiritual and moral quest so evident in the diary – the marriage was an expression of so many of the tensions and torments that now came to haunt him.

For, this book-obsessed man had married an illiterate woman and this socially mobile clerk had joined his fortunes to one of the labouring people of Rochdale. The occupations of Mary Ann's family in Rochdale are unknown, but they were undoubtedly of the background from which Waugh himself came. Almost from the start the marriage seems to have been a disaster. After almost ten years of being unable to live together or apart, and after three children, they finally separated in 1856. We begin to see some of the tensions and relationships that surface in the diary: those between the autodidact worker and the illiterate, the country and the city, and the worlds of manual and non-manual labour. We perceive also his situation of debt and economic insecurity. Waugh is well placed to help us explore the relationships suggested to us in the work of Rancière, those of work and the worker, the 'worker intellectual' and the mass of his fellows, and finally – in the guise of Waugh the artist yet also Waugh the diarist – that between the worker and both the creation and reception of representations of the social order.

We also begin to glimpse Waugh's 'character'. His only twentieth-century biographer has few doubts about this character.[32] He was 'impulsive', a man with money and women troubles all his life, something of a drunkard and a womaniser. Samuel Bamford, the renowned Lancashire radical and a fellow didact poet, called him a sponger and a drunkard.[33] In the late 1850s, until his death, Waugh moved in with a fairly well-off Irish widow in Strangeways, Manchester, a Mrs Moorhouse by name. It was Bamford's further charge that Waugh was living in sin with this woman while his wife and children were in the workhouse. The charges of being a kept man and a womaniser seem to have stuck: Waugh's biographer, unfortunately without citation, repeats the claim that he had an illegitimate child before his marriage. It is difficult, however, to know what this 'character' of Waugh's amounted to. Bamford in his turn was known for his jealousy, and Waugh was beginning to make his way in the literary world at the time when Bamford's charges were made. Waugh's fellow dialect poet, rival and companion both, Benjamin Brierley, was quite adamant that Waugh was not a drunkard, no matter what people said of him.[34]

There were several versions of Waugh's character, and the search for some distinct and unvarying character to the man is illusory. The varying constructions of Waugh are interesting, as is the hand he took in these constructions: more than most people, in his life, his diary, and his literary work, he was concerned to invent himself. This invention was related to the new social situation in which he found himself, overlain on the contradictions within him. One does not have to view Waugh as an

[32] M. Vicinus, *The Ambiguities of Self-Help: the Lancashire Dialect Writer Edwin Waugh* (Littleborough 1984). This pamphlet is an invaluable source of information on Waugh.
[33] *Ibid.*, pp. 11–14; see also the Diary of Samuel Bamford, 1858–1861, 19 September 1858, Manchester Central Library, Archives Department.
[34] B. Brierley, *Personal Recollections of the Late Edwin Waugh* (Manchester n.d.). The rancour of plebeian literary life in Manchester seems to have been marked. In the preceding diary entry Bamford writes that Dronsfield, another poet, said that if Brierley had confidence in Waugh he 'would betray him as soon as it suited his convenience to do so'. Waugh in fact seems to have kept in contact with his children, at least with his son Richard. In 1866 we find Richard writing, as his 'affectionate son', in order to meet his father on a visit to Manchester. He is sorry to say that he is not now in a Mechanics Institute or library, but he reports that, with other young men, he is setting up an 'Improvement class' in a chapel. Evidently, something of the father rubbed off on the son. See Letters to Edwin Waugh, L183/19 and 20, 29 October 1866, 20 December 1866, Manchester Central Reference Library, Archives Department.

unregenerate roué to be aware that he was a man of intense feeling, often proud, often sensitive to imagined slights, someone who liked 'company', and not at all a paragon of 'respectability'. Deeply interesting in the diary, as in the literary work, is the attempt of this lover of society to extol the virtues of respectability and the domestic hearth. In many ways he is a plebeian poet of the homely, and there is a keen pathos in this unhappy married man forever seeking an ideal of companionate domestic married love. Waugh's most famous early poem, 'Come Whoam to thi' Childer an Me' (printed in the appendix), concerned the plea of a wife to a drunken husband to leave the pub and return to the home. It was said, by Brierley, that this poem originated in Mary Ann's plea to her husband.

However, when we look more closely at the diary, we see that the Edwin who absents himself from the company of Mary Ann is more often snatching a few hours impassioned religious or political debate in a coffee-house, or a few hours earnest reading of Scott or Emerson, than he is some time in the pubs of Manchester and Rochdale. The profligate Waugh turns out on closer inspection to have been strangely innocent, transparent almost: what agitates his soul is likely to be a failure to pursue his studies, his taking of snuff or tobacco, his failure to behave in a godly way. And agitate his soul these seemingly unheinous failings did, for he was driven by inner demons, usually of his own making. Edwin was addicted less to alcohol than to the narcotics of sorrow and struggle. These he administered in order to comprehend the circumstances of his new life.

After the period of the diary he became a public man.[35] On leaving the Lancashire Public Schools Association Waugh applied for the job of librarian at the Portico Library, a 'gentleman's' library in the city. He was not successful, despite the support of many leading city educationalists. He then worked briefly as secretary to the head of the literary department of the *Manchester Examiner and Times* and for a much longer period as a salesman for a firm of letterpress printers, the same firm that did much of the Association's printing. One is aware of the network of patronage that distinguished the getting of work at all levels of Victorian society. But the break with the world of manual work was never complete: from time to time he returned to his trade as a journeyman printer. These occupations seem to have occupied his time up to his old age in the 1880s. But his real concern, and to some extent his occupation, was literature. He hawked his books around the city and the county, combining this at times with his salesman and jobbing printer work. He earned money from his published work, and later from giving dialect readings of his work within

[35] On Waugh's life, as well as on dialect literature, see also M. Vicinus, *The Industrial Muse: a Study of Nineteenth-Century British Working-Class Literature* (1974).

and beyond Lancashire. It was never very much, and his later life seems to
have been a financially insecure and uncertain one, just as his early days
were. In the 1880s, he moved to the seaside, near Blackpool, and died in
1890.[36]

During the period of the diary Waugh had already begun his literary
endeavours, publishing a literary journal with a colleague at the Association. He was criticised by his employers, these activities taking up an
increasing amount of his time. He published short articles and poems in
the Manchester press through the 1850s, as well as working for the press
for a time, as we have seen. In 1855 he borrowed £120 from a friend in
order to publish *Sketches of Lancashire Life and Localities*, and in 1856 he
sprang to a wider fame with the publication as a penny broadside of
'Come Whoam'.[37] During this time he had become closely associated
with various literary clubs in Manchester, first the 'Sun Inn' club and then
an informal group, the 'Shandeans' (motto: 'Plain living and high thinking'). Both were comprised of men like Waugh, autodidact working men
seeking to realise literary ambitions, but also clerks, newspapermen,
professional people, and some businessmen, a number of whom were
themselves of humble origin.[38] These circles overlapped with the *déclassé*
world of the subaltern, provincial intelligentsia of Liberal England, men
who were active in the press and publishing, and in the various Liberal
lobbies (especially education), as well as in literature, and local history and
folklore (above all dialect studies and writing).[39] Waugh was also a
founder member, in 1862, of the long-lived and very active Manchester
Literary Club.[40] The first edition of his works had been published in
1859, suitably enough dedicated to his fellow radical and townsman, John
Bright. Waugh went on to achieve great fame in the north of England, and
some fair notice in metropolitan circles also.

[36] There is extensive correspondence covering this later phase of Waugh's life, most of it
unrevealing on his personal life, but interesting on his literary activity. See various items in
Manchester Central Library Archives Department, esp. L183, Letters to Edwin Waugh;
and papers and letters held by the Edwin Waugh Dialect Society, Rochdale.

[37] M. Vicinus, *The Industrial Muse*, pp. 192–4, 203–14

[38] For biographical details of some of these see M. Beetham, 'Healthy Reading: the
Periodical Press in Late Victorian Manchester' in A. J. Kidd, *et al.* (eds.), *City, Class and
Culture: Studies of Social Policy and Cultural Production in Victorian Manchester* (Man-
chester 1985).

[39] For consideration of these circles, see P. Joyce, *Visions of the People*, pp. 272–6; also
M. Vicinus, *Industrial Muse*, pp. 203–6; and M. Vicinus, 'Introduction', *Broadside Ballads
of the Industrial North* (Newcastle 1973).

[40] On autodidact writers see also B. E. Maidment, 'Class and Cultural Production in the
Industrial City' in A. J. Kidd, *et al.* (eds.), *City, Class and Culture*; and 'Essayists and
Artisans – The Making of Victorian Self-Taught Poets', *Literature and History*, 9, (Spring
1983).

2   The struggle for the moral life

Edwin Waugh began his diary in May 1847, after pasting in a number of newspaper and other cuttings concerning the use of a diary, and the nature of the life the diary was designed to guide and build. For this man the confessional mode of the diary was a direct intervention in the world, a quite literal exemplification of the text constituting the world. The life that he aimed to build was above all a moral and spiritual life.

In his invocation of the magic of the book Waugh summons the presence of its high priests before beginning his own. 'Reading makes a full man, conversation makes a ready man, and writing an exact man', from Bacon's *Essays*, is followed by Emerson, 'The main enterprise in the world for enterprise and extent is the upbuilding of man' (as we shall see, Emerson the priest of education and improvement is for Waugh almost a god). Another tag he posts in the flyleaves of his diary is 'More people have gone to the gibbet for want of early instruction, discipline and correction, than from any incurable depravity of nature.'[41] Waugh is Enlightenment man, the archetypal 'working man' autodidact in his belief that knowledge is the key to freedom. He is well aware of the watchwords of his chosen path of the book; 'much reading' means 'an abandonment of society' is another of his tags, an invocation this time not of the high priests of the book, but of the received wisdom of his religion's practitioners, working men like himself.

But knowledge is only one key to freedom, and Waugh is more than Enlightenment man. He is a man of the greatest book, a product of the emotional religion of the eighteenth century in its plebeian forms. God is at the centre of his selfhood as well as the Emersonian enterprise of the 'upbuilding of man' in the world. The one is the reflection of the other: as Waugh writes in September 1848, 'The World is the College of God... The Universe is the Book of God, and God of Books.... The Universe is the magnificent reflection of the attributes of the Supreme Being.'[42] For this man of the book, the text of the diary, and the texts of his literary works later, gave access to the universe, to that text of texts, which was at once the Book of God and the God of Books. But before that text was inscribed in the world it was inscribed in him, and it was only by first looking inward that it was ultimately possible to look outward, and embrace the moral life in its fullness in the world and in the upbuilding of one's fellow man.

The moral life concerned the struggle of the autodidact to secure

---

[41] The diary of Edwin Waugh is in MS form in the Manchester Central Library Archives Dept (MS802), also on microfilm.
[42] Diary, 23 September 1848.

knowledge, and the struggle of the soul to reach God. Waugh talks of himself as a 'continual and secret sorrower', of 'holy sorrow'. Among his opening aphorisms he has chosen 'Sorrows are the pulses of spiritual life'. The grief at sin is the spur to the spiritual life. Man is a sinful creature, is continually spurred. Struggle is therefore the intrinsic condition of life, something always to be met with: as another of the young Edwin's tags reminds him, the 'tables of conscience and memory are everlasting'.

The table of ambition is also evident in the young man, and is as evident as conscience in the diary. The moral life was about another kind of struggle too, the struggle of the man of poor and obscure background to secure dignity and freedom by being released from the material needs of the flesh, needs that denied the poor a proper entry to their own inheritance, the world of high culture, the 'bourgeois' world, the workers' dream of 'a bourgeois civilisation without exploitation'. Altruism is the keynote, yet ambition is not a misplaced word. The young Edwin knows he has gifts, and that the cards are stacked against a poor man such as he. The opening aphorism of the diary again offers us a guide: he reassures himself that 'true merit' often 'shines to all but he who has it'. Self-doubt was, and is, the obverse of the autodidact's ambition, and Edwin assures himself that true merit lies behind his doubt. In still another sense the diary is a text intervening in the world, this time the means of the struggle to fend off doubt and realise ambition, to create a persona that will manage the manifold struggles of Edwin Waugh.

His mottos refer to the 'cruelty of disappointing reasonable expectations'. In September 1847 he tells his diary of 'the littleness of myself compared with my desire, and the littleness of the world I live in'.[43] It would be wrong to think that expectation and desire were not for fame, and perhaps for fortune: another of Waugh's introductory texts concerns 'The Secret of Becoming Rich'. Every man who lives within his means has such a hope. 'Independence is one of the greatest safeguards of honesty'. The diary had certain quite utilitarian purposes: arithmetical sums of fantastic complexity were attempted at the end of certain diary entries, and the diarist is clearly using the diary at times to practice his handwriting and his use of language, literal and imaginative. Yet all this is perfunctory. If anything, long diary entries make his hand worse not better (his employers complain of his writing), and the fruit of Edwin's mathematical ability is accounts of his ever-mounting debts and not his ever-growing savings. And, if Waugh sought fame, his pursuit of fortune through a literary career was a singularly inept choice. Even this fame has that innocent, transparent character so often evident: in July 1849, in one of

43 Diary, 6 September 1847.

his usual bouts of self-doubt ('I am no more than an insignificant and obscure scrawler') he none the less testifies to his ambition, but it is 'a restless, constitutional ambition to do something fit for the light, and for the good of the world'.[44] Ambition is in the end realised in moral conduct which exemplifies the moral life.

'The Use of a Diary' stands as the final tag before the door of the real diary. The purpose of keeping a diary in this account is explicitly said to be moral action. It is axiomatic that everything in a diary be put down with scrupulous honesty. Following this Waugh writes some lines 'To My New Book': he wishes he were spotless like the 'unsullied tome' that lies before him. The blank page preaches honesty, the virgin book preaches purity. Let us follow the diarist through the years of his search for the moral life. The tone is set as early as July 1847: all is folly, sin, hopelessness, 'my kernel is rotten', 'I am sick at the core'. The only release is in the grave.[45] A few days later, 'my life is a wild, incongrous dream', and not 'the expression of intellect and conscience'.[46] He prays to God the Redeemer for release.

Release is no nearer the following month: matters seem far worse, for now he has the intellectual conviction of God, but his heart's apprehension of the truth is 'but a cold, blind, groping about'. All could be borne if he had more.[47] It is now that what he calls 'the demon debt' begins to haunt him too.[48] In August he is repeatedly unwell, and out of work, severing his connection with Holden the printer after a quarrel. It is then that he contemplates work in a 'counting house', but his heart and head revolt at the thought.[49] A little after this, without success, he tries to get his old job back. Solace is to be had from books: Scott's *Antiquary* consoles him in one bout of sorrow. At other times it is the Latin lessons he is taking. The warmth of August finds him wandering the woods and fields: at one point he records languishing, reading, in Foxholes Wood, near Rochdale, at noon. There were diversions for the penniless young man. Nor does he seem to have been over-hasty in obtaining work again. One has a first intimation that the sorrows of young Edwin are perhaps sometimes something to be relished, the sign of the suffering, struggling soul, the mark of the romantic individual. November of 1847 finds him, as we have seen 'rejoicing' at his 'fast-abiding grief', luxuriating in his 'holy sorrow'.

Waugh was acutely aware of his life as struggle and sorrow, and one

---

[44] *Ibid*, 18 July 1849.
[45] Henceforth, unless otherwise stated, only dates for diary entries will be given; 21 July 1847.
[46] 24 July 1847.   [47] 13 August 1847.   [48] *Ibid*, see also 11 August 1847.
[49] 8 August 1847.

may glimpse him actively weaving the romantic figure into his own selfhood at this time. He speaks, in the terms of what was by then a cliché of the autodidact's drama, of 'the pursuit of knowledge under difficulties'.[50] He invokes *Pilgrim's Progress*, the language of which was to him 'life-like' and 'natural':[51] in common with other autodidacts he seems to have taken Bunyan's picture of struggle less as allegory than literally.[52] He also invokes the figure of his mother's struggle: 'That poor mother of mine that struggled in poverty and sickness, and obscurity, to teach her little colt of a lad to read in the Scriptures has tended more than all things to make me a Bible lover.'[53] If suffering creates the romantic protagonist, its source is the struggle for the moral life, as exemplified in closeness to God and service to one's fellow human beings. January of 1848 finds him with the usual fear and doubts: 'The world and its witcheries have led me astray and lulled me with its sweets awhile [I have] ... an embittering consciousness of its hollowness.' There is no home, no existence for him but God.[54] He continues in this vein throughout the year, and throughout the diary. Later in 1848 everything he does is 'sickled o'er with the pale cast of thought'. He finishes this entry with, 'Wrote some wretched rhyme, sighed over my ignorance and indolence, and went to bed.'[55] The demon debt again haunts him, just as the demon doubt. By September of the year debt seems almost a real presence to him; it 'torments' him, it is 'spawned in hell': 'Shun sin and debt, and you may defy men and devils to hurt thee.' These 'solder the collar of serfdom upon thy neck for slaves to engrave their names upon'. 'I would be a man', he says, in the eyes of the unerring judge, the Almighty. But being a man also meant the realisation of the 'noble power' within him: 'My only hope of happiness in this world is in the achievement of noble powers, and in a life of noble contemplation and action. But ah ... "Weak is the will of man, his judgements blind / Remembrance presents, and hope betrays."'[56]

There is something morbid and self-indulgent about all this suffering, real though it was. There is certainly something literary. In September he is being threatened with the law by a Unitarian minister he has not paid for the Latin lessons he has received. He is tormented by 'dammed suspicion and misrepresentation'. When he hears a foot on the stairs, 'my flesh creeps'. He contemplates suicide. Having summoned up Macbeth, he now summons Hamlet, and decides against it.[57] Somewhat later, 'I am

---

[50] 6 August 1847.   [51] 18 August 1847.
[52] D. Vincent, *Bread, Knowledge and Freedom*, pp. 192, 193.
[53] 18 August 1847.   [54] 5 January 1848.
[55] 9 September 1848. See also 22 April 1848.
[56] 9 September 1848.   [57] 12 September 1848.

nothing unless I unbosom myself and then I am worse than nothing.'[58] Towards the end of the year he notes that the recent past has been the worst time of his life, the experience of a weight of misery he believes he will never completely rise from again.[59] As will be seen, Waugh went about his life with some gusto in the period of the diary. Yet the narrative of suffering continues unabated right through 1850. Suffering and struggle had taken on a force of their own as indispensable sources of identity as the young Waugh lived through the changed circumstance of these days.

September 1848 finds him, as ever, resolving to 'perform what you ought, and perform without fail what you resolve'. This he translates into an invariably more rich, direct, and powerful vernacular (richer still in its dialect form): 'Brag's a good dog but holdfast is better.' There then follows his new régime: early rising, daily cold washing and 'friction', 'fit food in kind and quantity', 'proper recreation', and so on. In 'mental training' he will begin with arithmetic and history. 'Self denial' will be the order of his day.[60] Through 1849 the unceasing struggle comes to naught but 'bitterness' and 'self-hatred'.[61] In October of that year, when he is longing to see Macready as Othello, and discussing the character of various eating houses in Manchester,[62] he notes (in a romantic vein of representation), that his health trembled fearfully in the balance of life and death, and 'I walked about as silent and pensive as if I was following my own funeral.'[63] Through 1850 'madness and smouldering sorrow are eating at my heart',[64] and he is, as always, keen to begin life anew, to practice self-denial, miserable creature of habit that he is. He alternates despair with recklessness and frivolity, but underneath all is 'bitter desperation' of a pitch only he knows. His days are 'lost in brooding sadness'. As Milton says, 'ever to be weak is the true folly', for to be weak is to be 'the slave of folly'.[65]

In the figure of slave, and of 'the collar of serfdom', we begin to perceive something of the ends of moral struggle: the condition of freedom or independence that is the antitheisis of slavery. It is through Waugh's discussion of the sorrows his marriage brings him that we begin fully to grasp these antitheses, and to be aware of how deeply they were marked in his psyche and his spiritual life. Before considering the marriage and the insight it gives us into the ends of the moral life something remains to be said about Waugh's conjoint religions of God, Man, and the Book.

In late 1847 he is to be found going from church to chapel and back

---

[58] 15 September 1848.   [59] 5 November 1848.   [60] 16 September 1848.
[61] See e.g. 19 July 1849.
[62] 1 October 1849.   [63] 3 October 1849.   [64] 19 January 1850.
[65] See entries for 18–20 March 1850, up to September.

again in search of sentiments he feels worthy of the name of religion. In many respects his Protestantism is typical of the time: 'Every hour convinces me of the insufficency of man himself to preserve and uplift himself ... O God my life is fleeting and I am lingering helplessly in misery and slavery of mind and spirit', is how he writes in November.[66] This language of interior anguish is very typical of Methodism, something well and widely rehearsed in the Methodist chapels of Waugh's youth. It was a language conducive to the idea of the self having an interior centre, but at the same time – in the chapel – the self was directed outwards as a mode of communication, as an element constructing the 'social', in this case the imagined community of the gathered just. But in the same accounts Waugh describes being deeply offended by the character of the service he has just attended at an Anglican church: what is a beautiful service has been rendered in a 'comic' and 'inhuman' way. He talks of clerics such as the one he has just heard: '... when they come down from the altar and doff the surplice they talk with ten-fold the grace and fire about any twopenny-halfpenny affair, because they unconsciously speak from the fullness of the heart, and with warmth and earnestness'.[67] The cleric's religion is a 'counterfeit humanity'; Waugh's religion is a religion of warmth, and of the human heart's fullness, a religion of real humanity. Elsewhere he states his hatred of theological wrangling and the surge of 'invigoration' given to the human spirit by faith and prayer. We will meet with this cult of the heart, of the sincerity of unalloyed human feeling, later.[68] It helped construct another version of the 'social', this time not the gathered and justified, but the mighty collectivity of 'humanity'.

The link between the religions of God and humanity will be amply evident. God is realised in the heart, but also denied in the world of affairs. Waugh at this time inveighs against 'the tendency of the age to believe in itself and the sufficiency of its own achievements', its 'fitful effort to unite the worship of God with the love and pursuit of Mammon'.[69] As with the artisans of mid-century France with whom Rancière deals, the abiding sins are materialism and egotism. The rich trust their riches and not God, theirs is 'dust worship', 'pelf love'. In taking the golden calf to their hearts (saying 'We are the wise, We are the prudent') they deny the 'perfect freedom' found in the kingdom of God and realised in the human heart.

Later in November he went to a lecture on the subject of 'Reading' given by Ralph Waldo Emerson in Manchester. He writes that he was 'so influenced with love for this lofty-minded gentleman that I would have wept like a child when I began to think he would leave the county'.[70] He refers back to the miserable parson he wrote of earlier: 'that miserable man

---

[66] 6 November 1847.   [67] *Ibid.*   [68] 5 January 1848.   [69] 6 November 1847.
[70] 21 November 1847.

in the pontificals on Sunday would need his tone'. As he watches Emerson walk up to the lectern he thinks, 'How beautiful the feet of those who preach the gospel of peace ... My heart is with that man to its last beat.' Later on he talks of feeling 'Emerson's lecture taking root in my mind and whole demeanour as I walked about the streets thinking of man, of God, and of my relations to these. Emerson is turning upside down some of my schemes and questioning my plans for life. He has indeed given me great hints both in his books and in his lectures which my memory will linger over as long as I live.'[71]

It is difficult now to appreciate the great influence of men like Emerson (or of later prophets of humanity and 'the people', such as Thoreau, Whitman, and Tolstoy). Emerson's first lecture tour in Britain was such a failure that he handed over his arrangements to the artisans and clerks of the Metropolitan Early Closing Association. This was his natural audience, one he afterwards fondly referred to as 'my public'. He was received, and propagated, in the penny journals of the time as a man who combined transcendentalism and common sense, a man 'who knows the common thoughts and impulses of ordinary people'. And, as with Waugh, more widely it was the presence of Emerson the man that counted. This was above all a moral presence, one based on what was at the time called 'character'. Emerson was 'a man with a great soul', but one who was read, as his enemy *Blackwood's* put it, 'for the genuine confessions of one spirit to another', and (through the great soul thus democratised as one soul speaking among equals) 'for those lofty sentiments to which all hearts respond'. Even more in his speaking, was this 'great rhapsodist' of letters able to embody the religion of humanity which gave form to these lofty sentiments. For, more than anyone at the time, Emerson reconciled religion, philosophy, and morality, enabling men like Waugh to spiritualise all of life, and all mankind, and so retain a religious outlook and temper and yet reject the evident failures of so much organised religion. Emerson's transcendentalism presented mankind as sharing a common soul, and hence sharing in a divinity inspiring all creation. Mankind, especially mankind in nature, was a fit object for veneration, quite literally the centre of a religion of humanity.[72]

Emerson was only one influence among many working on constitutionally eclectic autodidacts like Waugh, but, through his speaking especially, a powerful one. Douglas Jerrold spoke of Emerson as combining in his speaking, *bonhomie*, earnestness, and a capacity for creating 'veneration' among his audiences. There is something more than this potent mix of the common touch, sincerity, and the quasi-religious, something almost sexual, in Waugh's ceding of his heart and love to Emerson. Women, in particular, for instance the Bright women who will be met with in the next study, flocked to see Emerson in order to witness moral beauty and greatness shine forth from the body of their hero (the Bright sisters also spoke of Carlyle, an influence on working men closely akin to Waugh, as 'most beautiful when descanting upon some character he admires').[73] But for Waugh the bibliophile preoccupations of the autodidact were no doubt uppermost.

'Reading' was, for Emerson, and Waugh, the way in which the 'up-building of man' could be brought about. Emerson was for Waugh a kind of demigod of the book, more than simply its high priest. As in the French case, the anti-materialism of the book, of literature, metaphysics, theology, is the inevitable recourse of the poor man seeking release from the material constraint of his condition. Waugh took most earnestly to Emerson's rejection of self, money, ambition, and his injunction to 'Go till the wastes of human mind'. For Waugh the figure of the poet was perhaps the greatest of all cultivators of the mind. His ambition was to be 'worthy in heart and head of the name of poet'. Not surprisingly, the Romantic poets most closely fitted this holy character: Wordsworth's death in 1850 called forth a eulogy on the 'poet and priest' from a stunned Waugh. Other poets were no less important: in 1850 Waugh was also a devotee of Milton, joining a Milton Club in the city.[74] The figure of Burns the plebeian poet of the plebeity was perhaps the most powerful of all to him.

The faculty of the 'imagination' was central, differentiating the poet, and Waugh himself therefore, from his fellows. In September 1848 he attended a soirée of the Lancashire Public Schools Association, mixing in the company of the upper-class people he was often, as we shall see, uncomfortable with.[75] Yet these 'most famed intelligent men in the county ... all seemed to me to be more remarkable for clear perceptions of what are called "practical affairs" than for fine imagination. There was more of brain eyesight than of fine perceptions of a delicate and intelligent enthusiasm – There were no men who thought and felt and spoke like Emerson ...' This 'fine imagination' he sought in the company of friends; talking, and drinking, into the night in earnest discussions of Burns, mixing in the bookshops Waugh sometimes felt to be almost a second home to him, in particular the shop of James Weatherley, which at this time seems to have been situated in the run-down, city-centre Shude-hill area of Manchester, the city's mecca for cheap bookshops and the

---

[73] When he visited their house in 1847; Bright Family Papers, Darbashire Papers 3, Priscilla Bright to Margaret Priestman, 19 September 1947.
[74] 25, 26 April 1850.   [75] 28 September 1848.

ballad trade.[76] It is to Shudehill that he would come to buy books when he could, or sell them, if forced to by some calamity. For it took great misfortune to make him dispense with his books: at several points in the diary he says he is forced to choose between bread and books, and chooses books. Quite literally, for this man, books were therefore the bread of life. But as we follow him into Shudehill, and into his pursuit of bread, we are aware of the daily life of the present pressing in on 'fine imagination', and on the pursuit of the moral life.

3   The ends of the moral life

The new situation Waugh found himself in after moving to the city was in very important measure dictated by his marriage to the illiterate Mary Ann. She is wanting 'even the barest school education' he reports. Only months after the marriage he is talking of 'the ignorant girl who has been ruined by a mother more ignorant than herself'. Petted and waited on by this mother, there is no living with her in order and cleanliness. It is all 'a miserably bad bargain'. Yet he defends her and her likes against the education à la mode of 'misbred' young ladies: she has the dignity that she can get her own living by her hands (as a sempstress) without much discomfort.[77] And this ignorant girl, this bad bargain, is also 'at once a pleasure, a revelation, a mystery and a misery' to him.[78]

By January he confesses to never having felt 'so soiled a thing in my life ... The day is eaten up with coarse cavils that make me disgusted and distrest for me and for her.' She is 'helpless', 'sluttish', 'miserable', unable to wait on herself let alone a home.[79] Mary Ann did not meet up with Edwin's expectations, expectations that seem to have been very much conventional for his time, whether with the poor or the upper classes: in 1849, when visiting the home of a seller of Chartist publications in Manchester, he notes how a 'clean and tasteful' home depends most of all on the wife. Women working in factories from early days do not make 'clever, cleanly housewifes'.[80]

About this time he wrote at some length of one of their frequent arguments, speaking of

that repulsive coarseness of deportment which she puts on so frequently to the utter damnation of all that is attractive in her appearance and disposition. She demeaned herself to me with an unfeeling rudeness that turned my stomach, and

[76] 23 September 1848 entry – Weatherley's diary is in the Chetham's Library, Manchester.
[77] 23 August 1847 and 6 August 1847.   [78] 4 October 1847.
[79] 20 January 1848.
[80] 16 July 1849.

let loose her vituperative tongue 'before folk' in a way that disgusted me, and filled me with smothered indignation and sorrowful hopelessness. She seemed hard and careless and as if she had no notion of having behaved in anyway wrongfully to me . . .'[81]

A frequent criticism of her, and of her family, was that of 'blackguard-ism', by which he meant in part the giving of false witness (as when his wife's brother brought an action against him, in which his wife appeared in court on the brother's behalf, or when her relative's 'blackguard' him to his employer). He also meant, and perhaps meant most feelingly of all, the 'repulsive coarseness' of which he speaks, and particularly its public unashamed display. It is not that she wants education so much, nor that she is a bad housekeeper, and least of all that he is not attracted to her (for through most of this he says he loves and is as 'jealous as hell' of her, this woman who is both a 'pleasure' and a 'revelation' to him), but that living with her in continuous strife breeds behaviour which wounds him to the quick, 'soils' him, 'disgusts' him, 'turns his stomach'. The public display of coarseness, 'blackguardism', seems to mortify him before all else in his relations with his wife. And this extended to his own behaviour as well, in his response to his wife. In November 1848, after calling on Mary Ann at her brothers at Lower Shore in Rochdale, and encountering her mother 'swearing, ripping and tearing', he begins to emulate her in 'filthy and disgusting language'.[82] 'The wind stood still and looked on in astonishment.' Pursued by brutal and public insult since before the marriage, especially by the mother, he replies in the same vein only to be consumed by self-disgust; 'my whole demeanour so warped from stern propriety. The worst that can befall me.'[83]

Let us examine further this worst that could befall Edwin Waugh. We could discuss 'stern propriety' as the stuff of which Victorian 'hypocrisy' was made. We would be wrong to do this. Certainly, Waugh was an exceedingly difficult man to live with, even on his own account, which reveals an ambitious, touchy person, bent on his own concerns. And we only have his account: Mary Ann is a mostly silent presence in the diary, the recipient of terms like 'ignorant' and 'sluttish'. It is impossible now to reconstruct her side of the story. Nevertheless, we can be sure that if books were the bread of life to Edwin, they were not so for the young Mary Ann, who before too long had three children to rear. In the diary accounts of his movements, Edwin is often out of the house, visiting his new friends in Manchester, or staying late into the evening at pubs and coffee houses. Although he does not seem to have led a dissolute life, necessary resources were spent on his socialising: at one point in the diary, in 1850 when she

[81] Cited in M. Vicinus, *The Ambiguities of Self-Help*, pp. 14–15.
[82] 5 November 1848.   [83] See also 3 October 1849.

went back to Rochdale with the children, Mary Ann says that she will go back to him if he will give her his earnings (she seems to have demanded *all* his earnings).[84]

It is the silences in the diary that are revealing. Waugh says little about his day-to-day life with his wife, except for graphic accounts of the quarrels. Just as his time is taken up with his life outside the home, so is the space of his diary. He has even less to say about his young child (it is not clear when the others followed, during or after the period of the diary). If the truth can not now be put together, whatever the truth was, then it is evident that the charges of selfishness and hypocrisy have some force: self-improvement was always to some degree about the self, and the concern with moral conduct was a concern with propriety in the public sphere as well as the conduct of the soul. The pursuit of the moral life sat easily with the gender presuppositions of the time: a 'clever, cleanly housewife' who would sit quietly in the home was a helpful adjunct to self-improvement. Such charges have force, but are in the end beside the point. The tradition of 'working class' autobiography, of which his diary is in part a product, takes us directly into the world of the self-taught worker, and hence of the 'working-class' activist and leader.

As David Vincent has shown,[85] the roots of popular autobiography in the nineteenth century lay in the seventeenth century, in the confessional diary and the religious autobiography. The narrative of spiritual development which these embodied had come, by the early nineteenth century, to involve a relationship between the soul and the world understood in terms of time and space, of the soul as existing in and through the world: 'The true state of man's soul could only be known through his experience of external reality. To discover God, man first had to discover himself.'[86] This knowledge came to be located in the individual's everyday life therefore. Above all, narratives of spiritual development were now based on the right of every individual to determine his own spiritual identity, an identity which was inseparable from his social identity. The force of the Protestant tradition is obvious: all that stood between a man and his maker was the Bible, which all men were privy to according to their own consciences. Waugh draws on this tradition, but his is not a spiritual narrative *per se*. In him, the social is even more intermixed than in the earlier tradition. But the all-embracing drive to determine identity is central: overriding family, wealth and fame were the desires of the individual to assert independence in the pursuit of independence, to be a free

84 See M. Vicinus, *The Ambiguities of Self-Help.*
85 D. Vincent, *Bread, Knowledge and Freedom*, pp. 14–19.
86 *Ibid*, p. 16.

man seeking the condition of freedom. These were the ultimate ends of the moral life.

Vincent notes the absence of discussion of private, intimate family life in popular autobiography.[87] This was partly because writers lacked a language, or practice in a written language, which would do justice to the emotions involved. But most of all it lay in the belief that much of home and family life was simply either irrelevant or subordinate to the central pursuit of improvement and independence. Waugh ignored Mary Ann not out of selfishness so much as out of conviction. In this he was no exception: as Vincent shows, wives and sweethearts were not seen as equal partners in the search for knowledge and freedom. Learning was in spite of, and not because of, daily life. Children were also unseen as part of this struggle: '.. they do not seem to feel that their interaction with their children had any measurable effect on their moral personality, or conversely that the fortunes of their children ... was any serious reflection of the autobiographer's moral strength and weakness ... they appear to have no desire to live their lives through their children ... They were not prepared to abdicate their hopes or their responsibilities in favour of the next generation.'[88] This did not mean that these men were not often, and usually, deeply affectionate to their wives and children. It was simply that the drive to determine identity was located elsewhere than in the circle of the domestic affections. It simply did not occur to Waugh that Mary Ann mattered, or, rather, mattered in the ways that subsequent generations have felt to be important.

In other ways she mattered greatly, and it is in Waugh's profoundly felt sense of the worst that could befall him, the fall from stern propriety evident in the 'blackguard' behaviour of his wife and her kin, that we gain insight into the workings of independence. It is the very force, the violence, of Waugh's reaction to 'repulsive coarseness' that helps us here. For, far from 'Victorian hypocrisy', the concern with 'stern propriety' went right to the heart of moral conduct, and hence the ends of the moral life. What was sinned against when propriety was contravened was the sense of order, itself linked to the capacity for control over one's self and one's condition of life.[89] This in turn involved an independence from things, from the constraints of disorder and ignorance, dirt and squalor. Waugh's quite dramatic response to 'repulsive coarseness' lay in the fact that for him the coarse was the ultimate denial of (and ever-present threat

[87] *Ibid*, pp. 40–6.   [88] *Ibid*, pp. 44–5.

[89] P. Joyce, *Visions of the People*, chap. 6, esp. pp. 151–6, see also pp. 297–300. But see above, pp. 12, 25–6, where I indicate the shortcomings of presenting 'poverty' and 'insecurity' as present in 'experience' prior to discourse, and so dictating a pattern of response in which a 'need for 'order' and 'control' are intrinsic to this supposed experience.

to) everything for which he strove; for the 'bourgeois civilization' that was the antithesis of the coarse. Waugh's sensitivity to the coarse was, however, only part of a larger pattern of oppositions that expressed his metaphysical struggle. It represents but one individual inflection of a pattern extending beyond his struggle to the metaphysical struggle of all the poor.[90] The coin of poverty displayed ignorance on one side, knowledge on the other, blackguardism as against propriety, the bestial and the spiritual, order and disorder, as well as the coarse and the refined, the barbarous and the civilised. These oppositions, to which were related dirt and cleanliness, defined the struggle for the moral life, and it was in their terms that the ends of this life come to be defined.

July 1847 finds Waugh inveighing against the 'crowd of electioneering guzzlers and creeping slaves' that hang around the skirts of the Tory party in Rochdale, and crowd the shop of Holden at election times.[91] A few days later he describes 'the chatter of whiskered monkeys, the fume of cigars, the clashing of pots, the splashing of ale, and the oaths and ribaldry of beasts ... I heard one of these pigs in the garb of gentlemen say ... "his insides wur as raw uz a collops".'[92] The motif of the slave is again evident, something apparent already in the diary, and echoed powerfully in 'the collar of serfdom' which sin and debt force the bondsman to wear. The creeping slave is equated with the beast here, and drink is seen, in these forms, to involve the enslavement of the condition of the beast. The pig is in the garb of the gentleman, gentility representing the antithesis of bestiality.

Waugh dwells on these terms throughout the diary. Two years later, he reserved his most venomous language for the (unnamed) 'swinish parson–magistrate' of Littleborough Chapel, near Rochdale. While waiting at a country pub be records joining in the collective abuse of this man, 'notorious for greed and guzzling'.[93] But it is the working man himself who perhaps most detains him in his concern with the condition of slavery. In August 1847 he went into a shop successfully set up by a working man, and notes how he had overcome 'that condition which to such masses of working men of like condition seems such a helplessly unconquerable condition of life-long slavery'. This man has won for himself 'more freedom and grace of position in relation to the ... selfish world of competing toilers and traders that he daily dwells among'.[94] For Waugh this 'freedom and grace of position' involved 'more pleasure and leisure, more physical happiness', but most of all it concerned 'intellectual improvement'.

The 'helplessly unconquerable condition of life-long slavery', 'the

[90] See below, pp. 74, 76–9.   [91] 29 July 1847.   [92] 30 July 1847.
[93] 20 July 1849.   [94] 6 August 1847.

selfish world of competing toilers', could be overcome however. What could be attained, 'freedom and grace of position', went beyond happiness and improvement to a realisation of the trueness of the human heart represented in the guise of the gentleman or gentlewoman. In a Deansgate shop in September 1848 Waugh was outraged by the owner, a shoe dealer, who abused a poor woman beggar who had come into the shop, begging timidly in her tattered dress. In a kind of epiphany Waugh describes being deeply moved by the 'gentlewoman', an 'angel of mercy', who followed the beggar to give her money: 'Deansgate never seemed so grand to me. God bless that gentlewoman's heart.'[95] Gentility represented a condition of the heart therefore, not a social condition: this gentlewoman's heart was but one manifestation of that true humanity all were heir to. In Waugh's literature, the real heirs to this humanity are often seen to be the poor, those nearest the harsh realities that reveal true nobility of character. This cult of the heart, of sincerity, is almost a religion in itself.

Other of the oppositions mentioned are also apparent, for instance that between dirt and cleanliness. There was no living in cleanliness and order with the wife of young Edwin. Several times in the diary he writes of his mother's house as a haven of cleanliness. He notes in his diary when he is praised, by his employer, for his cleanliness. The practical and spiritual significance of the contrast between dirt and cleanliness is obvious, given the economic (and environmental) condition of the poor at this time, just as the contrast of hunger and plenty went far beyond the immediate and practical to irradiate the whole symbolic universe of the poor.[96] Town and country, industry and agriculture, also served as a dramatisation of the condition of the poor and of their search for independence. From early on in the diary Waugh records the pleasure he takes in flowers (he provides long accounts of what he has seen on his walks).[97] Flowers bring a kind of peace of mind.[98] The city brings a kind of nightmare. Of the changes Waugh lived through at this time the move to Manchester was not the least important. Manchester was 'a hell of soot and stench'.[99] He speaks of 'the gin house routine of money grubbing Manchester',[100] and cites Wordsworth on nature as the educator of man. Nature has wisdom as well as reviving balm to give us. He took the same message from Emerson also. True release, true independence, was to be found in the realisation of human identity and spiritual purpose in the world of nature: the agricultural occupation was 'manly and sweetly natural', those in the city were 'slaves at the sedentary town crafts'. In seeking pleasure theirs is often a

[95] 19 September 1848.   [96] P. Joyce, *Visions of the People*, pp. 286–7.
[97] E.g., 25 July 1847.
[98] See press cuttings at start of diary.   [99] 18 September 1848.
[100] 26 April 1848.

kind of desperation, for they seek 'to suck all the pleasure they can get out of it, after the Manchester fashion, work while they work, play while they play'.[101]

In the city one was pent up, in the country free. The city taught what was artificial, the country what was natural. The book of nature was consulted by Waugh throughout his personal and literary life: it was in a mythical world of domestic-industrial production, close to nature, that he situated many of his more influential fictions. Nature revealed a spiritual and human essence common to all people. This notion of innate, immanent, qualities present in all people was especially evident in the political sphere, where the rhetoric of slave and tyrant was particularly evocative.

Waugh believed in 'man's natural instinct for liberty', a phrase be used in describing a lecture on Cromwell he attended in April 1848.[102] He went on, 'while I listened to his [the lecturer's] portraiture of the noble band of souls who confounded and crushed the despotic and despicable tyrant who set his infamous will against the liberties and lives of the people ... I felt myself nobly moved with a sense of the dignity and power of right principles in man's nature.' This made him hopeful of the destiny of his race, despite 'all the slaves on earth and devils in hell'. The 'instinct for liberty' has 'turned the world upside down' and 'smashed to atoms' the tyrants who would stand in its way.

Waugh further contrasted this instinct for liberty with 'the pettiness and disgusting meanness' of sectarianism, something against which he struggled in his working life.[103] The Wesleyans from which he sprang were not immune. They were, as he put it, 'proverbial for their pharisaical pride and intolerance'.[104] The invocation of the figures of slave, tyrant, and liberty drew both on present political and religious conflicts, and on the long history that had preceded these conflicts, and to which Waugh was so evidently an heir. But it also drew on his more immediate relationship to the economic situation of his day. In July 1849 he reported on the condition of factory operatives in Rochdale. Their lives were dominated by their employer, a 'manufacturing feudal lord' who was a 'griper and domineerer', of over-bearing manner to his operatives. They lacked everything but hard work, which was doled out to them 'on the principle of none at all or too much'. Their condition is believed to be fast approaching Irish levels (Waugh was greatly exercised by the inhumanity of the Irish Famine). Waugh cares for their bodies, but it is their moral and spiritual life that concerns him most. As long as they can weave flannel 'all else that enriches their possibilities may go to hell for aught the majority of

---

[101] 27 September 1849.   [102] 18 April 1848.   [103] 13 September 1848.
[104] 18 September 1848.

their employers care'.[105] It is absolutely characteristic of the time, of its religion of the heart, that it is the employers who are held to suffer for this as well as the operatives. *Their* human and spiritual essence is denied by their activity: the masters live in comfort, but 'cannot rid themselves of a kind of compensatory care that rides them continuously. They are not happy men. Ringing much employment out of the gains of the system . . . is no more than a pig's paradise . . . What they gain in physical enjoyment they lose in spiritual value.' This 'pig's paradise' was the opposite of the condition of true independence, and the access the condition gave to realising the religion of the human heart. It is to that religion, to what was in fact a cult of the heart, that I shall now turn.

4   The cult of the heart

As we have seen, Waugh drew little solace or pride from his work. Though he applauded the objects of the Association, and supported them strongly, he found the actual nature of clerical labour irksome. The particular terms of his work for the Association were doubly irksome: his wages depended on how many contributions he canvassed. This he hated, as it contravened the independence he so earnestly sought: he felt that he lacked the 'beggarly eloquence' necessary for this task.[106] There is little sign that he felt manual work to be any more rewarding in itself: as he says in September 1847, when he was working as a typesetter for the Tory newspaper proprietor Thomas Sowler in Manchester (the murders and 'police news' of newspapers he found disgusting), 'I have nothing for it but my labour – tis for the bare life.'[107] Work is seen without sentiment, as a necessity. However, as a necessity, it is to be valued in so far as it leads to independence of character: as was seen in Waugh's favourable comparison of his wife with idle, 'misbred' young ladies, hers is the dignity which comes of being able to get a living with one's own hands.

Want and the necessity it brings are also registered in an unsentimental way. Debt was at times a consuming concern. To some extent he brought debt upon himself, by his (mild) indulgence and his quite apparent lack of financial foresight. Near the end of his diary he gave an elaborate account of his debts: owing sums varying between 5 shillings and 6 pounds 10 shillings, he was in debt to twenty-eight people for a total amount of 60 pounds, a phenomenal amount for a poor man in his day.[108] None the less, though typesetting may have been reasonably well paid, his clerical

[105] 20 July 1849.   [106] 13 September 1848.   [107] 10 September 1847.
[108] 16, 19 March 1850.

work was miserably remunerated, especially for a man aiming to support a family.

Throughout this period the diary gives a fairly unrelieved picture of poverty, logging it in an almost neutral fashion. On Sundays he is frequently forced to stay in all day because he does not have clothes respectable enough to go to church in.[109] During one such acute period of poverty he complains that there are not two potatoes in the house to make a meal.[110] He is forced to choose between food, and the few books he has left. Later in the same year he is without a halfpenny worth of candle in the house to write by.[111] In spring 1848 he speaks of being 'uncommonly comfortable tonight', the cause being 'the luxury of a three-legged deal table, without paint, and four chairs, the first articles of furniture to grace our dwelling here' (this after some three months in their Manchester residence it seems). Previously they had made do with two, borrowed, deal chairs, and a table, itself almost unfit for use. It is not clear whether it was for the old or the new table, but his wife mended the frocks of neighbours' children in return for the use of a table.[112] As with labour, poverty is seen without illusion. But, again like work, it is always seen in moral terms, and always with the drawing of moral lessons, lessons which, as will be seen in the tale of his old and humble table, led directly into Waugh's elaboration of the cult of the heart, and hence his literature. It is only when the resources of Waugh's moral vision are brought to bear on poverty that it takes on its real significance for him (and for others).

So, we have a worker who does not dwell on the glories of work, mental or manual. However, like those French workers who invented the notion of artisan work and artisan traditions, this does not mean that mythical work is absent, even though real (intolerable and degrading) work so often is. Something of this may be understood by the ways in which Waugh depicts factory operatives in his diary, and his picture of hand-loom weavers and others in the semi-industrial, semi-rural 'country' districts of the south of Lancashire. The differences are subtle: he is quite capable of presenting a picture of factory operatives, such as his own relations in Rochdale, living in some comfort and, seemingly, in content-ment. But in other situations, when independence is not theirs, as in the case of the Rochdale 'manufacturing feudal lord' just described, they exemplify perfectly that 'helplessly unconquerable condition of life-long slavery' which Waugh found so marked in the ranks of the toilers: 'Among the labourers, who live in fear and trembling, from hand to mouth, there is

[109] 17 September 1848. See also 25 July 1847.   [110] 20 September 1848.
[111] 26 November 1848.
[112] 20 July 1849.

a vast amount of physical and mental suffering, which is for the most part unheard of . . .'

In accompanying his friend from the Association, Francis Espinasse, who went to deliver a lecture on 'The Education of Lancashire' to the Miles Platting Mechanics' Institute in July 1849, Waugh contrasted the 'dull-looking and uneducated factory workers' with 'a knot of men like handloom weavers' who congregated after the lecture to sing Wesleyan hymns.[113] It was into this cultural legacy that he was at once drawn, he and Espinasse joining in the singing, and his own childhood flooding back to him. By 1849 handloom weaving was long in catastrophic decline. The men Waugh identifies seems to have held on to some public signs of their calling none the less. He represents a living culture in decline therefore: his uncle Bob was a handloom weaver, and he reproduces his dialect speech with warmth and humour in the diary, but it is suggestive that this uncle is eager to take up with his nephew the possibility of a son getting a place in a counting house where he could be drilled in writing and business habits.[114]

Waugh also represented what was by the mid-century a swelling body of myth, that of the golden age of the handloom weaver. Whether the 'knot' of men Waugh saw in Miles Platting were weavers is unknown, but it is of some interest that if they were not, the spectator Waugh had a clear shape in his mind of how this occupation should appear. For the most part, Waugh's picture of this distinctive occupational presence draws its force from his account of the past, not the present. In describing the slavery of some modern operatives, he dwelt lovingly on his mother's life in her first marriage. The 'working folks' from which she and he came, made a living by weaving flannel for Newalls (putters out at Hare Hill, near Rochdale). The family had several pairs of looms, and employed a few workmen. The husband was Newall's huntsman, and kept a pack of beagles. His mother's home he judged to be the best furnished and cleanest in the neighbourhood.[115] As we have seen, Edwin Waugh gloried in the independence which he believed marked his family back through the generations, and which if mocked by the poverty of his childhood was none the less the aspiration of his kind, particularly of his mother. In representing a culture already in decline by drawing on his own knowledge, Waugh was already mythologising work, already fishing in the past for its meaning. This process was in turn to underpin the mythologising of work that went on in his literature, and in the literature of all the other dialect writers who, often even more than Waugh, were responsible for the invented tradition of the handloom weavers.

[113] 16 July 1849.   [114] 19 July 1849.   [115] 20 July 1849.

Waugh went beyond the weaver to characterise all 'country labour' as true labour. Let us move away from the diary to his unpublished notebooks and jottings of 1854, and to the north-east Cheshire village of Mottram, a place where agricultural, proto-industrial, and industrial pursuits were still mixed. He noted:

There is something fine and pure in the hearts of the people that live there thought I. And a whole world of beautiful cottage life that I know of among the class that live by labour in the country parts of the manufacturing districts ... the round of daily work cheerfully done, the sweetly-earned, and sweetly-eaten meals – the simple, hardy habits, – the traits of simple, sterling piety, – the purity and the independence and bravery that I have seen in some of the cottages of my native country, and I could not help thinking that such spots were sheltered from some of the worst dangers of earth, and nearer to heaven than the rest of the world.[116]

Waugh does not omit work, though it is less real work than invented work that emblematises class: he quite naturally adopts the terminology of class – 'the class that lives by labour in the country districts', the 'working folks' from which he came. Elsewhere work is given as a badge of identity: he writes of 'working men', 'the working people', and 'the working classes',[117] though it is true that on the whole 'class' is infrequently used, and never in the singular. Waugh therefore helps us understand what was earlier referred to as the dialectic of the acceptance and the rejection of class. Work, mythical work, was an assertion of the dignity and humanity of the worker in a world sometimes all too ready to deny these. Waugh was at all times keen to defend the humanity of the humble: the Rochdale workingman co-operator who befriended him in his early days, Charles Howarth, was for Waugh 'a king o' men, for a' that' (in Burns' parlance), even though he was humble.[118] Mythical work, and the class identity it represented, could be the basis of class distinctions when the worker's dignity was trampled on. But that dignity was expressed above all in being human, and work was in the end but a means to realising this all-embracing 'humanity'.

The heart, not the intellect, was at the centre of this condition. We have already seen the cult of the heart at work in Waugh's religion of God, Man, and the Book.[119] This involved always speaking from 'the fullness of the heart', a religion of true as opposed to 'counterfeit humanity', one warm and earnest in its feelingness. The denial of this by ranting parsons moved Waugh to a dialect denunciation in September 1849, which, if comic in tone, none the less summons up in the figure of Satan the force of his feelings,

[116] 'Unpublished Pieces', Manchester Central Reference Library, Archives Department.
[117] See e.g., 23, 24 March 1850.   [118] 23 November 1847.
[119] See above, pp. 41–2, 46–9.

I' th' seven, one day
Th' parsons ul pray
An rant an roar abeawt salvation
But th' tother six
Ur o Belangs owd Nicks
He may lap hiz tal round th' congregation.[120]

If the heart was the centre of humanity, its truest fullness was to be found in what was simple, genuine, honest, unaffected. All men and women were heir to this simplicity: the account of the Scots ballad heard on a Manchester street in 1850 which opened this study speaks of the universal appeal from the heart of a man to all hearts that beat after. The simplicity of Burns exemplified this, as did the simplicity of Bunyan and Cervantes. To Waugh, Cervantes' characters, Sancho Panza above all, exemplified the wisdom of goodheartedness and simplicity. If all people were heirs to this, it was the humble and the poor who had the most immediate access, not, it should be said, the 'worker'. It was they who were untrammelled by the 'witcheries' of the world, by 'dust worship' and 'pelf love'. It was Burns the 'ploughman poet', Bunyan the chronicler of Everyman, the servant Sancho Panza, who most nobly embodied the ideal. Transcending these, it was Waugh's mother, the archetypal 'working-class mother', struggling in want and obscurity who seems to have mattered here.

For it was these constructions put upon want that most eloquently taught the lessons of the heart, and it is here we return to Waugh's tale of a table. Writing his diary late at night, as was his practice, he dwelt not only on the luxury of the new table he had, but on the moral lessons of the old. In so doing one is aware of him transmuting the conditions of his life into the conditions of his art, for this moralising of the quotidian and exaltation of the humble was to be central to his later writing. He speaks of the affection that has grown up between him and the rickety red table that has been replaced, and explicitly draws a moral lesson from the 'forbearance and humility of the little deal table ... It bore with equal good will and faith my brown bread and my bible.' There was 'no sham about it'. He grieves that men do not treat their fellows as he has treated the table, knowing its weaknesses and treating it accordingly.[121]

Waugh's emphasis on the poor as the noblest embodiments of the heart's truth creates something like a 'language of class': a discourse about the condition of humanity is inflected with the accents of the poor and the simple; to some extent, but less so, also with those of work and the labourer. But, at least for this man, and I think for most of his poor contemporaries, this inflection involved an underlying aspiration to, and a

[120] 2 September 1849, second of three verses.   [121] 15 April 1848.

belief in, concord, a concord stemming from the conviction that all people were heirs to 'the workers' dream'.

In reporting his lack of social grace at this time, Waugh wrote of 'a sort of rustic akwardness about me', of being

never a deft fellow at those pantomime graces which are generally so largely incorporated with what is called 'good address'... I have always been conscious of a certain politeness by fits, no less astonishing to others than to myself, when I have thought about it ... from some sorts of people particularly, especially with rich men and men of authority, I felt a painful shrinking, as if all my sympathies were suddenly congealed. I was only tolerable and easy then, when left silent and still. If I attempted to speak and move it was generally akwardly and painfully.[122]

On seeking work at the firm of Brights in Rochdale in 1847 he also commented on 'the infernal diffidence' shackling him in such encounters, 'my confused ungainly manner in such affairs'.[123]

It was into the direct human encounter that Waugh carried his knowledge of the heart. The fundamental equality this knowledge betokened was a means of interpreting, rendering bearable, the painful shrinking, the congealed sympathies, the infernal diffidence, so evident not only to Waugh, but to very many poor people when they encountered their 'betters' in Victorian and Edwardian England.[124] The baroque complexity and oppressive weight of the rituals governing human interaction, and hence denying human fellowship (registered in the dismissive negativity of 'pantomime graces' and 'good address'), were both in turn instrumental in further validating the cult of the heart.

The cult became the major root of Waugh's writing, just as it was of his life. The 'life', the diary, and the work are indissoluble. The texts of the diary and the work were not reflections of the life therefore, but active interventions in it, shaping its course. As we have seen, the diary of the young Edwin, particularly in creating the personae of the sorrowing, suffering man, was a means of finding a way through the many tensions that beset his life. And the life became in turn a kind of story, in which were acted out the imperatives of his art, imperatives in turn drawn from the problems he faced and the cult of the heart through which he knew these problems. Nowhere is this clearer than in the later life of Waugh, when he began to adopt the rustic, homespun, honest personae of his characters, above all 'Besom Ben', the broom-maker of the Rochdale moorlands.

It was reported of him later in life that the old Waugh, 'a born gentleman', clothed himself in 'honest homespun', and invariably wore huge, unpolished boots, with a 'shepherd's plaid' thrown over his

[122] M. Vicinus, *Ambiguities of Self-Help*, p. 10.   [123] 18 August 1847.
[124] For a discussion see P. Joyce, *Visions of the People*, pp. 157–8.

shoulder, and a countryman's stick in his hand.[125] The personae of his characters were reworked in Waugh's public reading, and came eventually to inhabit the daily existence of the man. The cult of the heart was embodied in his material life, and through appearances Waugh strove to control the world of appearances, the realm of the public, the 'pantomime graces' of encounters between the socially high and the socially low. In the figure of the honest rustic Waugh was neither, not the condescending gentleman nor the coarse, 'blackguard' worker: 'Rather than compete socially, or fall back into the lower classes, Waugh took on the pose of an educated and humorous rustic. In time the world came round to him.'[126] He also seems to have come round to the world, for instead of the agony of the social encounters reported for his early life, at the end of his life it was stated that '... his bearing showed no timidity nor restraint in the presence of persons who were his social superiors'.[127]

The logic of the cult of the heart, however, was that those of superior position in the world who yet acted out the dictates of the heart were welcomed with a warmth which exceeded the coldness felt for the snobberies of the rich. Hence the seemingly disproportionate veneration for the true gentleman, and the true gentlewoman, in the diary (seen for instance in the case of the beggar and the lady in the Deansgate shop): such people had fought with just as much fervour as the humble poor to assert their true feelings. And they were to be praised for it.

Waugh provides revealing descriptions of his encounters with the better off in society. In July 1849 he visited the Oldham home of a fellow canvasser with the LPSA. His friend's father was the manager of Oldham Gas Works. Waugh is forcibly struck with the fact that though teetotallers, the family offer him a drink, as well as a cigar. He admires their courtesy, their delicate sense of his individuality,[128] in contrast to the 'ungraceful and repulsive' teetotal 'crew' with which he was wont to mix at Scott's Temperance Hotel in Manchester.[129] These were 'ignorant, carping, shallow brained', but above all 'frosty hearted' in their intolerant rejection of simple pleasure. Another young gentleman, this time closer to his heart, his friend Francis Espinasse, he criticises for contravening a different attribute of true gentility. In summer 1849 he frequented the Blue Bell pub in Strangeways, Manchester. There, with 'a ludicrously patronising air' Espinasse displayed his 'damned Scotch generosity', flinging down the change from a round of drinks for the waiter to take. The patronising Espinasse betrayed the central tenet of independence, and earned for

[125] G. Milner, 'Introduction', *Lancashire Sketches*, p. xxviii.
[126] M. Vicinus, *Ambiguities*, p. 36.
[127] G. Milner, *Lancashire Sketches*, p. xxxviii.   [128] 25 July 1849.
[129] 24 March 1850.

himself the mockery of the landlord's family, and of the much-amused clientele of the whole pub.[130] The mockery of the low born complemented the cult of the heart.

The sense of spiritual communion with his fellows that this cult created is perhaps best evident in Waugh's account of an excursion to Blackpool he went on in the September of 1849.[131] He woke at five, 'his wife not ready, nor disposed to be'. This time he will not let her incurable tardiness keep him at home. He walks towards Salford Station, bantering with some mechanics at a breakfast stall along the way, close to what was once Cobden's residence. To his delight he is slowly joined by a throng of excursioners, working people, especially working girls. Being taken up by the throng of upwards of two thousand people at the station he exclaims, 'I felt that the world was one house, and all men and women in it dear relations.' In the course of the day he reports delighting again in his 'dear relations', in the innocence and charm of children, in the good company he finds in his carriage there and back, the company of working women and an old teetotal reed-maker, also a 'modest-looking young man, seemingly of the clerk species' (though modesty is anything but the character of the Manchester clerk he says). From nature, from the sea, he derives pleasure, but most of all from the 'one house' of all the men and women of the world. When we turn from the diary to the literary work it is evident how the goal of independence, and the realisation of the trueness of the human heart this goal brought, were translated into terms which powerfully shaped the outlook of the labouring poor of the time, far beyond the ranks of the autodidact alone.

5   'God bless these poor folks'

To explore the hold of Waugh on the popular imagination needs consideration of his influence on other writers, particularly those who wrote directly for a popular audience. Waugh wrote in this way, though, true to his religion of humanity, he wrote for all people (he was certainly taken up by an upper class-audience, for whom expensive, annotated versions of his works were published).[132] In particular, Waugh had a profound influence on John Hartley and Joe Wilson, the two most influential writers

[130] 26 July 1849.
[131] 27 September 1849. See also Waugh's long, very interesting and very sympathetic account of the variety and gregariousness of Knott Mill Fair in Manchester, 6 April 1850.
[132] For discussion of the differing audiences of the dialect literature, see P. Joyce, *Visions of the People*, pp. 256–67.

in the two regions outside Lancashire which were the other great centres
of dialect writing, industrial Yorkshire and the industrial north-east.
Hartley said he had no thought of writing literature until he picked up a
book of Waugh's verse. Wilson also declared his vast debt to Waugh, as
did many of Waugh's contemporary authors in Lancashire, of his own
and subsequent generations. In the next section John Hartley, editor of
the big-selling Halifax *Illuminated Clock Almanack*, will be considered:
Hartley and his almanac (one of a large number of decidedly popular
publications in the West Riding), exemplified many of the concerns of
Waugh, and it is through it that one is aware how the cult of the heart, and
ideas about independence, the brotherhood of man, and the nobility of
the poor, were reworked for subsequent generations of the labouring poor
as well as for their laureates. But first it is necessary to consider in a little
detail the ways in which these themes were worked out in Waugh's
writing.

I can do little more here than offer a schematic commentary on the
themes exemplified in Waugh's verse and prose. I quote from the text of
his collected works, published in ten volumes in the 1880s and early
90s.[133] The themes that suffuse Waugh's work are evident throughout his
œuvre, and though this choice of his verse is selective it is not arbitrary.
First, the opening two verses and the last verse of 'God Bless these Poor
Folk' (the complete six verses are printed in the appendix).

> God bless these poor folk that are strivin'
> By means that are honest an' true,
> For some'at' to keep 'em alive in
> This world that we're scrambling through:
> As th' life ov a mon's full o' feightin',
> A poor soul that wants to feight fair,
> Should never be grudged ov his heytin',
> For th' hardest o'th battle's his share.
>   CHORUS – As th'life ov a mon.
>
> This world's kin to trouble; i'th best on't,
> There's mony sad changes come reawnd;
> We wander'n abeawt to find rest on't,
> An' th' worm yammers' for us i'th greawnd.
> May he that'll wortch while he's able,
> Be never long hungry nor dry;
> An' th' childer 'at sit at his table, –
> God bless 'em wi' plenty, say I.
>   CHORUS – As th'life ov a mon.
>   . . .
>
> Owd Time, – he's a troublesome codger, –
> Keeps nudgin' us on to decay,

133 Ed. G. Milner, *Collected Works* (Manchester, 1881–9, 1892–3).

An' whispers, 'Yo're nobbut a lodger;
Get ready for goin' away';
Then let's ha' no skulkin' nor sniv'lin',
Whatever misfortins befo';
God bless him that fends for his livin',
An' houds up his yed through it o'!
    CHORUS – As th'life ov a mon.

It is evident that the poor have the hardest fight, especially the poor who want to fight fair. As in the diary so in these verses: 'This world's kin to trouble.' Life is a matter of scrambling and striving, of struggle. It is the poor that are nearest the condition of 'fighting', which is here the generic condition of the life of a man. And it is through work, fending for a living, that one may realise the dignity life's hard struggles may bring. Work enables the worker to 'houd up his yed'. It confers dignity upon him, and enables the struggles of life to be borne with stoicism and endurance.[134] This exaltation of the poor was always embedded in strongly religious feelings about the transience of life on earth.

If the poor are exalted the essential note is one of forgiveness, reconciliation, and ultimately the realisation of human fellowship. Here are two verses from 'Forgive One Another';[135]

Like harp strings we're made of a different tone
And the minstrel, he sits up aboon;
To him every note of the garment's well known, –
Let's hope that he'll keep us i' tune,
To forgive one another.

Some liken to wrangle o'er nought but a name,
An' who wur their mams and their dads;
But gentle or simple, it ends up the same, –
'We're o' Johnny Butter'oth's lads!'
Let's forgive one another.

The saying 'We're o' Johnny Butter'oth's lads' was common in Lancashire at this time. What it meant was that all were the children of God Almighty, here incarnated in the Lancastrian flesh of 'Johnny Butterworth'.

'Tickle Times' tells of hard times, as do many other of Waugh's verses.[136] Verse two goes as follows,

But, when a mon's honestly willin';
An' never a stroke to be had,
And clemmin' for want of a shillin; –

---

[134] The dignity of work is evident in numerous poems of Waugh: see e.g. 'Come to your Porritch'.
[135] For another poem in a very similar vein, see 'A Lift on the Way'.
[136] See e.g. 'Hard Weather, Winter 1878–9'.

> No wonder that he should be sad;
> It troubles his heart to keep seein',
> His little brids feedin o'th air;
> An' it feels very hard to be deein,
> An' never a mortal to care.

The hardships of the poor are registered, and a protest is made. Yet the moral drawn does not entail social intervention and reform. It is the familiar one of the underlying unity of the human condition. This is verse five,

> There's danger in every station, –
> I'th palace as much as i'th cot;
> There's hanker i'every condition,
> An canker i' every lot;
> There's folk that are weary o' livin,
> That never fear't hunger nor cowd;
> An' there's mony a miserly craiter,
> That's deed ov a surfeit o' goud.

The message of this, as of his other poems, concerns the need for biding, for endurance. Yet it would be a mistake to consider this message as conservative, though it was certainly capable of conservative appropriations. Change is to be had, but it is essentially located in individual minds and hearts, in the intellectual and moral independence of the improving individual. The first task was to see to the soul not the social order. And the purpose of this attention was to make one privvy to the fundamental truths of human and divine nature. One sought first in the heart for that independence of character which would return one to a renewed sense of communion with all hearts.

Social intervention might be absent or at least secondary, but political activism was often very significant, for Waugh and for many an auto-didact like him. (Although Waugh kept political poems out of his published works, his 'Unpublished Pieces' contain bitter attacks on Toryism and Disraeli.) Political activity could unleash the forces of reason and progress, enabling them to overcome the ignorance, privilege, and darkness of Toryism: Waugh's early advocacy of educational reform was typical of this activism. And the roots of individualism, whether in religion, particularly the plebeian Protestant heritage, in Emersonian philosophy, or in its many other sources, such as the romantic conception of the artist, were often extremely radical in character.

Waugh published 'Cultivate Your Men' in standard English in the mid-1850s. It expresses the priority of tilling the mind, but the need for giving food to hungry men is just as pressing, if not quite so 'noble'. The first three verses are given here,

Till as ye ought your barren lands,
And drain your moss and fen;
Give honest work to willing hands,
And food to hungry men;
And hearken – all that have an ear –
To this unhappy cry, –
'Are poor folks' only chances here
To beg, or thieve, or die?'

With kindly guerdon this green earth
Rewards the tiller's care,
And to the wakening hand gives forth
The bounty slumbering there;
But there's another, nobler field
Big with immortal gain, –
The morasses of mind untilled; –
Go, – cultivate your men!

Oh, ponder well, ye pompous men,
With Mammon-blinded eyes,
What means the poverty and pain
That moaning round you lies:
Go, plough the wastes of human mind
Where weedy ignorance grows, –
The baleful deserts of mankind
Would blossom like the rose.

The sentiments of this are Emersonian, and Emerson's politics were close to those of Waugh and the millions of popular Liberalism. This bard of democracy was politically an independent, economically a free-trader. Committed to labour, a wider franchise, and a better distribution of wealth, Emerson was at the same time indifferent to organised social reform. It was the self-improvement of the individual that mattered, and, if in popular Liberalism social reform and a measure of state intervention were at times acceptable, this was chiefly a means to securing the fullest liberation of the individual. In line with the sentiments of his diary and his literary work Waugh's politics were radical, but this radicalism was anti-statist, and in its predominating moralism far removed from later variants of state socialism and social engineering. The concept of 'the social' in Waugh is a kind of void, in the sense of the social as a field distinct from, and yet embracing, the political, the economic, and so on. There is also no sense of the social as a *system*, independent of the moral, the political, and the religious. The latter categories constituted the social imaginary of Waugh's time, a concept of the social far removed from its later sociolo-gised manifestations, just as Waugh's – and others' – moral conceptions of the individual and of 'character' were far removed from later psycholo-gised understandings of the person.

In Waugh's writing it was not that poverty was inevitable, simply that it existed and had to be struggled with. That struggle brought the poor close to the realities of the hardness, also the fleetingness, of life, and so ennobled them, making them uniquely privvy to the knowledge that all life was struggle. In its moral eventuations, struggle also brought the poor to an understanding of the underlying brotherhood of mankind: all men showed the condition of struggle, its rewards and penalties. This is summed up in a verse from 'While Takin' a Wift o' My Pipe',

It's wise to be humble i' prosperous ways,
For trouble may chance to be nee;
It's wise for to struggle wi' sorrowful days,
Till sorrow breeds sensible glee;
He's such, that, contented with little, lives weel,
An nurses that little to moor;
He's well off 'at's rich, if he nobbut can feel
He's brother to thoose that are poor;
An to him 'at does fair,
Though his livin be bare,
Some comfort should ever be sure.

It is, however, not so much in these verses of reflection as in his accounts of the daily life of the working poor that Waugh best conveys the knowledge that the poor have an equal access with everyone else to the joys and tribulations of the heart. His poems of domestic life, by far his best, embody this democracy of the heart's truth rather than declaiming it. It was these poems, therefore, that had the biggest impact on his contemporaries, for they were proof that the poor could be written about in ways that dignified them as sharing in the human condition with all others. Before their time there was very little written that spoke of the poor in the same breath, and in the same ways, as the rich. Waugh did this, and what is more did it in a way that employed dialect, the mode of language most directly present to the intimate, daily life of his poorer readers.

In Waugh, and dialect literature more widely, this life was chiefly figured in terms of the home, and it is in his accounts of domestic sentiments and relationships that he conveys best the idea of the warmth and feeling of the poor. The full text of his best known poem, 'Come whoam to thi childer an' me', is given in an appendix. The evident sentimentality of this drew forth several dialect parodies, yet the poem had a huge impact. Sentimentality was at once embraced and undercut in dialect, and this capacity to comprehend seemingly contradictory tendencies is a sign of the suppleness of the literature. Elsewhere in Waugh the exploration of sentiment takes precedence over indulgence in sentiment, yet there is no denying the clichéd sentimentality of some of the writing, what later generations would frown upon as kitsch. Kitsch, for example in the self-indulgent sentimentality of Victorian *genre* painting, did form the basis of a truly 'popular' art, one embracing all social levels in the family of bad taste. None the less, Waugh wrote searchingly of subjects like childbirth and old age, subjects closest to an unsentimental knowledge of the daily circumstances of the poor.

In 'Down Again' the comic account of a husband managing the alarms of childbirth gives way at the end to a clear sense of the strength of feeling binding husband and wife (in Waugh's case, all the more poignant for being the expression of someone who sought, but failed, to sustain the relationship depicted here):

> I ran up in my stockin-feet;
> An' ther they lay! By th' mon;
> I thought i' my heart a prattier seet,
> I ne'er clapt e'en upon!
> I kissed our Betty; on' I said, –
> Wi th' wayter i' my e'en, –
> 'God Bless yo both, my bonny lass,
> For evermoore, Amen!
>
> 'But do tak care; if aught went wrang
> I think my heart would break;
> An if th ever aught in' th' world thou'd like,
> Thou's nought to do but speak;
> But, oh, my lass, don't lie too long;
> I'm lonesome by mysel';
> I'm no use without thee, thou knows;
> Be sharp, an' do get weel!'

'Owd Enoch' conveys another account of human love, this time the love of old age. The full text is given in appendix three, as the poem – one of Waugh's best – needs to be read in its entirety.

It is in Waugh's prose that we get the best idea of other of his major themes, those of independence and the mythical work held to embody this condition. It is, however, a poem of Waugh's, 'My Gronfaither Willie', that most succinctly conveys the idealisation of the old farming and handloom weaving days. The first four and the last of the eight verses best convey values that, as we have seen, Waugh took directly from his own knowledge of his family, past and present. The last verse suggests how this past might act as an anchor for the present, enabling the author in the present to 'walk like a man'.

> My gronfaither, Willie,
> Wur born o'th moorside,
> In a cosy owd house
> Where he lived till he died;

He wur strong-limbed an' hearty,
An' manly, an' kind;
An' as blithe as a lark, for
He'd nought on his mind.
Derry down.

His wife wur th' best craiter
That ever wur made;
An' they'd three bonny lasses
As ever broke brade;
An' five strappin' lads –
They looked grand in a row,
For they'rn six feet apiece –
That makes ten yards in o'!
Derry down.

My gronfaither's house
Wur a cosy owd shop,
An' as sweet as a posy
Fro' bottom to top;
Parlour, loom-house, an' dairy;
Bedrooms, greight an' smo';
An' a shinin' owd kitchen, –
The best nook of o'!
Derry down.

He'd cows in a pastur',
An sheep o'th moorside;
An' a nice bit o' garden
Wur th' owd fellow's pride;
With his looms an' his cattle,
He'd plenty o' wark
For his lads an' his lasses,
Fro' dayleet to dark.
Derry down.

As I journey through life
May this fortin be mine,
To be upreet an' downreet
Fro' youth to decline:
An' walk like a mon,
Through whatever betide,
Like my gronfaither, Willie,
That live't o'th moorside.
Derry down.

It is the prose however, in the form of Waugh's 'Besom Ben' stories, which best exemplifies these aspects. Ben is a besom maker, selling his brooms in the countryside, towns, and villages around his home on the moors outside Rochdale. These comic tales give an account of his encounters in his travels and his homecomings. Ben is also a celebration of domestic life – he is thirty years old (like Waugh at the time when the diary commenced), and has a young family. But the real object of celebration is the natural and cultural world of the 'country' districts, where weaving and farming in the old days went hand in hand.[137] In the stories Ben's travels are accompanied by long accounts of country customs and sports,[138] and of local notables, such as the 'Whitworth Doctors', noted surgeons who famously lived as ordinary country doctors; or the local gentry, such as one Colonel Chadwick, able to speak to the ordinary people 'in their own doric speech'.[139] Chadwick and his like were educated antiquarians, the author Waugh an autodidact of the species. In the stories he brought directly to bear not only his own experience of Rochdale and its environs, but his early passion for local history and folklore.

The picture he presents is a classless idyll in which rich and poor are all naturally a part of the unspoiled environment from which they spring. The economy he presents is far from the capitalist, factory economy of the present: it is what he calls a 'cottage economy', one where independence and individual effort are figured in the actual nature of production and exchange themselves, an economy of self-sufficient subsistence where people make their own furniture, their own clothes, their own medicine. Ben has relatively little to do with the towns, and Rochdale itself is presented more as a market than a factory town. Yet at the same time these fictions are rendered in such a way that this idealised version of independence is couched in the terms of realism, terms that endorse the minutiae of ordinary life, and the language which transacted this life. The substance and dialect language are those of the present, the subject that of the past.

Many of these sentiments were expressed in a letter the great radical and antiquarian, Samuel Bamford, sent to Waugh in 1854. Waugh shared Bamford's sentiments, both men, for instance, being deeply knowledgeable about the 'old halls' and 'old families' of Lancashire. Far from hating the old gentry they are an object of some reverence, but only because Bamford feels a part of this past. Bamford is proud of being part of the old Bamford stock, and he regrets never having seen Bamford Hall. He berates a landowner, James Fenton, for an 'act of vandalism' in pulling down his old hall (this, however, is preferable to turning it into a weaving shed, as some have done). Fenton comes in for blame, yet another current representative of the old stock, John Holt, is praised as 'a graidly, good-looking old Saxon'. The old families are acceptable when they remind us of a common origin in the 'old stock', yet their inevitable decay bears a

[137] G. Milner (ed.), *Besom Ben Stories* (Manchester 1892).
[138] See esp. 'Besom Ben and His Donkey' and 'The Old Blanket'.
[139] *Stories*, p. 210.

democratic message too: 'their descendants indistinguishable among the mass of their fellow countrymen, and perhaps all for the best, to learn us that all human pride and class conventionalities are vain; and baseless'.[140] The past and the present here are not sealed off one from another. Rather, the one is a means of interrogating the other.

This combination of imagined, independent pasts rendered in the accents, and with the preoccupations of, the present was to become a commonplace of dialect literature, and Waugh was instrumental in making it so. The everyman figure in the literature, so often the figure of the wise fool, was frequently the handloom weaver living in the semi-rural fold or 'fowt', most notably Brierley's influential creation, 'Ab o' th' Yate'.[141] I shall turn now to the broader currents of this dialect literature, tracing the legacy of Waugh as it developed, but also as it became changed, in the almanacs of the West Riding, the most important of which was John Hartley's Halifax *Illuminated Clock Almanack*, which enjoyed an uninterrupted existence from 1865 to 1957.

6   The legacy of Edwin Waugh

John Hartley was born in 1839, the son of a travelling draper and tea-dealer. His background and development were similar to Waugh in many respects, similar also to many among the ranks of the plebeian intellectual and artist. Though he lived through extreme poverty in his youth, there is the same background of small-scale economic independency in his father's trade. There is the same strong religious background on his mother's side (she was a Quakeress); the same legacy of artistic accomplishment. His grandparents were very active in Illingworth choir (Illingworth was a village outside Bradford, of a very similar kind to the domestic-industrial-agricultural environment Waugh grew up in). A mill half-timer, he became a full-timer at twelve, like Waugh taking up an occupation that permitted an opening to the high-cultural worlds beyond the workshop, in this case training to be a designer of worsted tapestries at the works of James Ackroyd and Sons.

He practised singing, reciting, speechmaking, and music at the Beacon Club near his home in Halifax, a young men's mutual improvement

---

[140] Letters to Edwin Waugh, L183/11, Samuel Bamford to Edwin Waugh, 9 November 1854. For the rehabilitation of the old Bamford as a truly radical figure see M. Hewitt, 'Radicalism and the Victorian Working Class: the Case of Samuel Bamford', *Historical Journal*, 34:4 (1991).

[141] For an account of Brierley see P. Joyce, *Visions of the People*, pp. 265, 282, 284–7, 298–9, and M. Vicinus, *The Industrial Muse*, pp. 192–3, 202–3, 205–7

society of a sort very common at this time.[142] In 1872 he threw up his job at Akroyd's and became a 'bohemian',[143] travelling and working in the US and Canada. At the age of twenty-three he had been converted by reading Waugh's 'Come Whoam', and five years later in 1867 he started writing for the *Almanack*. The first number he contributed to sold 5,000 copies in a week. He continued to write from the other side of the Atlantic, running the journal with his father-in-law, the owner of a hat shop in Halifax (under the sign of the illuminated clock), who began the journal in 1865.

From 1867 to his death in 1915 he almost single-handedly wrote the *Almanack*. None the less, he was still forced to work, for even reported sales of 80,000 per annum were insufficient to keep him, after everyone took their profit. On returning from the US in 1875 he ran a pub, going back to America periodically to work as a newspaper writer, a professional reciter of his own writings (to *émigré* Yorkshire people), and a carpet and upholstery designer. He developed a business as a designer, but this went bankrupt in 1894 when he seems to have returned to the West Riding for good. When in England, he seems to have travelled and worked around the country, though Halifax was always his home and the *Almanack*, it seems, his financial stand-by, if not his fortune (he appears to have died, as he was brought up, in poverty).[144]

Whether this was owing to his character is unclear, though, like Waugh, contemporaries were to speak of his impulsive, generous, improvident mode of life, a mode of life conducive, it was said, to the practise of literature, especially poetry. Descriptions of him at the close of his life suggest the same self-consciously literary persona as the public Waugh, the working man apart, the poet among, though also of, the poor.[145] A fellow almanac editor described his 'sensitive', 'artistic' temperament, that of a dreamer. What brought this to the surface was not, however, the aping of the high cultural tradition of standard English verse, but the sentiment and pathos of the poor's condition. Hartley is described as reading from 'Bite bigger, Billy', a comic–pathetic dialect account of poor, hungry children, and his fellow editor recorded: 'John put on his spectacles from the mantelpiece, and read us "Bite bigger Billy", his first literary attempt, written for the Halifax Beacon Club, a literary club, long years ago. John felt every word he read. Tears were hardly checked, and a

[142] On Hartley's youth see J. H. Waddington, *John Hartley, The Most Famous Dialect Writer: Sketch of His Life and Work* (Halifax 1939). On the Beacon Club see *Yorkshire Life*, March 1977.
[143] So he is described in F. Forshaw, *John Hartley, Poet and Author. An Appreciation* (Bradford 1909).
[144] W. J. Halliday, 'John Hartley', *Transactions of the Yorkshire Dialect Society*, 40:6, 1939.
[145] *Bob Stubbs' Yorksher Awmynack*, September entry, 1910.

lump in the throat threatened to get the mastery, but he went through with it, and we all felt we were in the presence of a master genius.'

Hartley enjoyed this sort of reputation locally, and the Halifax almanac greatly influenced the form and content of the other West Riding almanacs. The format of the Halifax example was itself unvarying, the 1930s ones being little different from the 1870s examples. The 1878 almanac is therefore typical:[146] a title page (with wise and elevating aphorisms), the two-page editor's preface, entries for each month with dates of famous events, details of the moon, accompanied by proverbs and sayings ('Grains and Chaff'), and for each month a one-page reflection on human nature and the passing year. These 'Ramblin Remarks for Every Month' were complemented by verse and short tales (the latter with titles like 'That Lass', 'Mi Fayther's Pipe', 'What Mi Mother Says', 'When the Heart is Sad', 'Hard Facts'). This section of verses and tales took up the majority of the almanac, the entirety of which was written in dialect (the title page and the January entry are given as examples in an appendix).[147] The whole thing was an extended meditation on the life of the poor, a compendium of popular wisdom recounted in a semi-comic way, at once reflective, sardonic, and amused.

As such it reflected very closely that exaltation of the poor as the great exemplars of human feeling, the cult or religion of the heart which embodied the brotherhood of man, that we have seen flowing from the self Waugh constructed, into his art, and thence into the self-image of his readers. In turn, men like Hartley, but also the many other laureates of poverty in his day, developed these images and motifs in their own way, forging new and changing relationships with their audiences. These can be traced through the history and pages of the Halifax almanac.[148] Walter Hampson succeeded Hartley in 1915 and wrote almost all the *Almanack* until his death in 1933. During his day it reflected the changed circumstances and susceptibilities of his readership. For instance, it seems to have been more overtly supportive of trade unionism, though before this time it was always sympathetic to the claims of labour, and Hampson, who was an active socialist, let his feelings be known on the page, even though

[146] For a discussion of the almanacs, see P. Joyce, *Visions of the People*, pp. 259–63.
[147] There are further examples in *ibid*, pp. 370–84.
[148] The almanac was started as a gesture of goodwill and a source of further advertisement by the Halifax hat-shop owner, Alfred Wilson. This was 'a common gift in those days'. After Hartley took it over it was printed in the offices of the *Bradford Observer*, the town's Liberal paper. It was published first by Hutchinsons of London and Wakefield, and then, after the Great War, by Watmoughs of Idle, who bought it in 1925. It carried much advertising after the war, but relatively little before, somewhat less pre-war than a number of the other dialect almanacs of the West Riding. See *Halifax Evening Courier*, 30 September 1978.

party politics was not pushed in a journal that depended on gaining as wide a readership as possible.

None the less, it is the similarities with the Hartley years that are striking, just as Hampson's background was very similar to aspects of Waugh's and Hartley's. If some emphases changed, then not only the basic form, but also the purpose and identity of this and all the other almanacs remained strikingly similar. The common denominator of 'as wide a readership as possible' among the populations of the great West Riding industrial cities and towns seems therefore to have changed little between the 1860s and the 1930s. (The same can be said up to the 1940s and 50s). The rhetorically created self-perceptions of the labouring poor, springing from the imagination of the worker intellectual, but shaped with an eye to the values of their fellows and readers, were therefore of striking longevity and uniformity. Despite change, writers and audiences for almost a century did I think express major continuities of outlook. There is no more striking instance of this than J. B. Priestley's editorship of the Halifax *Illuminated Clock Almanack* for a short period, also the connection with it in the early part of the twentieth century of two of the leading unionists and Labour politicians of their day, Philip Snowden and Ben Turner, both the offspring of pre-factory occupational cultures akin to their predecessors in the dialect tradition.[149] What is so often taken to be a Labour, and labour, tradition of the Edwardian and post-Edwardian years had deep roots in Victorian England, as did the invention of a particular kind of demotic Englishness in the case of Priestley.

Hampson was of a later generation than Waugh or Hartley, being born in 1864.[150] His was the same autodidact development however, despite the advent of the 1870 Education Act. His was the same knowledge of youthful poverty: he started mill work at the age of eight, and at the age of twenty began his graduation to the aristrocracy of labour with the Lancashire and Yorkshire Railway Company, eventually becoming an engine driver, the *crème de la crème* of the labouring poor. Like Waugh his upbringing was in a 'pre-industrial' setting, that of his father's cobbler's shop in the village of Normanton, outside Leeds. The background of economic independency was the same, as well as the setting. In Hampson's case, like that of the second most influential Lancashire writer Ben Brierley, radical religion and politics seem to have been breathed in with the air of childhood and youth (in his father's shop, as was the case with the village sociability enjoyed by Brierley's handloom weaver father).

---

[149] *Morley Observer*, 19 April 1984. Also, P. Joyce, *Visions of the People*, pp. 82–4, 156–7; 127, 264, 266, 301.

[150] On Hampson see *Yorkshire Life*, August 1959, and the obituary in the *Clock Almanack*, 1933.

Waugh, Hartley, and Hampson followed superior occupations, and followed them in a similarly adventurous way. The railwayman Hampson travelled throughout the country in his work, and always took his holidays abroad. Like the others, too, Hampson was reared in what seems to have been a rather gifted family, whose gifts, again musical ones, went back a number of generations.[151]

Hartley's work embraced a good deal more than the *Almanack*. He was as well known for his dialect verses and tales. His most popular character in the tales was Sammywell Grimes, also his wife Mally, who were near in spirit to Brierley's Ab o' th' Yate, and Waugh's Besom Ben, examples each of life in the fold or 'fowt', a pre-factory, pre-urban, setting which continued to evoke the ideal of independence (Grimes was however rather less a figure of the past than the other two). It is, however, the *Clock Almanack* of Hartley and Hampson that will be considered here, and the 1878 number is as appropriate as any.

Hartley's preface sets the tone: as he says, 'a lack o' prosperity gives birth to a lot o' philosophy'. This philosophy fills the pages that follow. The January entry informs us of the key to happiness,

Few wants an' just enough to meet em is most likely to produce happiness, not havin' moor nor we know what to do wi'. Aw can honestly say 'at aw nivver saw a rich man 'at seemed any happier nor misen, an aw'm poor enough, goodness knows! If a chap wants happiness ther's one or two things he mun have, an ther's some things he mun be withaat. Good health, summat to do, a gooid tempered wife, an one or two bonny bairns, are all things to help to keep him cheerful an' contented; but drink an idleness, enjoyin' another's position astead o' making one for yorsen ... are just enough to make a chap declare 'at th' sooner th' end o' th' world comes an' th' better.[152]

There then follows a brief story about one Joe, like whom 'Ther's monnya chap ... goon through this life disheartened becoss he doesn't get what he wants, when th' faults his own, for not gooin th' reight way about it.' As in Waugh's work, and in dialect writing as a whole, the theme of 'biding', of stoicism, is central: it is necessary to put up with things that cannot be altered. The September remarks tell us that, 'To be comfortably lodged an' weel fed isn't such a little slice o' gooid luck as we're apt to think. To be, "too proud to beg, too honest to steal, to know what it is to be wantin' a meal", is a deal commoner thing nor some fowk fancy.' The brief tale

---

[151] For other authors of dialect almanacs who shared a number of these formative experiences see the cuttings files of Leeds Public Library on Thomas Blackah, the *Nidderdill Olminac*, and Charles Rogers, *The Bairnsla Foaks Annual or Pogmoor Olmenac* (Nidderdale and Barnsley), esp. E. G. Byford, 'Bairnsla's Best, Wi a Bit Abaght T'Others', *Yorkshire Dialect Society*, 1925, on Rogers.

[152] 1878, p. 5. The *Almanack* is available in Manchester, Leeds, and Halifax Public Libraries, and at the British Library.

here goes on to embellish the message – though we will never be content because we are made up of wants, it is better to be contented with what we have than dissatisfied by what we have missed.

The theme of stoical endurance, putting up with the necessary limitations of poverty, suffuses the almanac literature as a whole: recurrent sayings, mottos, are embroidered in the following fashion: 'If it is little you get it is little you need', 'Mak t'Best o' Life', and 'Humility Inherits the Earth'.[153] We seem here to be at some distance from the 'workers' dream', that desire to embrace all of high, 'bourgeois' culture as an assertion of the worker's dignity, that concern to deny egotism and materialism in favour of the higher verities of literature and metaphysics. 'Few wants an' just enough to meet em' is a decidedly more modest aim. Something to do, a good wife and children, good health, are the riches of the poor, of those who are 'too proud to beg, too honest to steal'. Not envying the lot of others more fortunate or energetic than oneself is the counsel. There is here a limitation as to ends, an awareness of tangible, immediate needs, a sense of the limitations life itself imposes on people's hopes. There is, in short, the real tragedy of class – the closing down of aspiration, the trammelling of vision, the self-policing of hope. The almanacs tell this story as well.

They tell another one too. For, when we look closer, behind the elements of self-limitation there is the same idealism, the same utopian longings, that are evident in the workers' dream. There is the same dream, for in the cult of the heart and the fellowship of mankind there are still played out, in a new key and a new form, the longings of the worker intellectual, longings perhaps in some ways strengthened by their contact with the visions of the people. Despite the sense of the stoical, there is a clear sense that we are all responsible for ourselves. Translated into the parlance of the poor, this notion of independence becomes a matter of making something of yourself and not blaming or envying others. But what one made of oneself involved far more than improvement in a material sense. The message was as much against materialism and egocentrism as the seemingly more exalted message of the autodidact's struggle: 'few wants' and not having 'moor nor we know what to do wi'' was the key to happiness in Hartley's remarks. As in the struggles of Edwin Waugh, what was sought was a moral, religious, comprehension of the world.

In verses called 'Dooant Forget', forty years after Hartley wrote, Hampson recalled his readers to a version of the higher verities that was all the more powerful because of its humility:[154]

---

[153] P. Joyce, *Visions of the People*, p. 296.
[154] *Illuminated Clock Almenack*, 1918, p.14 (*ICA*).

> It's grand to be a heearo in a great an' glorious cause,
> To feight for human liberty, an God's eternal laws;
> It's grand to know yo'r honour'd bi greet noblemen and kings,
> But doant forget 'at life's made up of lowly, little things.

The verse goes on, telling its audience not to forget that 'th' human race consists o' fowks 'at's poor', 'th' race would dee if sombody didn't wark', 'men's bodies need sustainin' wol ther heearts', and 'a man may be fulfillin' God's commands/Performin' life's most humble tasks 'at's nearest to his hands'. Forty years on, the message of forty years before is substantially unchanged: the humble things that concern the great majority of people, the poor, are nearest to the truths of life. They are nearest because, like work, they engage with the realm of necessity that teaches real wisdom. As other almanac aphorisms have it – those born in clover do not know what it is to 'rep a bare pasture'; love is free and cannot be bought by money, whereas, as Hartley put it in 1878, he can honestly say that he never saw a rich man happier than himself. Riches distort the nature of happiness and betray the underlying truths of the heart and of human kinship: again the almanac aphorisms have it; 'Muck in a cart and muck in a carriage are the same', 'Ther's monny a thing born in a stable 'at doesn't turn aght a horse; – it isn't where a man's life begins but where it ends 'at proves him.'[155] There are also the numerous variants on the sentiments evoked by the parable of the rich man, the camel and the eye of the needle.

In Hartley's words, poverty makes evident that it is kind hearts and not cunning heads that matter, and that when religion is on the tongue it is usually missing in the heart,[156] exactly the sentiments of Waugh. And, as in Waugh, it is the cult of the home that reinforces that of the heart, in turn proclaiming the essential unity of all people. Hampson described the purpose of the *Almanac* in 1918,

For aboon hauf a century its been teichin fowks to love one another. It's allus tried to show 'at God intended mankind should be happy an' live kindly together, it's helped thaasands o' fowk to see 'at ther's a lot o' reeal pleasur' an' fun i' life, even tho' they may be i' th' poorest circumstances. It's helped monny a fayther an' mother to shoolder th' burdens o' family life wi' mooar pluck an' determination than they otherwise would ha' done, an' its helped to knit them an' their bairns cloiser together i' that domestic love 'at's made th' cottage hooams of owd England of mooar valley than all her gold.[157]

The cottage homes of England, knowingly or not, echoes earlier versions of a pre-factory, pre-urban industrial pastoral. As in those versions of independence, a utopia is summoned up in which the extremes of poverty

[155] For amplifications P. Joyce, *Visions*, chap. 12, esp. pp. 295–6.
[156] *ICA*, 1878, p.6.
[157] *ICA*, 1918, p.2.

and riches are to be avoided. The line from Waugh is a direct one – a 'modest competence' is the best realisation of underlying humanity, and, while poverty is the best teacher, it is the 'middle state' that is aspired to. As the *Weyver's Awn Comic Olmenack* of Leeds put it in 1881, 'T' middle state is t' best; for gurt riches bring gurt cares, dangers an temptations; an failyer an poverty weigh as hevvy on t' heart as they du on t' stummock.'[158]

A few pages after asserting that the cottage homes of England were worth all her gold, and in the depths of the Great War, Hampson gave voice to sentiments that would have found a ready place in the mental universe of Edwin Waugh. I quote from the last two verses of 'Things Wodn't Ha' Bin Noa War To-day' (War: Worse),[159]

> Hed Roman, Saxon, Dane, an' Jute
> An' Roman left ahr isle alooan,
> Hed English Kings but follered suit,
> An' ne'er to forrun lands ha' goan –
> Hed they thowt moor of Peace an' Reight,
> An' less of war, an' pomp, an sway, –
> Why, coom, aw think yo'll own up streight
> Things wodn't ha' bin noa war to-day
>
> Sun, mooin an' stars, – this dancin sphere,
> Ocean an' river, vale an' hill,
> Sweet flaars an' Songburds is evrywhere,
> An teemin' meads for mon ta till –
> Noa slothful rich, nor clemmin poor,
> One God to whom to sing an' pray, –
> If fowk hed nivver wanted mooar
> Things wodn't ha' bin noa war to-day

We have therefore something of the self, or the selves, of Edwin Waugh as these took form. This form depended greatly on the technology of the self (in the next study oratory will be considered as just such a technology, though in Bright's case a technology of the public self). At the moment we have the clearest sight of Waugh the diary is the self's technology.[160] W. J. Ong has described diary keeping as 'a heightened expression of a psychology shaped by written language, with its nervous movement backwards between self-as-author and self-as-audience, and its devices for the "internalisation of consciousness".'[161] Some diaries are more heightened expressions than others, and Waugh's is a peculiarly sophisticated variant,

[158] August entry.   [159] February entry.
[160] See the extracts from Waugh's diary in appendix six.
[161] W. J. Ong, *Orality and Literacy: the Technologising of the Word* (1982), pp. 102, 152.

an essential expression of the autodidact's spirit, itself an essential spirit of the Victorian era.

Where the engagement with standard English, and hence with the great resources of high culture, was less marked than in Waugh's case, the selves that were constructed in writing by the poor are less elaborate, less nervous in the movement between self as author and audience. In her *The Radical Soldier's Tale*, Carolyn Steedman has examined John Pearman's diary.[162] The command of standard English this soldier and policeman had was far less assured than Waugh's. Steedman explores Pearman's representation of his life in terms of the relation between standard English and Pearman's own linguistic resources.[163] The result is fascinating and Pearman's creativity is great, but by comparison with Waugh this creation of a self is two-dimensional. Paradoxically, before a really positive dialect literature could develop the standard had to be fully and confidently assimilated. In comparison with most 'working-class' autobiographies and diaries, including those of autodidacts, Waugh's account is singularly sophisticated. These differences can only be gestured at here, by comparing Waugh's diary with a recently published, and greatly revealing diary and family history, that of Benjamin Shaw, of the village of Dent in the West Riding, a man who was for most of his life a mechanic in Preston.[164] Here the account of the self is one-dimensional, without any sense of interiority at all. Shaw taught himself writing and reading, slowly and painfully, whereas Waugh was taught. Shaw, of an earlier generation, represents an earlier and much less complete opening out to writing by the poor, and the possibilities for the creation of the self it offered. Waugh, by contrast, represents the apotheosis of new technologies of the self, ones increasingly available to those so long deprived of them.

The diary is Waugh's laboratory of the self, its confessional nature the ideal way to try out new personae as he scuttled between self as author and self as audience. It was the arena of his sorrows and suffering, where these could be at once played out and spectated, released and savoured, or expressed in pain and apprehended with condemnation. Sorrow was a kind of coloration, or medium, of Waugh's emerging selfhood, spanning the various theatres in which he rehearsed the self, whether these be the literary, the religious, the philosophical, the political, and so on. These theatres offered him a variety of roles, also an overarching figure of the self as agent. It is not known if Waugh had read Goethe, but the model of a

---

[162] Carolyn Steedman, *The Radical Soldier's Tale. John Pearman 1819–1908* (1988).

[163] *Ibid.*, chap. 5, esp. pp. 68–9.

[164] Ed. Alan G. Crosby, *The Family Records of Benjamin Shaw, Mechanic of Dent, Dolphinholme and Preston 1772–1841*, The Record Society of Lancashire and Cheshire, 130, 1991.

sorrowing young Werther was certainly in the ether of Romantic literature, which Waugh breathed in from his early youth. Other models were
to be found in his love of Wordsworthian simplicity and Milton's high
seriousness. Spanning these was the figure of the self as agent in the world
conferred by literature, the poet as priest and seer. Religion, especially
Methodism, also gave him many models of how the person might conduct
a moral, and sorrowing, life, from the great forebears of the faith, with
whom his kin had connection, to this kin themselves. The overarching
figure was that of the self as soul, in struggle and sorrow before God,
playing out the narrative of providence. Methodism also gave him part of
his language of interior anguish, Romantic literature another part. Both
contributed to the religious note that reverberates throughout his life and
his very influential work, that note of exaltation, uplift, and spirituality
that found its most important expression in what I have termed the
religion of humanity and the cult of the heart. His debt to Emerson, and
probably to Carlyle too, obviously contributed mightily to all this, while
also representing a move beyond sorrow to affirmation.

This move was intimately tied up with the narrative of the autodidact,
one in which the individual's pursuit of knowledge is seen to be part of the
great historical scheme of reason's unfolding in progress. The self as
autodidact is the most central source of models and figures of the self in
Waugh, as the aim of the seeker after the light of knowledge is liberation
from dependence, escape from the cage of want into the realm of
independence, the workers' dream of embracing all of culture the better to
realise the equality of all people as human. The autodidact self handles the
gendered self of husband and father, and in turn takes definition from it
(as we shall see independence is predicated on dependence, and women
and wives were cast – to varying degrees – in situations of dependence
within the home). The governing self, or the principle of the self's
governance, is, however, the improving self of the autodidact. T
psychic economy is that of knowledge.

In representing the workers' dream this economy dictated loss a:
gain. The man who half leaves in order to find out that he be
severed from, as well as joined to, his fellows. The cost of represer
poor man's aspirations is to be unlike the poor man, for to be a .
culture and to enter 'bourgeois civilisation' may be to distance oneseu
from those whose 'repulsive coarseness' cuts them off from 'stern propriety'. The desire to enter civilisation might be bred out of discontent
with an intractably material, daily situation and the unregenerate poor
who surrounded one. In representing the immediate culture of his formation he was most effectively of it, the more of it because of his
self-imposed exile from it. His was an essential voice of the poor's

condition, involving and constructing the 'social' identities of 'mankind' and 'humanity' by means of which the poor could measure the respect due to them by others and by themselves.

In considering Edwin Waugh, and John Bright, it is apparent that the sense of the self, and the broader sense of the social – particularly of agency within this imagined social – were secured by narratives, by stories that patterned 'experience' into coherent and satisfying, or unsatisfying, wholes. We can see this in the religious narrative of the soul's journey to God, in the narrative of knowledge that was the autodidact's concern, and not least in the historical narratives underpinning Waugh's politics. Narratives patterned the life of the person, just as it patterned the meaning of the social. Before considering this it is however necessary to turn from a man who can be said to have had a crucial, if unacknowledged, role in the making of a supposed 'working-class' identity, to one who had an even more crucial, but this time acknowledged, role in the construction of what is usually taken to be 'middle-class' one.

II John Bright and the English people: a study in 'middle-class' identity

2 John Bright in later life

II John Bright and the English people: a study in 'middle-class' identity

How clear cut is the sturdy image evoked by those two eloquent Saxon syllables, 'John Bright'. Once the rallying cry of the masses seeking enfranchisement – the trump of doom to Whig and Tory in possession – the name in memory has since become the symbol of an honest man in politics ...

... And so he lies, 'as he himself would have wished it', not under Gothic arches hung with conquered flags and echoing back the organ's peal, not among warriors and princes, and the statesmen who played for fame and power, but under the northern sky, in front of the humble houses of peace where he had worshipped as a child, in silence sometimes broken by the sound of workmen's footsteps up the steep flagged street, he dwells among his own people.

(first and last sentences of G. M. Trevelyan,
The Life of John Bright (1913)

We feel that Mr Bright is entitled to a higher eulogy than any that could be due to intellect or any that could be due to success ... the character of the man lay deeper than his eloquence, deeper than anything that can be described or seen on the surface, and the supreme eulogy which is his due I apprehend to be this, that he elevated political life to a higher elevation, and to a loftier standard, and that he has thereby bequeathed to his country the character of a statesman which can be made the subject not only of admiration, and not only of gratitude, but of reverential contemplation.

(W. E. Gladstone, House of Commons, 29 March 1889)

Farewell Father! May I never
Dim the brightness of thy name
But with heart unsullied ever
As thy course be mine the same.

(John Bright, 'Lines written on leaving home', aged 21 years)

History is only dimly aware of Edwin Waugh, but it knows John Bright with certainty. He is the Rochdale mill-owner, the great radical who championed free-trade, peace, and franchise reform; the Quaker who struggled against the Established Church. He is the man who hated the aristocracy. Above all he is the absolute bourgeois, the very image of bourgeois identity and the champion of the bourgeois virtues, the virtues we traditionally describe under the headings of 'individualism' and 'self-help'. These were the virtues of *Manchestertum,* and it was from the cloth of *Manchestertum* that Engels cut the figure of the historic bourgeoisie. In many regards we are still Engels' children, not least the most sophisticated students of the historical formation of subjectivities, alive to the complexities of the textual positioning of subjects, but borne down by the leaden weight of an obsolete view of class in which 'individual' is the sign of 'middle class',[1] a 'collective self' that of 'working class'.[2]

Merely a glimpse at the struggles of Edwin Waugh convinces us this must be otherwise. How can we disallow the terms of 'individualism' in considering these struggles, as his sinful soul confronts God, and as the autodidact fights his way towards knowledge and improvement? He is the very emblem of the search for self-discipline, and a form of independence that begins within himself. Yet he is 'working class'. By the same token, the 'bourgeois' Bright will be seen to evince versions of the self incontrovertibly 'social' in character, and versions of the social rooted in the sense of the individual self. The logic of post-structuralist conceptions of identity would lead us to expect nothing else: the absence, or 'trace', of the individual self is always present in the collective self, and vice-versa. The 'self' and the 'social' are always mutually defining.

In the case of Bright this reveals an understanding of social identity at variance with Engels' persistent inheritance (just as Waugh's juxtaposition of self and social gives us a new view of 'working class'). The understanding begins by allowing supposed contraries to define one another; and by seeing that the important thing about 'class' identities is that they are invariably defined in relation to a shared discursive subject, and that this sharing produces a sense of social similarity as well as social difference. In the case of Waugh it was apparent that the personal and social relations he entered into were transacted through the language, the metaphysic, of humanity, through the cult of the heart. When we come to consider Bright we find that he talks much the same language. As will be seen, the 'language of class', of social relations described in the explicit vocabulary of 'classes', was important. But the discourse of the human heart was arguably more hidden, more subtle, more urgent. This was the

[1] Regenia Gagnier, *Subjectivities; A History of Self-Representation in Britain, 1832–1920* (New York 1991).
[2] Felicity A. Nussbaum, *The Autobiographical Subject: Gender and Ideology in Eighteenth Century England* (1989).

major ground of social distinction, the script of the social, through which resemblance and difference were played out.

We discern a language of the social that not only accentuates human resemblances, but is shared by people in different conditions. Paradoxically, the route to understanding human difference lies in understanding human similarity. And the similarity matters as much as the difference, the emphasis on fraternity, on some human essence going beyond the company of men alone, yet still heavily masculine in conception. Equally, all emphasis on similarity may be a means of making difference, just as all emphasis on difference presupposes criteria of similarity against which difference can be judged. The idea of the human is defined against the 'other' which is not human or not fully human, the cult of the heart against bestiality.

Waugh and Bright shared much in common, lives that made them subscribe with deep feeling to the metaphysic of humanity, and emphasise what all people had in common. Waugh was born in the same town six years after Bright. Both men were reared in Rochdale, and the stamp of this remarkable nineteenth-century English town was upon them. They both experienced, for instance, the tumult of radicalism in the town, from Peterloo in 1819 to the 'Church Rates' controversy around 1840, in which Bright took a leading part. They crossed each other's paths, in the Rochdale Working Men's Educational Institute, in which Waugh was heavily involved. The town was the conduit through which the rush of national events reached them in the eventful years of the early nineteenth century. Quite simply, the two men were formed by the same forces, from romanticism and Evangelicalism to radicalism. Waugh dedicated the first edition of his works, in 1859, to Bright. This formation makes them specially revealing to consider: what differences emerge, what similarities? They form a kind of laboratory in which we may experiment on social identity, these men who read the same books, who walked the same streets and woods.

The differences of the two men were of at least equal importance as the similarities. Formed by similar forces, they were none the less made in different moulds. Bright was a man of property, Waugh a poor man. It was Waugh who petitioned Bright's father for work, not the reverse, suffering in the process the anxieties of self-presentation we have seen to be so frequent in the encounters of the socially high and socially low in Victorian England. In meeting Jacob Bright, Waugh suffered the 'infernal diffidence', the 'confused and ungainly manner in such affairs' which always dogged his steps. Waugh was the dependent one, not John Bright, and it was through the Brights' support that Waugh got a post in Manchester: Samuel Lucas, John Bright's brother-in-law, was the chairman of the Lancashire Public Schools Association. As we have seen, Waugh and his successors, gave a particular, 'plebeian', caste to the ideas of humanity and independence. In his turn, Bright was to give a particular 'class' inflection to this common language, in which the dependent, including women, were the 'other' against which the 'human' was defined. However, very many working men, including Waugh, joined him in doing this, sharing an understanding of who the dependent were and why they were so. Differences of origin remained, but they were often transformed by the unifying potential of the available social languages of the time. To understand something of how this might have been so let me turn first to the origins of John Bright. This man of property yet had certain strong plebeian characteristics. In this he was not untypical. The 'industrial bourgeoisie' of his day had a much more ambiguous social origin than is often thought, one not unlike Waugh's beginnings in a state of 'competence' and independence. These commonalities, real and mythologised, were a basis upon which the unifying potential of social languages could work.

Bright, however, is history's Bright, unlike Waugh. We need to know what history has made of him, from his own time to the present. In confronting Bright we confront many selves, not the personae through which Waugh conducted his struggles, but the selves of history, biography, hagiography, political advertisement, and 'improving' literature. We are aware of history's Bright, which, in its pre-1945 form, and especially its pre-1914 one, became something like the cult of the plain man and his democratic mission. The demotic version of the public self constructed by others, particularly in the popular biographies, was also constructed by Bright himself, in the self projected in his oratory especially. For in this era of the still-youthful democracy of print, the spoken word continued to be of great significance. Doubly so for Bright, as he left no writings of any worth, nor wished to leave any, for he was an orator first and always (if one keenly aware of the workings of the printed speech). We begin to be aware of a silent collaboration at work, one between the representations of Bright made by himself and others.

The collaboration becomes even more evident when we consider the 'private self' created by Bright, for this too, or much of it, was made in such a way as to be the stuff of the public, the historical, and as such the makings of the mythology of a nascent mass democracy. In this construction of demotic, not necessarily democratic, man, we are aware of something like a circle of representation in which it is often difficult to see where others start and Bright stops, so caught up are both parties in the myth-making that they produced and which answered to the needs of a new democracy. The results of this myth-making contributed to the creation of the democratic imaginary, which itself was perhaps the major contemporary version of the social imaginary.

The circle of representation I describe begins in the 'private self' Bright constructed from childhood on. This self was not only the raw material of the public man, but also answered – as in Waugh – to particular circumstances and dilemmas. These I consider in 'Making the self', which is followed by a consideration of the social forms created by Bright out of the personal self. The study concludes by looking at his deployment by others and his place in the democrataic imaginary of his time, chiefly in the practical uses of the cult of the plain man.

7   Plain man's prophecy

John Bright's family originated in Wiltshire, where in the seventeenth and early eighteenth centuries they were farmers, woolcombers and serge weavers. His great grandfather migrated to Coventry, where John's father Jacob was born in 1775. Jacob's parents died in poverty when he was young, and charitable Friends sent him to the Ackworth Quaker school, near Pontefract in Yorkshire.[3] Jacob was at Ackworth from the age of nine to fourteen, this concern with education and the poor, especially those of their Society, being a particular interest of the Quakers. Jacob was then apprenticed to William Holme, a Friend who had a small farm and a few looms weaving fustian. Holme's sons set up a mill, at home in Derbyshire, before moving to Rochdale in 1802, where Jacob followed them. In 1809 two other Quaker businessmen, this time in Manchester, went into partnership with Jacob. They provided the capital, he the knowledge. Greenbank Mill was the result. Jacob's story is akin to the classic success story of the industrial entrepreneur, his route being from poverty through apprenticeship into partnership and success (complete to the last detail of this social narrative, Jacob marrying the daughter of his master). These are hardly the ways of the unrestrained market: at every step Jacob's career went forward through the agency of the Quaker connection. John was born in 1811, by which time Greenbank was beginning to prosper. Yet he was only a few years distant at birth from Jacob's struggle, if not his poverty. Brought up in a household becoming daily more comfortable, he looked back through his knowledge of his father to a legacy of poverty and of the 'yeoman' condition of the farmer–artisan (a legacy not unlike Waugh's). This legacy was of powerful effect, because Jacob was to have such a profound influence on his son. Jacob's second wife, John's and the other children's mother, was the daughter of prosperous Bolton trades-people. In old age, in 1851, Jacob took a third wife, after Martha Wood. Again a devout Quaker, she was the family governess, and the daughter of a Wensleydale farmer.

John therefore stood at what he and contemporaries felt to be an historical divide between the 'common people' (from which he came) and the propertied and respectable (which he, his siblings, and his children became). In this sense, like Waugh, he was a marginal or 'liminal' figure. Out of this marginality was generated the force that gave his myth such purchase on Victorian and Edwardian England. The myth was related to what I have called the circle of representation constructing Bright, a term

---

[3] For accounts of John Bright's early life and ancestry see William Robertson, *Life and Times of the Right Honourable John Bright M.P.* (1877), 6 vols., I; John Bright, 'John Bright's Memoir of His Youth', in R. A. J. Walling (ed.), *The Diaries of John Bright* (1930).

denoting the hermetic nature of his 'life'. There is a sense in which all biography is ultimately self – or auto – biography, the subject writing themselves. However ingenious and indirect, the biographer is subject to the texts and narratives the subject leaves behind, whether these be words or behaviour. In Bright there is a more direct sense in which this is true. Compared with the spectacularly interiorised self of Waugh, Bright seems to have had only an attenuated inner life, seemingly without such deep conflicts or struggles over identity. Bright is a supreme example of the self formed within religion. It seems almost as if he were stamped at birth with Quakerism and that the stamp endured unchanged until his death. He seems utterly one-dimensional at times, such is the apparent conviction of his faith. This is only partly so, however, because his conceptions of the self and the social were not simply given to him, but actively constructed by him out of his religion. He can be said to have invented his religion, in the sense of using one kind of Quakerism to create another kind. The conflicts he did have, between authority and liberty say, were none the less played out in terms of a religion which proffered a conception of self without an unknown centre within, a centre in which doubt and confusion might reign. In terms of emotional space, conflict was lateral, 'flat', confined, and in the end contained by religion. He was transparent to himself. He was also transparent to his contemporaries: this, like his 'marginality', was what gave his myth such power at the time. The transparency enabled a singularly direct and unmediated persona to be bequeathed to his contemporaries, one without silences and depths, one that in its elemental force and simplicity lent itself to the mythology of the plain man and his prophecy.

However, there was also a more mundane way in which Bright intervened in this biographical circle. He either changed the record himself, quite literally, or caused it indirectly to be changed. He edited his speeches before publication. Bright said that his life was in his speeches. He meant the public life, and that the private life was of no interest before the public one. To the extent that this is true, it can be said that Bright quite literally wrote his public life. He also wrote himself in further ways: in at least one case biographies were sent to him for correction and additions.[4] His own writing on his early years and his family was, until the twentieth century, the chief source of information on his formation. In the nineteenth century this was supplemented by reference to Robertson's monumental six-volume *Life* of 1877, written by a Rochdale man and a fitting tribute to the deities of hagiography.[5] Robertson made no effort to do anything

---

[4] B. Rhodes, *A Popular Sketch of John Bright Statesman and Orator* (London and Manchester 1884), foreword.

[5] W. Robertson, *Life and Times*, I, chaps. 1 to 6.

but retell stories about Bright's early life that fed directly into the public myth of the common man already by then well in place, partly assembled through the considerable influence of the Bright family in the town, of which Robertson was a part.

By the time of Trevelyan's great biography, deeply sympathetic but not hagiography in the nineteenth-century mode, it seems we have gone beyond Bright's capacity to reproduce the biographical circle. Not so, for, as the Bright family papers reveal, Bright reached from beyond the grave to influence events. His son, John Albert, was always the most dutiful of Bright's children, the most made in his image and concerned to burnish this image. The correspondence with Trevelyan in 1913 finds the two men collaborating to 'put John Bright's reputation where it should be'.[6] John Albert selected and provided correspondence for Trevelyan. Letters to Bright sought out his advice, and all the chapters of the biography were submitted to him. The two men shared the profits, which were not inconsiderable (Trevelyan made 700 pounds on it well within a year of publication).[7] It was a book designed to make a reputation, one that was in more senses than one posthumous. In turn, in the twentieth century, despite work on the family papers, the imprint of Trevelyan's work has powerfully shaped subsequent historical accounts of Bright.

Trevelyan's life can be understood as the summa of all the biographical works that went before, the arch of the edifice constructing the cult of Bright.[8] The edifice itself was built by the voluminous works of 'biography' before Trevelyan's book of 1913. The first thing to emphasise is just how numerous were those works. The second, just how great was Bright's reputation as an orator, a statesman, and a tribune of the people before 1914. The Great War and the disintegration of Liberalism destroyed this reputation. It is difficult now to imagine the renown of Bright, the reverence with which his figure was perceived (though, as we shall see, there were some who were not so reverent). I use 'biography' here loosely, to refer to all considerations of Bright's life in newspapers and pamphlets, as well as in the large number of books.

These works bore titles such as *John Bright: The Tribune of the People*,[9] published for a penny probably in the 1880s, and *John Bright as Statesman and Orator* (1911),[10] the latter presenting the invariably triumphalist narrative of liberty fought for and now gained. In the *Life and Opinions of*

[6] Bright Family Papers, Street, Somerset, in the possession of C. and J. Clark Ltd: Darbashire Papers (hereinafter titled such), Packet 14, Letters of G. M. Trevelyan to J. A. Bright, 13 July 1913.
[7] Trevelyan to Bright, 31 December, 1913. See also 8 October, 1912.
[8] G. M. Trevelyan, *The Life of John Bright* (1913).
[9] J. P. Hutchinson, London n.d.   [10] Francis W. Hirst, London 1911.

the Right Hon. John Bright, An Illustrated Edition (1880s)[11] Bright is again caste in the familiar role of the warrior for liberty. But he is also a man above politics. He does not believe in 'the mystery of politics'. Politics is simple when honestly looked at by the honest man. Honesty is kin to simplicity and a particular kind of Englishness: the author takes up a persistent theme in representations of Bright, that of his body and visage (his 'broad, powerful Saxon face', for instance) expressing a force and depth echoed in the English language itself. Of his oratory it is observed, 'In the finer passages there is the same expression that so often affects us in our English Bible – the expression of elevated human passions in common words . . . whose force we never feel until we find them used in this manner'.[12] The 'great human passions are rendered directly in their natural garb', the common tongue of the English, and not the unnatural garb of the learned tongues (or the foreign vernaculars). The plain, preferably Saxon, Englishman complements the plain English tongue in revealing the peculiar force of English versions of the human.

This emphasis on elemental and powerful human passions, basic to all people, being rendered best through the means of the common tongue and the honest, plain man, the common man, is perhaps the basic theme: the simplicity and force of the man, and his medium, speaks to the simplicity and force of the basic passions. In *A Popular Sketch of John Bright, Statesman and Orator* published for sixpence in 1884,[13] religion is fused with this theme; Bright, of 'a large mind' and 'an honest soul', being here the expression of 'God's good providence'. The author cites John Morley on Bright and Cobden, on how the public is powerfully struck by these 'two plain men' giving themselves up out of integrity to 'a great public cause', and leaving their homes and businesses to do so. There is, for Morley, 'something apostolic' in this, far removed from the stereotyped ways of political activity. Again, there is the theme of the dead, arcane, faction-ridden worlds of politics being conquered by the virtues of the plain man, who now carries the aura of providential holiness with him as he goes on his 'pilgrimage'.[14] It is apparent that the Liberal intellectual Morley is little different in his understanding of Bright from the 'low cultural' representations of the popular biographies. Both streams conceived of Bright as quite literally the prophet of democracy, a man fusing, and reconciling, the divine and the secular, the old testament of religion and the new testament of 'the people'.

Robertson represents the high watermark of the low cultural stream, Trevelyan that of the high, and again there is nothing to separate the two

[11] F. Watts, London n.d., 1880s?   [12] *Ibid.*, p. 311.
[13] B. Rhodes, *A Popular Sketch*, p. 4.
[14] *Ibid.*, pp. 13–14.

understandings. Robertson's first volume opens with an extraordinary encomium on the common man, accompanied by a page-long list of the great of England and the world who were of common origin, common origin here being those who were neither born wealthy nor above the station of the 'middle class'. The poor and the middle class are all ranked together in this commonality, which includes the obvious success stories of the day (Stephenson, Arkwright, Peel, Gladstone), and a small army of English writers and thinkers. Beside these are figures like Luther, the son of a miner, Homer, a beggar, 'Virgil the son of a baker', Columbus, a weaver, and so on.[15] There then follows a bitter attack on the claims of blood and birth:

The fantastical claims of high birth merely confers learned ignorance and the groping in the dark of Heralds College ... Fantastical is the vanity which, while it cannot deny to the beggar at the gate the privilege of being descended from Adam and Eve, rests its own claims to superiority upon being enabled to prove a fiftieth part of the same antiquity, struts, like a bird in the fable, in others finery, and piques itself upon the actions of its ancestors, instead of its own. 'No matter what his race, but what he is' is preferable to being only the shadow of a mighty name.[16]

Robertson goes on to make the common connection to Englishness, and to what was perhaps the major cultural totem of that Englishness in the nineteenth century, the English tongue, especially its Saxon elements, as expressed in a great literature.[17] English blood was, says Robertson, always an amalgam, and this blood flows through the veins of Shakespeare and those who wrote the English Bible. Men such as these, a tongue such as this, will counter the fantastical claims of high birth. As the above quotation indicates, they, and we who come after, may do so by recognising our kinship with all people, the beggar and the poor included. Here Robertson sets together the generalities of the virtues of Protestant Englishness – shared, as we have seen, by Edwin Waugh – with the particularities of Quakerism. The poor partook of the Godhead as much as the rich, sharing in the Inner Light with all people. The Inner Light was perhaps the central tenet of Quakerism, the source of communion with divinity that lay within all people, and which made the mediations of other men and institutions redundant. Quaker teaching laid great stress on humility and simplicity, virtues which the poor were often seen to exemplify. Robertson expressed Bright's Quakerism in verse: 'Taught by no priests but by their beating hearts/ ... in the silent bodily presence feel/ The mystic stirrings of a common life, which makes the many one.' The range of meanings given simplicity, plainness, is deepened, extending

[15] W. Robertson, *Life and Times*, pp. 8–9.   [16] *Ibid.*, pp. 9–10.
[17] P. Joyce, 'The People's English' in R. Porter and P. Burke, *Language, Self and Society: A Social History of Language* (Cambridge 1991).

beyond the nation to religion, connecting with their ultimate destination in 'the people' and 'democracy', those secular expressions of the mystical urgings to a 'common life'. It is the teaching of the 'beating heart' that leads to this communion. And so, by a somewhat different route, we are again in the territory of the human heart, itself, as we have seen, the object of its own cult.[18]

Robertson's account in turn invests this potent mixture with the associations of home and homeliness. He cites Waugh's 'Come Whoam To Thi' Childer' to make his point. He gives a long account of the 'half patriarchal, half democratic' mill régime of Jacob Bright. The 'mill as home' becomes a model for economic and social relations. Striking in this context is how 'owd Jacob', and his kin, exemplify in their behaviour towards, and advice to, their workers the virtues of a particular kind of homeliness, one marked by kindness, gentleness, a tenderness to the poor and to children (yet also marked by firmness towards those who stray). Jacob is among his 'own people', and again there is the emphasis on communion with the common people. Particularly apparent here is the idea that these simple, homely feelings are the great 'natural' emotions, to which all are heir. We come full circle to the idea of elemental human passions, passions, in this case, bearing the marks of simplicity and kindness, marks deeply etched by Quakerism.

This Quaker legacy, as we shall see, was in turn part of a broader emphasis on sensibility and feeling coming out of the eighteenth century and given a new lease of life in the nineteenth. Bright was heir to this: for Robertson he early on shows 'tenderness of heart', 'loyalty', 'firmness of purpose', but yet a 'fancy easy to excite'.[19] The heart is here the centre of the affections, an inflamed sensibility its expression, and its text the fundamental human passions, especially those expressed within the hallowed walls of the home or in the extension of the home, the mill.

Trevelyan gave the most eloquent expression to almost all these themes. This is the last paragraph of his biography,

And so he lies, 'as he himself would have wished it', not under Gothic arches hung with conquered flags and echoing back the organ's peal, not among warriors and princes, and the statesmen who played for fame and power, but under the northern sky, in front of the humble house of peace where he had worshipped as a child, in silence sometimes broken by the sound of workmen's footsteps up the steep flagged street, he dwells among his own people.[20]

The book opens with the words,

How clear cut is the sturdy image evoked by those two blunt Saxon syllables, 'John Bright'. Once the rallying cry of the masses seeking enfranchisement – the trump of doom to Whig and Tory in possession – the name in memory has since become

[18] W. Robertson, *Life*, p. 13.   [19] *Ibid.*, p. 38.   [20] G. M. Trevelyan, *Life*, p. 465.

the symbol of an honest man in politics, a 'strong, kind face framed in venerable white hair'.

Above all, Bright uttered 'his plain man's prophecy', a prophecy rooted in 'the broad human joys and sorrows, the common weal and woe, the great homely things of life and death, which drew men and women to this most formidable giant of their time with a personal affection, quite alien from mere political gratitude'.[21] His was 'a strong simplicity, learnt neither in academies nor senates, but springing direct from man's common experience on earth, and reaching thence straight upwards into the sphere of a faultless and noble literature'.[22] This common experience for Trevelyan also took the form of a particularly powerful view of British history, one extending from late whigs like him to the English Marxist historians. The second paragraph of his first chapter begins:

But the long, quiet, rustic centuries were drawing at length to a close. The impulse of the English folk – wandering, which has, with rapidity ever increasing up to our own day, everywhere uprooted the peasant families from their ancestral lands, early laid hold of the Brights.[23]

Bright comes from his own people, the English peasantry, and returns in death to his own people, the Quakers and operatives of Rochdale, the latter a new urban peasantry.

In Trevelyan's account Bright's 'plain man's prophecy' is firmly rooted in the sense of place; the different 'homes' of his house 'One Ash' in Rochdale, of the Quaker Meeting House, as well as the home that Lancashire itself was. Bright is a lover of the traditional stories and local customs of his county and neighbourhood, a teller of dialect tales. Waugh deified Bright, but Bright also thought very highly of Waugh's work, and the dialect revival explored in the study of Waugh exemplified much of the feeling for place Bright had. In many respects he too can be seen as sharing in many of the currents that shaped Waugh and his literature, the interest in local history, for instance, and in the local language (a Saxon language of course). In the domestic home itself Bright is seen to exemplify the straightness of Lancashire: he is a man who loves home and misses it, a man who never tries to be what he is not, a man who tells his daughter Helen, when she is thirteen, that she must never write with irony![24]

---

[21] *Ibid.*, p. 2.   [22] *Ibid.*, p. 1.   [23] *Ibid.*, p. 5.

[24] pp. 134–5. For corroboration of the importance of the cult of the ordinary in the nineteenth century, one owing much to a reworked 'Puritanism' see Raphael Samuel, 'The Discovery of Puritanism, 1820–1914: A Preliminary Sketch', in Jane Garnett and H. C. G. Matthew (eds.), *Revival and Religion: Essays for John Walsh* (1993). I am grateful to Raphael Samuel for allowing me to read the proofs of his article, which arrived after this study was written.

8   Speaking Bright

It has been suggested that perhaps the central theme in the biographical representations was the idea that within all people were elemental feelings. Language, and a man like Bright, could bring these feelings to expression: English might be the 'natural garb' of these passions, Bright in his access to 'the great homely things of life and death' their natural spokesman. Here are the elements of a theory of oratory, speech being that which makes the inner outer, the personal public. It is the speech of the great orator that taps into this reservoir of universal human emotion, because the great orator is, through his nature and his voice, in sympathy with a universal humanity. Therefore, simply by orating, the orator translated his human essence, part of all human essence, into the tangible and the known. He put his interlocuters into contact with themselves, each other, and – to the extent humanity expressed divinity – into contact with God himself.

A full understanding of Bright's, or any, oratory before the coming of recorded sound is beyond our knowledge. Oratory is in its essence evanescent, as perishable as the moment it is spoken. We can never know how such oratory was apprehended by contemporaries in the past, and it *was* a matter of the spoken as experientially present; being there, being part of the emotions of those moments, was what oratory was about. If we can not know this 'experience', we can at least appreciate – as historians have not usually done – that it was the experience that mattered. Bright's speeches were invariably printed, and reached a vastly greater audience than ever heard him speak. The first and the most profound, quasi-religious, effect of oratory was, however, aural and immediate.

Contemporaries aplenty referred to the power of this direct exposure to Bright's oratory. Wemyss Reid spoke of being moved to pity and indignation by Bright, of the ineffable and unforgettable effect of hearing him speak. The ineffable could not be explained, it had to be known directly.[25] One experienced *with*, alongside, the speaker: for instance, Bright's oration on his great and lamented friend Cobden, in Bradford in 1877, found the audience 'struggling under the influence of deep and strong emotion', as the speaker told the 'story' of his grief. To hear Bright was to rediscover the novelty of long familiar emotions. It was also something unique in itself. In this sense, it was not the politics or the morality that mattered, but Bright himself. He was the experience: Trevelyan described his particular oratory as follows, 'He was singular among orators for his want of gesture: there he stood foursquare, and sometimes raised his arm.

---

[25] W. Reid, *Politicians of Today* (1880), p. 201.

His oncoming was as the surge of the full swollen tide, not of the sea in storm; he awed his listeners by the calm of his passion, a terrible steed restrained by a yet stronger hand. Thus he uttered his plain man's prophecy to his fellow citizens ...'[26]

The audience therefore both experienced with the orator and experienced the orator himself (the orator was always a man, the attributes of oratory masculine). Waugh's engagement with Emerson can be said to be transfiguring in both ways, the figure of Emerson moving him as profoundly as Emerson's message. Bright himself gave testimony to the magical effect of oratory in the sense of experiencing with the orator, this time the unknown and exotic, instead of the known emotion rekindled and re-experienced. In 1833 a visiting lecturer spoke on 'Palestine and Egypt' at the old theatre in Toad Lane, Rochdale (Toad Lane was later the first home of the Co-op movement). Bright's account of this lecture series finds him describing it as if it had enabled the lecturer's audience to actively know the unknown themselves. He went on, 'We have ascended the giant pyramid, and from its summit surveyed ... the glorious sun rising in the east ... we have viewed with astonishment the lofty cedar of Lebanon ... From the summit of a neighbouring hill we have beheld Damascus in all its beauty', and so on. The whole thing offers, 'intense delight', 'unspeakable interest'.[27] All this has been known through the eloquence of the speaker, he says. We might say that Bright's oratory did not reflect 'experience' but make it, in the process actually extending the range of what 'experience' might itself mean for his contemporaries.

The ideal combination was, therefore, to experience with the orator and *through* him, living him as the incarnation of what it was he had to say. This seems to have found expression in contemporary teaching about oratory. The orator was literally the instrument of truth, not least the orator's body. Cicero was cited to explain how the orator must convey authority through his body, as well as through his mind.[28] This might involve gesture, but where gesture was not in evidence, as with Bright, the face became significant: 'Since he did not deal in gesture men all the more watched his face. He once said to a friend, "An orator should be shaved", and certainly the play of his lips was very fine.'[29]

There is no historical study of the theory and practice of oratory in the nineteenth century. It is a very important subject. If we seek for the technologies that governed the social in the past, and the technologies of the self, then these will be found in the spoken, as much as in the written, word. In the case of Waugh the diary has been identified as one technology of the self. Oratory is another. This account cannot be more than a

[26] Trevelyan, *Life*, p. 1.   [27] Robertson, *Life*, I, pp. 63–4.   [28] *Ibid.*, p. 62.
[29] Trevelyan, *Life*, p. 385.

brief and inadequate look at a subject of real importance.[30] Its importance may be measured by the popularity of elocution books and reciters in the nineteenth century, also the popularity of recitation, at home and in public, quite apart from public speaking itself, and the many manuals and guides that attached to it. 'Reciters' often combined extracts from great public speeches and great prose and poetry: as late as 1907 Bright's speeches were published as models of oratory and literature in the 'popular-classical' Everyman's Library.

Bright was schooled in the art of 'diction' at Ackworth and the other schools he attended.[31] Ackworth had a special reputation for teaching diction, its teaching being based upon a firm grasp of grammar, through the printed grammar of Lindley Murray, the most influential grammar text of the century. Lindley Murray was a Quaker.[32] The emphasis on diction in a localised educational setting seems paradoxically enough to have involved removing the peculiarities of local speech from public address (unlike Peel and Gladstone, his fellow Lancastrians, widely viewed as the great orators of their time along with Bright, Bright did not speak with a Lancashire accent in public, though in other contexts he was attached to the dialect). Bright's education in speaking was continued in the Rochdale Literary and Philosophical Society, of which he was an avid member in his youth, as well as in the Temperance Society orations he gave in the town. Speaking in the Meeting House was a major source of his training, and Bright was of the conviction that the greatest speeches he ever heard were at the Quaker Yearly Meeting in London, not in the House of Commons.

If we cannot turn to a helpful history of oratory and public speaking we can turn to accounts of contemporary speakers, especially Gladstone.[33] Of Gladstone it was noted, by W. T. Stead, how his voice, his use of the preposition, the eloquence of his gesticulation, the movement of his chest even, all produced a situation in which 'the whole of the man's energy was concentrated in a single act'.[34] Through this energy the speaker gave material form to the immaterial. Both intellectual concepts and faith were materialised, and the audience was 'Gladstonised' (as a contemporary put it), for those who lived it an unforgettable happening. This involved feeling the faith, but also feeling reason as itself a form of faith: as has been

---

[30] For some very interesting remarks see James Vernon, *Politics and the People: A Study in English Political Culture c. 1815–67* (Cambridge 1993), pp. 117–26.

[31] J. Travis Mills, *John Bright and the Quakers* (1935), 2 vols, I, chap. 5.

[32] Patrick Joyce, *Visions of the People: Industrial England and the Question of Class 1840–1914* (1991), pp. 203–5.

[33] Eugenio F. Biagini, *Liberty, Retrenchment and Reform: Popular Liberalism in the Age of Gladstone, 1860–1880* (1992), chap. 7.

[34] *Ibid.*, pp. 390–2.

persuasively argued, the tenets of Gladstonian Liberalism involved the rationality of free and informed public discussion, and this was expressed in the serious and didactic nature of Liberal rhetoric, which was calm, logical and reasoned. The ideal of a free press gave expression to this idealisation of reason.[35] But reason seems to have been experienced by the faithful as the affirmation of entrenched beliefs, the exemplification of the spirit of Gladstonian faith.[36] Gladstone's audiences experienced the logic of his speeches emotionally. His was a function akin to that of the revivalist preacher, securing adhesion to the faith, this time the faith in reason. The atmosphere of sacrality and prophetic revelation hung heavily over Gladstone's speeches.

It hung just as heavily over Bright's. He, too, spoke in measured tones, marshalling his evidence with enormous care for the veracity, as well as the effectiveness, of his arguments. Yet even more than Gladstone, emphasising faith itself rather more than the emotionality of reason, Bright tapped into the religious feeling in which the age was suffused. What was it like to be Brightised? As with Gladstonisation it involved being invited to share with and through the orator a sense of communion, with God but also with history. Here he, or she, might find faith, succour, justice – a profound discovery for people shut out from these in their everyday life.

The historian Justin Macarthy echoed Trevelyan's account of the leashed power of Bright's speaking: 'His style of speaking was exactly what a conventional demagogue's ought not to be. It was pure to austerity. It never allowed itself to be mastered by passion ... [it had] superb self-restraint.'[37] But however restrained, passion was felt and broadcast in Bright's 'oncoming', 'the rage of the full-swollen tide', if not the sea in storm. This calmed passion owed a great deal to Quakerism, where one approached the Lord in silence and stillness, moving within oneself towards the Inner Light. Trevelyan remarked how Quaker witness involved expressing the deepest thought and emotion in stillness. In speaking Bright therefore can be regarded as moving inwards in order to bring truth outwards, the distinction between the inner and the outer being obliterated in oratory, the truth within each being made known to all. And that truth was a moral and religious one, the distinction being important. A rhetoric fired by religion reached many for whom its religious messages were secondary to its broader moral appeal. Both forms of

---

[35] P. Joyce, *Visions of the People*, pp. 40–4; H. C. G. Matthew, 'Rhetoric and Politics in Great Britain, 1860–1950' in P. J. Waller (ed.), *Politics and Social Change: Essays Presented to A. F. Thompson* (1987).

[36] E. F. Biagini, *Liberty, Retrenchment and Reform*, p. 391.

[37] Anon., *John Bright the Tribune of the English People* (Rochdale 1911), p. 52.

appeal were held to be expressive of Bright's innermost 'character'. For Augustine Birrell his character flowed unmediated into his speeches and public letters, it 'exploded' in his talk, and formed his 'marvellous style'.[38]

The Congregationalist cleric and intellectual Page Hopps testified to the force of the religious truth Bright found within: 'One of the characteristics of John Bright's speeches, even in the House of Commons, was the grave and reverent undercurrent of reference to a supreme Being, to the real king of the nation, to someone who had a right to rule ... the rightful king of all.'[39] Bright compared his own speaking to the work of the cleric: 'I consider that when I stand upon a platform as I do now, I am engaged in as solemn a labour as Mr Dale' (the renowned Birmingham Nonconformist cleric). One contemporary observer noted how Bright was telling his audiences that they, with him and like him, could have the same access to the Inner Light, and hence to truth. This light was, however, popularised as conscience, the tribunal God had set up in man. The religious law was translated into the human terms of a moralism more pervasive in its effects than religious truth alone. The voice of the Old Testament spoke, in terms of a stern moral code governing actions in this life. As Bright in his Birmingham speech went on to say, 'It was not only upon the affairs of the other world that men must be true to themselves and to their consciences.'[40]

When Disraeli congratulated Bright on his famous 'Angel of Death' speech on the Crimean War, and wished that he had made it, Bright replied, 'You might have if you had been honest.'[41] For Bright the matter was as straightforward as this; 'True eloquence' (he said, citing his hero Milton) was 'none but the serious and hearty love of truth'.[42] Religion spoke the great moral truths of life, and the orator could give these voice only when he too was of moral character. In the popular estimation of Bright he was felt to be uniquely placed to voice moral truth because he was morality incarnate, again like an Old Testament prophet. As Robertson put it, 'His arguments were practical and made what was merely a commonplace duty appear as a glorious and elevating work; they touched the hearts of his hearers as religion and poetry would touch them.'[43] It was Bright's elevation to the personification of the eternal

---

[38] John Bright, An Address Delivered at Rochdale on 16 November 1911, by the Rt. Hon. Augustine Birrell M.P. (Rochdale 1911).

[39] John Page Hopps, John Bright, A Study of Character and Characteristics (n.d., 1880s?), p. 20.

[40] W. Reid, Politicians of Today, pp. 87–8.   [41] G. M. Trevelyan, Life, p. 245.

[42] Cited in Loren Reid, 'John Bright: The Orator as Teacher', The Southern Speech Communications Journal, (1975).

[43] W. Robertson, Life, I, p. 62.

moral law that was near the root of his popular appeal ('Be Just and Fear Not' was his motto, and that of the multitude of working men who followed him).

Gladstone's Commons eulogy after Bright's death is well known but bears repeating,

> We feel that Mr Bright is entitled to a higher eulogy than any that could be due to intellect or any that could be due to success ... the character of the man lay deeper than his intellect, deeper than his eloquence, deeper than anything that can be described or seen on the surface, and the supreme eulogy which is his due I apprehend to be this, that he elevated political life to a higher elevation, and to a loftier standard, and that he has thereby bequeathed to his country the character of a statesman which can be made the subject not only of admiration, and not only of gratitude, but of reverential contemplation.[44]

Collini has recently observed how Bright gave particular expression to the 'language of character' in which 'high' Victorian political thought was registered from the 1830s and 40s.[45] There is more to it than this, for Bright did not voice the language of character, he *was* the language of character, an icon, a talisman, the object not of mere admiration but of 'reverential contemplation'. In being this, he translated the language of character from high politics to low.

Finally, in the public projection of Bright the 'character' that voiced the moral law was ineffably the plain, homely man. As Trevelyan observed,

> His greatest passages are those in which his sense of poetry and of grandeur came closest to his vision of homely, common life, which was to him, as it was to Wordsworth, the source of high thoughts and great imaginings. Thus, in his other Crimean speech, he leads up to the death of Colonel Boyle by telling how he lately met the Colonel at 'Mr Westerton's, the bookseller, near Hyde Park Corner', a place well known to the Member whom he was addressing, and how his late Colleague had there told him his fears as a husband and father at going to the war. Then came the thunderous climax – 'the stormy Euxine is his grave; his wife is a widow, his children fatherless' – which quite overpowered his hearers.[46]

Moral grandeur made homely, made part of 'common life', this was the recipe by which the 'prophecy' of this plain man gained such a purchase on contemporaries. He engaged the intensely powerful moral sense of his age by relating it to the ordinary things of life and to ordinary people, so harnessing the strength of that sense in the cause of the very people he had so exalted. He became the prophet of democracy by making the moral law

---

[44] Commons Speech, 19 March 1889.
[45] Stefan Collini, *Public Moralists: Political Thought and Intellectual Life in Britain 1850–1930* (Oxford 1991), chap. 3.
[46] G. M. Trevelyan, *Life*, p. 385.

itself demotic. Behind this achievement lay the achievement of his own self.

9   Making the self

RELIGION

A good deal of the public myth of Bright was constructed out of what contemporaries took to be the marginality of his position as the wealthy, established son of a man who had known poverty at first hand and was of 'humble' origin. To the extent that his oratory expressed a view of the man as voicing the moral law, and hence passions and feelings common to all people, Bright can be seen as producing a public self that corroborated this cult, the Bright of history. If history's Bright was constructed out of his assumed marginality, his private self was constructed out of religion, out of the Quakerism that was the most important element in his formation. For, if Bright was 'socially marginal', he was also religiously marginal: he spanned the old dispensation of Quakerism and the new, the quietism of the eighteenth century and the Evangelicalism of the nineteenth, being not quite completely of either. This religious outlook can be seen as expressing his indeterminate social position. The historian of Victorian Quakerism has observed that the quietist indictment of the Evangelical current in Quakerism was as much social as theological.[47] What was objected to in the new emphasis on engagement with the world in order to save souls for God was the worldliness believed to be initiated by the change, a fear of the world not unconnected with the increasing wealth and status of Quakers in the early part of the century. In Bright's case the social and religious worlds of the eighteenth century which he inherited were analogous: the stress on humility in the latter directly echoed the humble condition of the former. The successful man of the worlds of politics and business can be seen as living out the consequences of what he felt was a changed social position therefore, a situation similar to many of the 'middle class' who were like him (the term 'middle class' in fact registered this perception). The danger of a reductive reading of religion is however considerable: Bright created a self out of the materials of religion, and religion, not some putative 'social' dilemma, dictated the creation of this self. The narrative of his self's creation can not be adequately given in terms other than those it which it was written.

The observation that Bright was given the Quaker stamp at birth and

---

[47] Elizabeth Isichei, *Victorian Quakers* (Oxford 1970), chap. 1.

that this endured thereafter, is true to the extent that the Society of Friends did dominate the whole life of the member, from the earliest days. A 'particular people' demarcated themselves by dress, speech, personal demeanour. By the early eighteenth century the wearing of black, the standardised clothes, the standard use of the personal pronoun, the refusal to observe titles and the nomenclature of the calendar were all well entrenched. These marks of humility and simplicity were the material manifestations of the doctrine of the Inner Light, the notion that God dwelt within all people and could be directly approached without benefit of the intermediaries of the world. This was a world in which 'hat worship' was despised, the doffing of the hat at the time being a primary expression of social deference. Here we seem to have the root of Bright's later attack on privilege in the name of the masses, the people. It was, but only because Bright made it so. There was nothing immanent in Quaker-ism dictating the political and moral character it was to have in Bright's hands. For all the 'totality' of the experience of Quakerism it was more neutral than this. It may be thought of as a resource that might be used in different ways to create different kinds of self, still enjoining choice on an acting subject.

When we begin to penetrate the world of traditional, quietist Quaker-ism in Rochdale we are aware that something rather different from what Bright and posterity constructed is evident. The hatred of privilege was not related to a political awareness. The small-town Quakerism of Roch-dale was intensely introspective. The society of the Society involved a special care for the education of fellow Friends. Yet, rather than an education in some assumed Quaker tolerance, one alive to broader his-torical contexts, the education Bright had was extremely narrow, and in many respects highly intolerant. This was most of all evident at Ackworth, one of the most important Quaker schools in the north of England. In Bright's day Ackworth seems to have alternated a rule of almost monastic severity, and more-than-monastic elaborateness, with periods of anar-chy.[48] The school was akin to a monastery: monthly walks were taken, apart from which the pupils lived in isolation. Waterloo, for example, went completely outside their knowing, and they had hardly any connec-tion with their families. The school-day itself involved compulsory cold bathing, which Bright remembered to the end of his life, particularly the occasion when he was forced back into the water by a besom in the face, directed by a master.

In his 'Memoir' of youth, he remarked 'I was a timid and docile boy,

---

[48] For accounts of his schooling, J. Travis Mills, *John Bright and the Quakers*, I, chap. 3, and J. Bright, 'Memoir', in R. A. J. Walling (ed.), *The Diaries of John Bright*, pp. 5–7, hereafter 'Memoir'.

and with older and wiser control I should have escaped much of the unhappiness I suffered while at Ackworth.'[49] He suffered greatly from the assistant masters, older boys who 'had authority wholly inappropriate to their years': his was an experience of 'much annoyance and injustice which seemed almost like persecution'. Far from Quakerism schooling him in the fellowship of the persecuted just, it is evident that in this manifestation it was the active source of a sense of persecution. It also schooled him in the need for liberty, without which authority was oppression. The sleeping accommodation was barbaric. Not until 1829 did the pupils have single beds (Bright left in 1823), and not until 1832 were nightshirts provided. In 1832 provision was made for daily washing; before then the boys washed when they could in a trough in the cellar, the water being changed once, after 90 boys had washed. Bad sanitation brought frequent disease into the school. There was little heating. The food was intolerable. The education on offer was of a piece with the conditions: aside from the rigours of Lindley Murray's *Grammar* the emphasis was heavily upon works of religious instruction, especially Quaker instruction. Geography and history were not taught at Ackworth until the 1820s and 30s.[50] Bright was taken away from the school early, and completed his education at smaller and kinder Quaker establishments. And his father, and subsequently his mother and second wife, thereafter took a direct hand in the reform of Ackworth. None the less Ackworth was a major Quaker school at the time, and this seems to have been the régime for decades before reform. This time at Ackworth registered very powerfully with the young boy, as his 'Memoir', written in old age, testifies.

The historian of Bright and Quakerism, J. Travis Mills, presents a revealing picture of the quietist traditionalism in which Bright grew up: a third of the small congregation in Rochdale were manufacturers or merchants, and their families (usually of no great standing), the others mostly prosperous 'tradesmen'.[51] These were narrow in their outlook, their world being bound by the Quaker system of Meetings, extending by tradition into the Pennine uplands of Yorkshire, Derbyshire, and Cumberland, as well as Lancashire. Theirs was an educational régime sometimes even less enlightened than the Ackworth one. This Pennine association seems earlier to have extended into a constituency among the weaver-farmers of these areas, but the description of the social composition of the congregation given above, for the first decades of the century, suggests a growth

---

[49] *Diaries*, p. 6.
[50] For a very interesting account of the reading provided at Ackworth see Travis Mills, *John Bright and the Quakers*, I, pp. 194, 197.
[51] *Ibid.*, I, chaps. 3, 4, 10, esp. 3 drawing on the journal of Joseph Wood of Newhouse.

of the influence of the relatively wealthy. Whatever the case, this was a milieu considerably more restrictive than that of a number of the more prosperous Quakers in the bigger cities. Travis Mills described it as both religiously and socially conservative.[52] Quakerism has usually been characterised by reference to socially highly visible groups, whereas this small-town narrowness was probably just as typical.[53]

In relation to Bright Quakerism has also been characterised in a singular way; in the hagiography, as we have seen, but also in the twentieth-century historical writing that we shall consider later. William Robertson, for instance, dwelt lovingly on how Quaker mysticism permitted a communing with what was common in mankind, Quaker humility permitting a particular closeness to this common human identity. The demotic implications of this rendering are plain here, as they are in Trevelyan's biography, and as they are among twentieth-century historians. There is a direct connection in these readings between the simple Quaker and the tribune of the people. However, both figures are alike inventions, operations on a reality that was altogether more neutral than this, and in many respects quite counter to these constructed identities.

In order to consider the democratic credentials of Quakerism we must look at its awakening from its quietist traditions, a change that initiated argument long after the early nineteenth century. Bright is a good example of this continuing internal quarrel, though there is no doubting his move away from the restrictions and what he felt to be intolerance of the old dispensation. The persona Bright constructed came, therefore, out of this relation between the old and the new. His was a made Quakerism, through which he handled not only the 'social', but also the familial and personal relations of his day. His revolt against the old may be briefly substantiated.

We know most about his reaction to the Society, least about his personal theology, of which, especially in later life, he seems hardly to have spoken at all. Those who saw him at Ackworth already detected a definiteness of character unlike the run of Quakers, something manifested in a lack of respect for some of the leading Friends of the day.[54] In his account of his other schools he dwelt on the 'kindness', and 'gentleness' of the school régimes, in contrast to Ackworth. At William Simpson's School in York he came into contact with the Tuke family, founders of The Retreat, a Quaker-run lunatic asylum, also of Bootham's School, both in

---

[52] *Ibid.*, chap. 9 for his extended discussion of the character of the Rochdale Friends from 1808 to 1889.

[53] On the narrowness of small-town and village Quakerism see Margaret Howitt (ed.), *Mary Howitt. An Autobiography*, (1889), 2 vols.

[54] Travis Mills, *John Bright*, I, p. 56.

the town. The family exemplified the Evangelical current sweeping through Quakerism, the new emphasis on the régime of kindness and 'sympathy'.[55] This involved a diminution of the place of the Inner Light, and a greater emphasis on the Bible as a source of revelation, when compared to the authority of the 'primitive', early worthies of the Society, and to the promptings of a mystical inwardness. There was a turning outwards from the quietism of a 'peculiar people' to an engagement with the world in the form of an intervention to secure the moral betterment of mankind. The theology of the Atonement, in which salvation needed to be actively pursued, for oneself and others, tended to displace the light within as the assurance of being saved. Bright seems to have assembled his perspective on the world from these two points of view. This involved distancing himself from what he felt to be the unnecessary grip of mere convention in his religion. His sister Priscilla was excluded from the Society for forty years for marrying out, and John suffered life-long distress because of this.[56] Others of his brothers and sisters were also excluded, including his brother Jacob, for non-attendance. The Quaker régime in Rochdale seems to have continued in a fairly conservative fashion throughout John's lifetime. For instance, marriage was directly vetted by the local Society, candidates for marriage having to present themselves to the Men's and Women's Meetings for approval. At the same time John was more rooted in the past than almost anyone else in the family. Only he and his brother Thomas, who ran Greenbank, stayed in connection with the mill (his son John Albert continued the line of filial devotion in the next generation). The others grew up and out, out to a reading of books that worried 'owd Jacob' (Emerson and Carlyle for instance, or the Lake poets), outwards too to an appreciation of music. This was especially the case with the Bright women, his sisters and daughter, however, rather than his wives. They, along with his brother Jacob, who was latitudinarian to the point of unbelief, point forward to the next generation of Quakerism, to the liberal theology of the 1880s and 90s, a development in many cases presaging a radical politics linked to advanced liberalism, and ultimately to socialism and feminism.[57] Bright was located somewhere in the middle, between this new world and the eighteenth century. His loyalty was to the latter. But this does not mean he avoided the present. Quite the opposite. He was a child of the political and religious tumult of the early nineteenth century, a product of, and an agent in, the opening up of Quakerism to this ferment. His loyalty to the past was a product of his engagement with a troubled present. The

---

[55] *Ibid.*, I, pp. 232–6, II, pp. 316–23.   [56] *Ibid.*, I, chap. 6.
[57] E. Isichei, *Victorian Quakers*, chap. 2.

making of a self for Bright involved this negotiation of the present by means of an imagined past.

On the question of the assumed democracy of Quaker organisation the chronicler of Rochdale Quakerism said, 'To attach importance to the wise words uttered by wise men rather than to the impulsive demonstrations of a uninformed majority, that at least was the desire and purpose of the Society of Friends during John Bright's youth and throughout his life. Quakerism might still preserve the forms and formulae of democracy, but in all essentials for 200 years in the sphere of its own government it was aristocratic to the core.'[58] Quaker Meetings exemplified this: the Clerk of the Meeting counted the weight of the words spoken, not the number of hands raised. A few words from a Quaker elder or minister of repute 'might for generations outweigh the utterance of a dozen of the rank-and-file'. The social standing of speakers counted as much as their wisdom.[59] The Clerk took the final sense of the Meeting and the Clerk's word was final. The ethos was one of submissiveness, the emphasis being on humility, on 'submitting to each other in lowliness of heart'. Quaker counsels might therefore in practice be removed from the ideal of a government based neither on birth nor wealth. None the less, the ideal remained, and if the result was not a democracy but an aristocracy of the faithful – or better perhaps a meritocracy of the faithful – the desire that faith should tell before birth or wealth always gave Quakerism a more radical potential than most other beliefs.

This mixture of practice and ideals in church government seems to have been reflected in conceptions of political governance too. These are William Penn's words in his 'Preface to the Frame of Government in Pennsylvania',

But I chose to solve the controversy [between monarchy, aristocracy and democracy] with this small distinction, and it belongs to all three: any government is free to the people under it, whatever be the frame, where the laws rule, and the people are party to the laws . . . let men be good and the government cannot be bad . . . But if men be bad, let the government be ever so good, they will endeavour to warp and spoil it to their turn. The great end of all government is to support power in

---

[58] Travis Mills, I, p. 17.
[59] E. Isichei, *Victorian Quakers*, pp. 79 ff. It should be emphasised that the doctrine of the Inner Light was a spiritual doctrine and not a moral or philosophical one. While it could lend itself to such applications the 'Inner Light' should not be confused with 'conscience' or 'reason'. It was first and last about seeking Christ within. So much is clear from Quaker teaching. See *Christian Faith and Practice in the Experience of the Society of Friends* (London Yearly Meeting of the Religious Society of Friends, first printed 1960), 'The Spirit', sections 163–82; see esp. 'George Fox's visit to North Carolina' (167, from 1672), and section 170, from the Yearly Meeting for 1879. I wish to thank Professor A. G. Dyson of Manchester University for directing me to this work.

reference with the people and to secure the people from the abuse of power ... for liberty without obedience is confusion and obedience without liberty is slavery.'[60]

These are Bright's words in a Birmingham speech of January 1882,

I do not pretend myself to be a democrat. I never accepted that title, and I believe those who knew me and spoke honestly of me never applied it to me. What I am in favour of is such liberty as will give security to freedom, but I am not in favour of that freedom that would destroy it ...'[61]

The aim of both men was to secure liberty with obedience, consent with security. Bright always sought to balance the interests of all groups and classes, allowing none to preponderate over the interests of the 'nation', 'the people', and liberty itself. And, as with Penn, the aim of government was to make people moral, for if they were not moral then good government would never prevail.[62]

If we turn from Quaker government to other aspects of their teaching we find the same difficulty in identifying 'democratic' elements, the same desire to secure liberty with obedience. I shall consider their teaching on the care of the poor, and on servants and employees. Rich Friends were expected to exercise a stewardship of wealth, and show care for their poorer brethren, to whom they are connected as partakers of the Inner Light. Within the Society a spiritual equality of sorts obtained, albeit often with deference to men of standing and wise words. Humility of mind could mean mere submissiveness, though the ideal primacy of spiritual criteria before other standards often meant a strong sense of fellowship with the poor, expressed in the injunctions to simplicity and 'lowliness' of mind. Simplicity was the condition that brought one closer to God, because further from the things of the world, which by their nature impeded this closeness. One needed no intermediaries with God, and the poor and the 'lowly of mind' were idealised representatives of this closeness. The major figure in Rochdale Quakerism in Jacob Bright's day was Joseph Wood, a rough farmer–weaver, without learning. He gave expression to this sense of the fellowship of the humble by speaking of the Rochdale Friends as 'the People', a term that for John was to assume enormous significance in another field.[63] But the connection between the two senses was close, as was the depiction of both as often suffering persecution.

In all this, however, there is no quarrel with the existence of riches and poverty. The rich simply have duties of guidance towards the poor. Perhaps the best guide in this matter is the *Minutes and Epistles of the Yearly Meeting* from its first institution, published in collections in 1862

---

[60] cited in Travis Mills, I, p. 21.   [61] Cited in *ibid.*, II, p. 289.   [62] *Ibid.*, p. 290.
[63] *Ibid.*, p. 137, and accounts taken from Wood's journals, pp. 131–65.

and periodically before and after this date.[64] Christian practice and
discipline were regulated in this fashion. Here the poor may be an
'ornament to our society' when properly cared for, but that care involved
the moral guidance of the rich: 'The children of the poor are to have
useful employment to keep them from vice and looseness.' In ministering
to the poor, care should be taken not to wound their feelings (this
emphasis was important), but it was clear that the poor's first duty was to
help themselves: '... we would remind our poor Friends, that it is their
duty, by frugality and industry, to use their strenuous endeavours to
maintain themselves and their families ... and not to be dependent on
others'. The children of the poor should minister to them and not throw
the burden on others.[65] This last epistle was dated 1833 and shows the
nice mixture of Quaker sentiment and early Victorian self-help.

These sentiments were directed to the Society, but much else in the
Minutes and Epistles is aimed at mankind generally, the injunctions on
'Liberality and Benevolence' for instance, 'concerning the whole human
race'.[66] The movement outwards was necessarily the case with the
'Counsel to Employers'. Here the concern with moral and religious
tutelage was even stronger than in the case of the poor. The emphasis on
liberty arising from a recognition of a common condition in which all may
share is correspondingly less evident than in the case of the Quaker poor,
as subordinates are involved. There is a similar emphasis on 'sympa-
thising' with servants and employees, rendering them happy. However,
there is an even stronger emphasis on securing obedience. Obedience is
seen as being to the moral law, the Law of God, but, just as in Bright's
own justification of political activity, the moral law and the obedience it
secures is designed to create 'security' alongside liberty.

The social regulation of the servant is to be through religion: 'pride and
idleness' should be discouraged in them, and the way to do this is to
encourage them to worship. The care of all masters is to 'teach and
restrain ... all those whom Providence has placed under them'. An
account to God must be rendered for one's servants, an account given in
the terms of keeping the minds of 'those placed under them' attentive to
the truth, especially through the reading of the scriptures (as the injunction of 1805 had it).[67] The young George Fox had long before revealed
the contradictions of wishing to embrace both fellowship and authority:
you must treat your servants as yourself, and 'in patience and meekness'

---

[64] *Extracts from the Minutes and Epistles of the Yearly Meeting of the Religious Society of
Friends Held in London ... From its First Institution to the Present* (1862).
[65] *Ibid.*, 'Christian Discipline XIV – Care of the Poor'.
[66] *Ibid.*, 'Christian Practice VIII'.
[67] *Ibid.*, 'Practice XI'.

show them their 'place and service'.[68] Impossibly, one must be brother and father.

Quakerism was the medium of John Bright's selfhood, from his earliest days. And yet, in this examination, we seem to have no 'self' before us, at least no 'inner self', certainly not a self like that of Edwin Waugh, deeply riven by sorrow and struggle. Perhaps this is because there is no revelatory diary and correspondence that has remained? But Bright kept a private diary throughout most of his life: written in a minute hand, in fading pencil often, it does not look as if it was designed for publication. It is flat, translucent, nothing like Waugh's diary. Similarly, he had a vast correspondence throughout his life, but this dealt with family and political affairs, not with a personal self, in struggle or not. One is forced to the conclusion that no interior drama of the self is evident in the sources because no interior drama of the self was present in the man. This relative absence of interiority is in part owed to the fact that the language in which Bright constructed a personal self was innately a 'social one': it concerned 'Friends', who were in a 'Society', the self being by definition in a social relation, however spiritual the understanding of the social entity. The self took form in relation to a situation of the social governance and moral regulation of the extra-personal collectivity.

Set within the larger society and polity of England, the ordinances and sympathies of the Society had no necessary broader meaning. They permitted many views of the 'social' and the self. As the introverted Society of the eighteenth century impacted on the political and industrial turmoil of the early nineteenth century, Bright shaped a particular view of his religion to both understand and command this ferment. If religion was the language of the self, its schools were economics and politics. And, in the invented self of Bright, history and politics were to be inseparable, Bright constituting himself as a living principle of both in the form of the plain man transmogrified as a persecuted demos struggling towards liberation.

Bright's first and most important school of economics was the family mill. Greenbank Mill was the arena in which Quaker principles were put to work, the figure of the patriarch Jacob exemplifying these principles, particularly for his eldest son. John left school at the age of fourteen. Thereafter, until his entry into local politics in the early 1830s, his education was that of the mill, supplemented by his autodidacticism while at work (again, from a different vantage he shared experiences with Edwin Waugh). Like all the sons, John was taught all the branches of the trade, and not merely the theory but the practice, including the different manual trades such as weaving.

[68] For a discussion of 'Bright in Business' on business ethics, see Travis Mills, II, chap. XVI.

Jacob exemplified the Quaker teachings on servants, combining sympathy with guidance. Something like a 'circle of representation' is evident with 'owd Jacob' as well as his son: in Robertson, Trevelyan, and other biographies the same stories of the mill régime are recycled.[69] The mythology extended to Edwin Waugh: in the 'Besom Ben' stories we have looked at, Jacob figures more than once (he is rendered in dialect), as does the 'plucky lad', his son John. The same motifs come up again and again in these accounts: Jacob's rule is one of kindness, his overlookers do not use the strap, and he directly dispenses charity to those who are deserving, but also to those who may not be, so kind is his heart that he does not enquire too closely. On winter nights Jacob is said to have lit his workchildren's way home himself, dispensing sweets to them in the day.[70] There is no reason to doubt these stories: long after his death the benevolent mill régime of Jacob was remembered with affection in the town. None the less, 'moral suasion' was also evident, educational and religious provision being made and personally directed by Jacob and his family. This was even more apparent with John, who, before his entry into the Anti-Corn Law League agitation, inherited his father's mantle as the eldest son, the coming patriarch. John erected new houses for workers in his youth, ran a school, and – sign of the increased force of moral suasion – started the Fieldhouse Educational Institution in 1832, which organised 'improving' lectures for the workers. On his seventieth birthday John looked back to his youth, when he claimed to have known all at the mill, following their lives (and their moral progress), and personally paying their wages. Strict economic logic was not always followed in the time of Jacob, and later: when new mills were built in the 1820s and 30s, the old ones were kept running at a loss in the interim period, and the firm seems to have run at a loss in the cotton famine to prevent workers being thrown on poor relief.

This philanthropy was only possible because, unlike Edwin Waugh and his like, John Bright was not exposed to the vicissitudes of actual want. We must remember here the extent to which this mythology of the common man was accompanied by the condition of plenty, not want, however taxing was the business competition of the early cotton industry. Unlike some working men, these representations involved not present dispossession – except for the dispossession of the father – but possession, in the sense that between his father's time and his own those who had nothing had acquired wealth. For Bright and his like, for 'middle class' people, the sense of security was as telling as the sense of insecurity was to many of those sometimes called the proletarians. 'Security' was culturally

[69] W. Robertson, *Life*, I, pp. 183, 257–8; G. M. Trevelyan, *Life*, 17–18.
[70] Rev. Robert Collyer, 'Capital and Labour: A Lecture', *The New York Tribune*, 'Extra', no. 61, n.d., pp. 4–5.

constructed, but the construction was all the easier in a situation not marked by economic deprivation. Security was constructed through the symbols of freedom from want, by possessions, in Bright's case by property, chiefly the property of the mill. And the 'experience' of security was inseparable from the exercise of authority: to have property was to have authority. The Quakerism Bright constructed for himself was therefore so much about the exercise of authority, authority in the mill, the meeting house, and the home, and beyond these authority in the democratic polity. Ontological security was to be had in these different spheres, including the 'economic', but the economic in this reading less of production than of consumption and exchange.

Bright's conception of the self and social was therefore forged in the arena of Quaker principle. And it begins to appear that John's father was the central figure in this arena. The drama played out by this figure was that of the father of the mill, in daily contact with his children-workers, and in close sympathy with them because they were of his own family, the family of the common folk. When it came to the school of politics, Jacob was again the central figure. Long before the pre-Reform Act agitation and the time of the League John's introduction to politics was in the form of his father's 'persecution' for refusing to pay church tithes. The first of a series of distraint warrants arrived in 1811 and continued to at least 1832. The father's goods were on several occasions seized. In his 'Memoir' John claimed that his early experience soon taught him he was of the 'stock of the martyrs'. Yet the emphasis on martyrdom and persecution, central to his make up, was of his own creation and not the product of some Quaker Unconscious. The patriarch among his 'own people', as Trevelyan gloried in putting it, became the persecuted patriarch, reaching back into a Quaker past rewritten to serve the needs of the day, a past in which the 'commons' of England again figured prominently.

For generations many quietist Quakers, rather ignobly, had simply paid up for a quiet life. And a quiet life they seem mostly to have had, not least in Rochdale. A history of unrelieved oppression is belied by Travis Mills' account of the town in the late eighteenth century.[71] The vicars of Rochdale and the local magistrates seem to have acted to protect Quaker meetings, and clerics in the town offered their homes to Quakers visiting for meetings. The immediate political context of the post-Waterloo years seems to have been the spur to Bright's creation of the long pedigree of Quaker suffering for truth. This in conjunction with the persecution of his beloved father, who, left to himself, tended to the quiet life. Jacob was never involved publicly in politics, even though he was a moderate radical

---

[71] Travis Mills, I, pp. 119–21.

in his sympathies.[72] The real goad to John's passion may have been the fact that the absentee Vicar of Rochdale during his father's persecution was the chairman of the magistrates who ordered the 'Peterloo Massacre'. The 'Peterloo Butcher' was one link connecting Bright's religion and his growing political radicalism. As we shall see, he learned much of his politics at first hand from the Greenbank hands.[73] He could hardly fail to do otherwise: the mill was on the verge of Cronkeyshaw Common, and the common land of England was at the time a potent symbol as well as an important meeting-place of the common people of England, and Cronkeyshaw was no exception. Bright would have witnessed many great meetings in his youth. And, while he may have learned radical politics, he seems to have kept out of the way of direct involvement. What mattered more was the persecution of his father. It was this that brought him into the violent and bitter conflict over Church Rates which convulsed the town in 1839–40, and in which he was the leading figure. The stories repeated at this time bore the powerful imprint of justice hung high on a cross: for instance, it was believed the bailiff minions of the Vicar of Rochdale spent what they seized on jovial living, while at the same time persecuting poor dying weavers, descending so low as to appropriate the only, and dearest, possession left to them, the family Bible.[74]

Bright took upon himself the mantle of the protector of handloom weavers such as this, the common people of England. He did this through a process of conscious identification with a fictive Quaker past. He named his house One Ash in commemoration of the village of Monyash in Derbyshire, the birthplace of John Gratton. According to Travis Mills Bright was John Gratton reincarnated.[75] Gratton was a renowned Quaker preacher of his day, righteous, courageous, frequently imprisoned for his belief. The first words of the Minute Book of the Monyash Meeting describe Gratton as ministering to 'an unworthy and despised' people among the valleys and hills of 'the High Peak country'. He ministered to a flock in wild places, part of the Pennine uplands that were also the wild ministry of the quietist Quakerism of eighteenth-century Rochdale. Bright reached past that quietism, back to a seventeenth century by means of which he recreated the vanished, or vanishing, legacy of the humble, unlettered Quakerism of his youth. This tie to the past was one of blood too, albeit blood also rekindled in the imagination. Gratton's granddaughter was his father's grandmother. The past Bright reached back to

[72] *Ibid.*, pp. 260–1.
[73] W. Robertson, *Life*, chap. 4, 'Popular Agitations', and pp. 64–5.
[74] For the best account of the Church Rates controversy in Rochdale see Travis Mills, II, chap. 14.
[75] *Ibid.*, I, pp. 99–100.

was that of the plebeian seventeenth century, that of George Fox, a shoemaker and cattle dealer, and earlier still the past of the mystical Jacob Boehme, 'the inspired cobbler of Görlitz'.[76] The first preachings of Fox were in the hamlets and farmsteads of the Pennine uplands. These northern districts were seen as 'the true cradle of Quakerism', especially by northern Quakers. The drama here, part of a sweeping historical narrative of at once personal and social identity, was that of unpolished and unlettered men going forth, always in the teeth of persecution. Their reward might be found in the English cradles of their faith, or in America, the symbol of a Quaker utopia long before it came to figure, especially in Bright, as the symbol of nineteenth-century democracy.

FEELING AND FAMILY

John Bright was decidedly the child of the early nineteenth century as well as of the seventeenth, particularly of those currents of thought character-istic of the time of his youth, Evangelicalism and romanticism. What these offered, particularly Evangelicism, was a new access to 'feeling' through which the self and the social could be addressed in novel ways. Evangeli-calism is as interesting for this, as for its directly religious tenets. As G. M. Young observed,[77]

We are in an age when, if brides sometimes swooned at the altar, Ministers sometimes wept at the Table; when the sight of an infant school could reduce a civil servant to a passion of tears; and one undergraduate had to prepare another undergraduate that a third undergraduate had doubts about the Blessed Trinity – an age of flashing eyes and curling lips, more easily touched, more easily shocked, more ready to spurn, to vaunt, to admire, and above all, to preach.

Evangelicalism had much to do with this. According to Young the certainties it ushered in gave a licence to feeling not available to gener-ations bred in doubt.[78] Reared in 'seriousness', and moral 'eagerness', licensed feeling overflowed in sentiment, invective, in tears and flashing eyes. These were the emotions of exalted self-righteousness. But there was a darker side too, for the consciousness of sin, and the possibility of damnation, might lead to extremes of fear and despair. None the less, the essential characteristic was licensed feeling, restrained excess. We enter the world of Edwin Waugh's sorrows, though these are not to be Bright's. Even so, he drank at the same fountain of feeling and its truth.

    A more recent student of Evangelicalism than that of Young informs us that the 'vitality' evident in Evangelical religion sprang from its dual

[76] Ibid., pp. 1–8.
[77] G. M. Young, Victorian England: Portrait of an Age (2nd edn., Oxford 1953), p. 14.
[78] Ibid., p. 13.

nature, the belief in the natural depravity of man coupled with an awareness of the joyful prospect of salvation.[79] Rightly I think, this is seen to be at the root of what John Vincent called the 'visceral thrill' of Liberalism,[80] the 'sublime self-righteousness that gave Gladstone's Liberalism and Bright's radicalism their common *élan*'. This, perhaps, is to over-emphasise the self-confidence bred by religion, and to miss the necessity of making certain that feeling was controlled and did not run away into anarchy; that it was 'licensed' in the double sense of that term, permitted and regulated. Hilton emphasises how, for the 'moderate', 'post-millenarianist' stream in Evangelicalism, salvation was not assured.[81] To be morally at ease with oneself was to be unsafe. It followed that to be potentially safe one had to feel uneasy. Therefore doubting one's own sincerity bred the desire for real sincerity, a desire that as often as not manifested itself as the wish for spontaneity. The emphasis on feeling, 'vitality', had a root in doubt and anxiety, as well as in certainty. One looked inward to the self for the spontaneous, moderate Evangelicalism condemning all behaviour which threatened the autonomous self-action of the self.

It is difficult, and perhaps impossible, to know what combination of Evangelical strains were evident in Bright (and in practice both strains were often present in different combinations within Anglican Evangelicalism itself). The pre-millenarian strain, with its greater assuredness of salvation, would have put less emphasis on doubt and anxiety as a necessary burden on the way to salvation. And Bright's Quakerism, in its certainty about the Inner Light, was nearer to this strain than the 'moderate' one. Correspondingly, the emphasis on preserving the autonomy of the self would have been less strong in Bright, and it is evident that Bright's religion did not lead to the production of a strong sense of interiority, of a self anxious about and defending its own autonomy, and hungering after spontaneity and sincerity. The communion of Friends, and through this communion with mankind more generally, turned on a less absolutist, more 'socialised', concept of the self than in other sorts of religious sentiment. But it still led to a discourse formed around metaphors of inwardness, if not an inward-turning and anxious self. This was because, in all Evangelical strains, religion was felt to be 'natural'.[82] And the natural was felt to be as much within man as within his world. As the

---

[79] Boyd Hilton, 'Gladstone's Theological Politics', in M. Bentley and J. Stevenson (eds.), *High and Low Politics in Modern Britain* (Oxford 1983).

[80] John Vincent, *The Formation of the Liberal Party 1857–1868* (1966), pp. 96–118 for his discussion of popular Liberalism in Rochdale.

[81] Boyd Hilton, *The Age of Atonement. The Influence of Evangelicalism on Social and Economic Thought, 1795–1865* (Oxford 1988), pp. 18–19.

[82] *Ibid.*, p. 19.

Evangelical sentiment had it, 'Natural religion is ... written in these feelings of the human heart'.[83] And here we apprehend the powerful religious root of what later grew into 'the cult of the heart' (Edwin Waugh's Methodist beginnings partook of this Evangelical influence also).

The leading Quaker Evangelical J. J. Gurney commented on the Anglican Evangelical Thomas Chalmers that he was a man of 'child-like simplicity'. It was constantly said of Bright that he was a man of great simplicity. Commentators and acquaintances felt him to be child-like too, 'quite like a boy' in his sense of good spirits.[84] He represented the 'natural' and 'spontaneous', and – as will be seen – he exemplified these characteristics in his behaviour. The reference to the boyishness of Bright is telling, for this language of feeling was gendered to its centre. The emphasis on sensitivity and naturalness, was intimately related to new notions of manliness in the early nineteenth century:[85] these have been seen by some scholars to be 'middle class', but their remit was much wider and more complex than this notional social basis. The new sensitivity led to sympathy for the weak and helpless; slaves, criminals, the insane, and in certain settings, workers, women, and children. If it sought to avoid the 'macho' characteristics of what was often taken to be a 'gentry' idea of manliness, it strove equally to avoid the dangers of 'effeminacy'. We are aware, therefore, of how the release of feeling inevitably involved the problem of controlling this release. The borders of manliness had to be patrolled in order to prevent the licensing of feeling running away into licentiousness and anarchy. If morally and spiritually equal before God, women were none the less held to be in a position of necessary dependence, and their sphere was the home.[86] Women's feelings might be rather *too* close to the realms of 'nature' (as seen in the introduction 'woman' at the time was equated with nature): 'nature' denoted the spontaneous and the sincere, but, in opposition to 'culture' and 'society', could in its unrestrained forms denote chaos and disorder. We are aware here how the new emphasis on 'feeling' mapped out selves around a series of axes of difference, the manliness–femininity relation being articulated with others.[87]

We must not forget that emotionalism could be its own reward, almost an end in itself, rather than solely an index to the self. In the case of Edwin Waugh we have witnessed a man at times luxuriating in his own grief and sorrow. In this and very many other cases, the emotionalism involved

[83] Cited by Hilton, *Age of Atonement*, p. 19.   [84] K. Robbins, *John Bright* (1979), p. 24.
[85] Leonore Davidoff and Catherine Hall, *Family Fortunes: Men and Women of the English Middle Class 1780–1850* (1987), pp. 108–13.
[86] *Ibid.*, pp. 114–18, also 81–106 on Evangelicalism and 'serious' Christianity.
[87] For some interesting but brief remarks, *ibid.*, pp. 25–8.

became a narcotic, the purpose of feeling being feeling itself, and the 'fix' it gave the *habitue*. From this vantage, we can look back to the nature and experience of Victorian oratory with a better understanding. Oratory was concerned with bringing to expression the great, universal feelings of mankind. The emotionalism of everyday conduct meant that such feelings constantly pressed for expression, bursting continually into conduct. The orator – through his words but also through his being – had at his disposal an eminently workable raw material, whether he worked it by violence and declamation to further arouse emotion, or whether – as in Bright's case – he worked it by restraint, controlling it all the better to reveal its huge force. The orator can be seen as akin to a musical conductor, emotionalism his music. And, as in music, the meaning of the medium lay in its experience, in being part of it, rather than in extracting a literal significance from it, either before or after the event.

All this bears very much on that other current feeding the new emphasis on feeling as the medium (to some extent the substance) of the self: romanticism. Rather than stern Protestantism and romanticism being opposed, they complemented one another. This fusion is a commonplace of Victorian intellectual history. In Bright's case it may seem a little unexpected, so stern was the moral code, so suspicious the understanding of a number of the arts, especially theatre. But Bright was a lover of Byron, even though the Bible and Milton seem to have taken first and second place. It was said that Bright's speeches were often 'Byron in solution', so close was his reading of the poet.[88] In 1832, in Rochdale market-place, he is said to have thrilled to the rebellious spirit of Shelley's 'Masque of Anarchy'[89] (itself written after Peterloo). However, just as in the case of religion we discern a less interiorised, less individuated, self than was sanctioned by religious emotionalism in others, so too with romanticism. There the upsurge of feeling characteristically took an 'external', political bearing, as in Shelley's influence, or the combined political–religious form of Bright's highly romanticised picture of the Mediterranean as the home of the Judaic and Greco-Roman cultures to which England was heir.

Gladstone, Cobden, Newman, Disraeli, and many others of their class, took the same route as Bright. In 1835 Bright did Rochdale's version of the Grand Tour as a twenty-four year old. He saw the Mediterranean through a Byronic haze, dreaming of Greek liberation as he lazed in the Ionian Isles. Rather than introspection and self-knowledge as an aim, this was a romanticism that presented England as ancient Greece re-born. At the zenith of her powers, Britain was now to be the liberator of the world,

[88] J. Travis Mills, *An Orator's Library: John Bright and His Books* (1946).
[89] G. M. Trevelyan, *Life*, p. 20.

romantic struggle being enacted between modern Greece and despotic Turkey. He was perhaps even more moved to eloquence by the experience of the Holy Land, while at the same time condemning its contemporary 'backwardness' (and taking copious notes on local trading conditions and prices).[90]

Yet it is in the home and family that was played out the full force of feeling as the medium of the self. It has been seen how Bright's religion and politics pulled him outwards to a less autonomous, or at least less interior and conflictual self than might elsewhere have been the case. The family can be seen to work in a rather different direction, towards a more individuated self as head of an individual household. What is probably more correct is that the family functioned as a kind of junction, and to some degree a terminus, for many views of the self, re-combining, or transacting, some of those fundamental elements of difference noted earlier, such as society and nature, work and home, also the public and the private.

Bright's diary, and especially the Bright family papers, give more than ample testimony to the power of feeling in his life. A diary entry for 1846 runs as follows: 'I have a heart to feel emotions far more tender than I can give utterance to, and I often long for that sympathy which is only possible in the union of hearts and interests which I seek.'[91] Elizabeth Leatham, his second wife, whom he was courting at the time, provided this sympathy – she was pure and benevolent, but 'warm in heart' in particular. Lest one think emotion was contained only within the family, this is how he described his state of mind after speaking to the House of Commons immediately after Cobden's death: 'I sat down sobbing with grief, trembling with excitement and passionate sorrow.'[92] Shortly after he describes how he spent two hours alone in Cobden's library, the dead friend lying in his coffin beside him.[93] When Cobden is laid to rest he is again racked by 'passionate sobs and tears'.[94] As he grows older, he says, he grows ever softer.

None the less, it is within the circle of the family that deep emotion is usually expressed. And the dominant emotions are so often 'kindness' and 'tenderness': we recollect the 'timid and docile boy' at Ackworth, and the deep impression left on him by the experience of the opposites of these attributes. When he came to write his 'Memoir' he said that he recollected little of his early days but for the overwhelming sense of the 'unceasing care and tenderness' of his parents. His mother's early death, when he was a boy, was a profound blow: 'the calamity of her loss' is described, 'from

[90] For accounts see Keith Robbins, *John Bright*, pp. 12–16; R. A. J. Walling (ed.), *The Diaries of John Bright*, chap. 2.
[91] *Ibid.*, p. 84.   [92] *Ibid.*, p. 287, 3 April 1865.   [93] *Diaries*, 4 April 1865.
[94] *Diaries*, 7 April 1865.

which sprang many of the troubles and disappointments which disturbed us in later years'. The loss 'cannot be measured or described'.[95] When he described his schooldays it was again kindness that was remembered, again in contradistinction to Ackworth.[96] This kindness he associates in the 'Memoir' with the experience of nature as renewing and refreshing (his schools were in some sublimely beautiful parts of England, such as Newton-in-Bowland in the Forest of Bowland).

There is striking evidence for the malevolent role of feeling throughout his life. For much of it he lived on the edge of physical breakdown, sometimes fearing mental breakdown as a consequence. The first breakdown, followed by a long period of complete inactivity and much seclusion, was brought on by his opposition to the Crimean War, when he was often a lonely and isolated figure in the country as well as the House. He told his wife before the breakdown that he feared his 'disgust' at the opposition might bring on an 'injury to his temper'.[97] The second breakdown was in 1870, in the aftermath of the great Reform Act agitation, when he no longer had Cobden at his side. In 1865, in the midst of the turmoil, he had to retire from parliament for much of the session in order to prevent a breakdown. Significantly, it seems to have been the rigours of public life rather than personal or family difficulties which brought him to the edge. None the less, superabundant emotion certainly contributed to his difficulties, even if these seem to have been the result of an excess of conviction rather than an excess of doubt and inner conflict.

Within the family it was perhaps in relation to his parents, and especially his father, that some of the strongest emotions were expressed, emotions that tell us most about the place of the family in his concept of self, and his projections of the social. The following is from John's 'Lines written on leaving home', prior to his Mediterranean departure in 1833, aged 21:

> Farewell Father! may I never
> Dim the brightness of thy name,
> But with heart unsullied ever
> As thy course be mine the same.[98]

This is his daughter Helen's account of his very last day, perhaps hours, in 1889:

He was very sweet in the night. Said tenderly 'Blessings on thee' ... and 'It was a very touching observation of Forster's when he said the Church of my Fathers had

---

[95] *Diaries*, p. 3.   [96] *Ibid.*, pp. 5–7.

[97] D. Read, *Cobden and Bright. A Victorian Political Partnership* (1967), pp. 13–14, also J. Vincent, *Formation of the Liberal Party*, pp. 166–7.

[98] Darbashire Papers, Packet 19. See also Bright Family Papers, Whiteknights MSS., Box 39, Bundle 3, John Bright to Elizabeth Priestman, 15 October 1838.

not forsaken me . . . if he had not forsaken the Church of his Fathers in some things he would have been saved from those things that were the great mistakes of his life . . .'[99]

Towards the end of his life his sister Priscilla wrote to his daughter Helen that his son John Albert, the eldest, was, like his father, the only one among their respective siblings who showed the same 'adhesiveness' in family matters, the same 'reverence'.[100]

As the words 'Church of my Fathers' indicate, religion and the figure of his father were inseparably connected in his understanding. His 'reverence' was to both. The father emblematised his attempt to relate old and new, the old and the new in his religion, and the old and the new in what he understood as his social condition: in the end, he adhered to a past constructed around the father. In this he reproduced the rule of the patriarch, the patriarch in heaven above, the patriarch in the Meeting House and the patriarch in the mill. A particular kind of masculinity, and a particular ordering of family relations, can be seen to connect family and religion, and these in turn connect with the realm of work, of production as opposed to the home and reproduction. At the very centre of his emotional life, in the family and before the sacred image of the Father, were played out the tensions that we have seen to characterise his religion, particularly the difficult connection of authority and liberty. At home authority told, as it ultimately told in the sphere beyond home. As John Vincent has brilliantly observed, 'The Achilles Heel of his Liberalism lay in his creed of the family. His household suffrage amounted to a confederation of absolute despots; and in his opposition to Home Rule, he was applying the principles of family life to Irish insubordination.'[101]

The home rule of Jacob drew forth the remark from John's brother Thomas that their father was an 'absolute stranger' to any feelings of Christian charity and liberality.[102] The reason was Jacob's Quaker strictness, typically manifested in his refusal to attend the marriage of his daughter Margaret, who had found a partner outside the Society. The patriarch could not stand against the tide of youth, but young John, the eldest son, seems none the less to have taken on the father's mantle, repelling the suitor of one sister, not even letting another sister know of a proposal made to her. As Priscilla his sister later observed '. . . he never could bear women to assert themselves', his aim being 'feminine deference to the power of men'.[103] He did not think his sisters had a right to

[99] Whiteknights MSS., Box 30, Bundle 13, Miscellaneous Items.
[100] Priscilla Bright to Helen Clark, cited in J. Vincent, *Formation*, pp. 209–10.
[101] *Ibid.*, p. 209.   [102] K. Robbins, *John Bright*, pp. 24–5, and 22–3.
[103] Letter cited in note 100 above.

think for themselves as regards offers of marriage, and felt that daughters had no right to legacies if these could be of use to brothers in business.

Yet the same man wrote endlessly of politics to his two wives,[104] and to his first wife's mother.[105] His first daughter Helen – by his first wife – was both his favourite and his political confidante. Women might have a role in political affairs therefore, but within the home only: he foresaw 'evil consequences' for women who entered politics.[106] In this the church of his fathers supported him (though in the hands of women like Helen it was to change in this from the time of his old age). Despite its reputation for liberality, evident in women preachers and separate Women's Meetings, all important decisions, at national and local level, were made by men at the Men's Meetings, without reference to women.[107] The line between authority and liberality was drawn here by John Bright in the traditional way, just as the effusion of emotion in public life, seen for instance in his reaction to Cobden's death, had to be kept under control, for fear of manliness spilling over into femininity. None the less, the 'feminine' side of a man's nature was given full expression in his family life, and – in the mode of the leashed power of emotion – in his public, political life.

The family papers give many examples of his great tenderness towards Helen when she was a young child. He does not write to an adult in miniature, but to a child with child-like feelings he respects.[108] Despite his involvement in finding her a suitable partner in later years, the match had in the end to be one of 'love'. Perhaps his greatest love was for his first wife, Elizabeth Priestman. He felt her loss terribly, and continued to feel it always, despite a happy second marriage. It is very moving to read in his private papers voluminous notes taken very late in his life from a certain 'Book of Spectral Experiences'. These concerned accounts of spiritualist contact with the dead, particularly of a case strikingly similar to his own situation.[109]

This was a powerful testimony to the bonds of family, all the more remarkable for his second wife being made privy to his devotion to the first. If the operations of family authority were highly gendered, it was the case that male authority always operated through an emphasis on the family (and it was inevitable that such authority became diluted in the

[104] See the faithful, and voluminous, correspondence with his second wife Margaret Leatham in University College Library, London; Ogden MS. 65.
[105] Whiteknights MSS., Boxes 29/30, correspondence to the Priestman family, esp. Box 29, Bundle 2.
[106] J. Vincent, *Formation of the Liberal Party*, p. 209.
[107] E. Isichei, *Victorian Quakers*, pp. 107–10.
[108] Whiteknights MSS., Box 29/1, childhood letters to Helen from John Bright. See also Darbashire Papers, Packet 3, Priscilla Bright to Margaret Leatham, 16 October 1844, on Richard Cobden's son as Helen's playmate.
[109] British Museum Additional MSS. 43392.

process). Within the household, the collectivity of the family took precedence over individual actions, another curb on the supposed 'individualism' of a bourgeoisie. The meaning of family for Bright can be understood from his correspondence – long continuing – with the parents of his first wife.[110] These are unselfconsciously called his 'father' and 'mother'. In a similar fashion he addressed Cobden as his 'brother' in his diary. Friends, not only within the Society, could in this sense become family, the boundaries of 'family' and 'friends' being still relatively fluid at the time.

10   Bright makes the social

We can talk of a self made; we can also talk of a self deployed in the public realm (from whence it is returned to the subject in a new form). Bright deployed himself, and was in turn deployed by his contemporaries. What models or conceptions of the social order can we see Bright himself deploying? Perhaps the most revealing one is a vision of independence that was almost the exact social analogue of the personal self. The created self of the common, plain man issued in a social utopia of the plain man. The understanding of his father's condition as of the common people produced a social vision in which the imagined society of the patriarch was reproduced in an imagined social ideal, that of what might be termed the urban yeomanry. This social vision had no fixed social base or constituency: it could and did appeal to men of many social conditions and 'classes', not least men of the 'working class' for whom a vision of social, moral, and political independence was of quite crucial significance.

When men of the 'middle class' spoke of what it was to be middle class, especially in the first half of the century, this dimension of independence was central to the meanings given these words. Benjamin Armitage, a rich and powerful Manchester merchant and close friend of Bright, was described by W. H. Mills as a man who saw the urban present as a rural utopia, an Eden based on nonconformity and plots of three acres, ruled over by village Hampdens, in which all would have unfettered liberty to shoot anything that flew over their land.[111] The rural dimension to this is no accident, though the description also reflected a pressing political situation in which Liberalism was turning its attention to that last bastion of dependence, the English (and the Irish) countryside. Bright himself looked back to a northern plebeian heritage in which 'industrial' and rural

[110] Whiteknights MSS, Box 29, Bundle 2.
[111] W. H. Mills, *The Manchester Reform Club 1881–1921* (privately printed, Manchester, 1922), pp. 8–9.

pursuits were closely linked. Industrial employers generally, were concerned at this time to connect the idealised social relations of an imagined rural past with the troubled present of the sprawling town and the insubordinate mill[112] (especially great employers of labour, as we have seen in Bright's case).

But the imaginary was inseparable from the real. As recent research on the Manchester middle classes has shown (and the point goes for the other English cities too) many of the new crop of prominent merchants, manufacturers, and professionals in the first half of the century – and later – came from decidedly rural backgrounds, or from rural backgrounds in which the transition to proto-industry had already long been made.[113] Such men loved to describe their origins as in the English 'yeomanry', or in the ranks of the Scots equivalent (the Scots infusion in Manchester being very significant). When such families set up colonies or residences outside the town, or in the new suburbs, they were decidedly *not* aping the gentry. The *rus in urbe* they created often harked back to their own pasts.

However, it took men like Armitage, Bright, and Cobden to give this background a public and social meaning. To the great extent that they created a powerful, and enduring, meaning for the term 'middle class', this meaning was inseparably connected to a sense of yeoman independence, and to a sense of injustice, persecution, and dispossession. These men helped forge the uncreated conscience of their race, which was not alone the 'middle class' (this they might quickly tire of) but the 'working class' English too, for whom the theme of dispossession was of quite central significance (feeding, as will be seen, the narratives which powered politics and shaped social identity). Bright looked back to a persecuted father and learned a sense of justice from it. Cobden looked back to a father turned off his land when the boy was only ten years old (the same age as Bright would have experienced injustice to his father). In fact, the farm may have been lost as much by incompetence as by anything else, but this was of no account. In a most revealing phrase Cobden saw the family farm as his birthright: the farm was the 'hearth of my fathers held by honourable title'.[114] Bright's social imaginary was produced by cleaving to the church of his fathers, Cobden's by cleaving to the hearth of his.

Cobden's most recent biographer describes his idealised view of his childhood, again, like Bright, one produced by the awfulness of his school experience, which involved long periods of separation from his beloved

---

[112] Patrick Joyce, *Work, Society and Politics: the Culture of the Factory in Later Victorian England* (Brighton 1980), esp. chaps. 1 and 5.
[113] Simon Gunn, 'The Manchester Middle Class, 1850–1880' (Manchester University Ph.D., 1992), pp. 102–4, 109–11, also 199–216 on suburbia.
[114] Nicholas C. Edsall, *Richard Cobden: Independent Radical* (1986), p. 28.

parents.[115] This was followed by the humiliations of his early, clerking career, before the move to Manchester and economic success. In all this time Cobden never lost his West Sussex accent, and thought of himself as a countryman. Robertson's biography of Bright presents Cobden in a similar vein: the family are seen as living in Dunford since Henry VIII's time, 'substantial yeomen of the old school'. Since Cobden's early days the area has seen havoc among small farmers. He reports Cobden as saying that if he had stayed he would have been poor, his playmates of days gone by now sunk to labourers breaking stones upon the road.[116] After the Repeal of the Corn Laws Cobden bought the Dunford farm back, retiring there to live the life of the small farmer.

With some justice, Cobden saw the small farmer as the natural ally of the 'working classes'. Both were interested in low taxes and cheap food. In the 1830s and 40s he fixed the meanings of the yeoman upon the 'shopocracy', particularly of Manchester. Later on, these were to drift towards the 'working' or industrious classes, or at least the honourable and independent 'artisan'; the man who, unlike the dependent poor (and women), most deserved the title of yeoman. The term 'industrious classes' denoted a social constituency in which all the productive classes, masters, and men, were to be counted together. From its earliest days the language of class was open to the utopian meanings described here. Those who least often deserved the honourable name of yeomen and 'independent' were the wealthy, and Cobden was constantly at pains to emphasise the dangers of an aristocracy of wealth, particularly in the Manchester of the 1850s and 60s.[117] The real aristocracy were even greater sinners. All aristocracies, for all their power, displayed a particularly heinous form of dependence, dependence on the material rather than the good (again 'materialism' is seen to be a charged term of social criticism). The rural poor were alike dependent, and Bright and working-class radicals were deeply suspicious of this dependence.[118] For Bright and the radicals, the labourer's deepest loss was that he could not be his own man. The vision of independence took form in relation to this understanding of dependence, as did the view of the urban dependent, the 'residuum' of the criminal and dangerous classes. Bright coined the term around the time of the agitated public discussion that accompanied the Second Reform Act. However, if the aristocracy were often sinners who could not be saved, the labourers, especially the rural labourer, were sinners who could. Much of late nineteenth-century popular Liberalism was about this attempted

[115] Wendy Hinde, *Richard Cobden: A Victorian Outsider* (1987) pp. 2–3.
[116] W. Robertson, *Life*, I, p. 86, and chap. 7.
[117] N. C. Edsall, *Richard Cobden*, p. 29.
[118] E. F. Biagini, *Liberty, Retrenchment and Reform*, pp. 268–9.

salvation. All emphases on social unities were at once principles of social exclusion and sources of social difference – speaking in the name of a universal manhood was inseparable from making these exclusions.

This view of utopian independence was intimately linked to the ideas of family and home. The two merged in the Anti-Corn Law League agitation. This is how Bright gave an account of Cobden's words to him on the death of his first wife in 1841, when the agitation was at its height. Bright spoke at the unveiling of a statue to Cobden in 1877, itself an occasion when the 'feeling' involved was utilised to political effect by Bright, the inner man being brought to the outside through his oratory:[119]

the light and sunshine of my life had been extinguished. All that was left on earth of my young wife, except the memory of a sacred life, and a too brief happiness, was lying still and cold in the chamber above us. Mr Cobden called upon me as his friend, and addressed me, as you might suppose, with words of condolence. After a time he looked up and said, 'There are thousands of houses in England at this moment where wives, mothers and children are dying of hunger. Now', he said, 'when the first paroxysm of your grief is past, I would advise you to come with me, and we will never rest until the Corn Law is repealed'. I accepted his invitation.

The peroration continued, building the events that led up to Repeal into an expression of historical inevitability, and ending

and finally the barrier was entirely thrown down. And since then, though there has been suffering, and much suffering in many homes in England, yet no wife and no mother, and no little child has been starved to death as a result of a famine made by law.

To the rhetorical trope, 'the homes of England', was married the powerful symbolism of bread (the symbols of the big and the little loaf were central to a later popular Liberalism, and were of great effect in the Repeal cause). Maintaining the homes of England from starvation, and hence from dependence, became the aim of the Anti-Corn Law League. The appropriation of 'England' was always a major element in Bright's deployment of the social idea of independence. He presented himself as the man who throughout his life was an outsider, outside the classically trained culture of the Victorian ruling classes, and superior to it.[120] He was made by an English culture, by English literature and English history, by Milton and Milton's libertarian seventeenth century. As his most recent biographer declares,

Jowett's translation of Plato's Dialogues produced more admiration for the industry of the translator than for the wisdom of the philosopher. John Bright never lost his family's belief that Rochdale had more to offer the nineteenth century than Balliol College, Oxford.[121]

[119] Bright's speech at Bradford, 25 July 1877, cited in G.M.Trevelyan, *Life*, pp. 43–4.
[120] K. Robbins, *John Bright*, p. 8.   [121] *Ibid.*, chap. 1.

The English constitution was one embodiment of this independent spirit of the English, Lancashire another.[122] Briggs has described the great pull of locality on Bright. Rochdale, exemplified this, also the widely prevalent contemporary view of Lancashire as the home of gritty independence.[123] Bagehot described Lancashire as 'America-with-water', and in the 1860s Liberals, including Gladstone, loved to think of it as the exemplification of independence in the cause of liberty. However, as we know, there were limits to the endurance of the operatives in the cause of the North during the Cotton Famine, and when the results of the Second Reform Act were seen in the county they showed anything but a steadfastly 'independent' electorate.[124]

In deploying this utopian viewpoint, Bright most often presented himself not as a spokesman of a class, but of humanity itself. 'Humanity' might correspond to 'the people', but the associations of 'humanity' carried their own weight and had their own history, associations that connected them to what has been called 'the metaphysic of humanity' and 'the cult of the heart', in the case of a working man like Edwin Waugh. In his first election campaign, in Durham in 1843, Bright addressed the electors with the words, 'I am as much a working man as any one of you ... my father was as poor as any man before you.'[125] He came before them as one of their class, as one of the people, as one of the poor (the terms were very often used interchangeably). In later life he described his political principles in the following way '... from earliest youth I have learned to feel for these men' – the 'lowly' who suffer – 'to feel for them a sympathy I have never been able to express in words, and of which I can find no proper expression in my outward conduct'. We have no reason to doubt the reality of his deep sympathy and identification with 'the multitude, the millions who formed the nation'.[126] They were the true example of the human condition.

Nor should we doubt his claim that the Anti-Corn Law cause was never a question of class, only of suffering and hungry humanity. In his Covent Garden speech of 1847 he maintained, 'We, the masters, were not hungry. I never had a meal the less however my countrymen suffered, and my business always yielded some profit.' Historians in the twentieth century have persisted in seeing the League as a 'middle-class' movement, *the* middle-class movement. But this is avowedly not how contemporaries

---

[122] See below, pp. 192–204.
[123] A. Briggs, 'John Bright and the Creed of Reform', in *Victorian People: A Reassessment of Persons and Themes 1851–67* (1954).
[124] P. Joyce, *Work, Society and Politics*, chap. 6.
[125] Cited in full by Trevelyan, *Life*, p. 113.
[126] *Ibid.*, pp. 193–4.

involved in the agitation saw it.[127] Theirs was a humanitarian movement, a movement of 'philanthropy' designed to feed the hungry of England, and bring justice to the land. Priscilla Bright, one of many women active in the League, saw the League as breaking down oppression and raising up justice. She saw the passionate feeling for justice evident in the great League congregations as the fervent conviction that animated meetings (a feeling made 'electrical' when John Bright got up to speak).[128] For Bright in 1843 'injustice' was the publicly expressed driving force. He had no sympathy for the 'middle class': they could help themselves, and if they put their necks 'under the heel of the landed oligarchy', then so be it.[129] The Corn Laws were never a 'middle class' question he claimed, but rather that of starving working men. Bright took much of his Anti-Corn Law feeling from the rhymes of Ebenezer Elliot, and his depiction of the 'bread-taxed weaver' and 'the homes of England'.[130]

Bright's own picture of the 1842 'Plug Plot' disturbances in the north-west corroborates this view of a suffering humanity, rather than a class, as the object of his understanding. He wrote to his political confidante, 'his dear Mother, Rachel Priestman', Elizabeth's mother:

They are reported to be peaceable and firm, but alas hunger will tear down all barriers which reason or morality or religion oppose to violence and outrage.

And again,

The quiet and the timid and those who never study politics, and who seem content if the people are in the fangs of the aristocracy will have a severe lesson now ... Suffering caused by law has made the whole population a mass of combustible material.[131]

Unlike many of his respectable contemporaries he regarded 1842 as 'a passive resistance revolution', inherently right and reasonable if maddened to violence by a corrupt aristocracy on the one hand and a few unscrupulous agitators on the other.[132] 'A population formed for great and good purposes are marred, brutalized, made barbarous by men who trade in famine.'[133] These traders were 'a savage aristocracy', and Peel and Graham, 'Famine and Co.'.[134]

It is quite apparent that Bright fervently believed all this. Subsequent generations of Liberals were to believe it equally fervently: the myth of the 'Hungry Forties', like the myth of Peterloo as a Liberal happening, was to

[127] The new work of Alon Kadish on the League makes this plain (forthcoming at the time of writing).
[128] Darbashire Papers, Packet 3, Priscilla Bright to Margaret Priestman 7 February 1843.
[129] Trevelyan, *Life*, p. 53.   [130] *Ibid.*, p. 51.
[131] Darbashire Papers, Packet 3, John Bright to Rachel Priestman, 14 August 1842.
[132] Darbashire Papers, 3, Bright to Jonathan Priestman, 'my dear Father', 11 October 1842.
[133] *Ibid.*   [134] On 1842 see also K. Robbins, *John Bright*, pp. 37–9.

be one of the most enduring and energising political myths of the century. The people were driven mad by hunger, to be rescued from want, and the clutches of demagogues and aristos, by the League and free-trade, also – in many accounts – by a virtuous 'middle class', fulfilling its historical mission as the bearer of democracy and progress. Unlike many who came after him, Bright was aware how strong at the time, including 1842, were the political aspirations of popular movements. If driven by hunger, he knew it was the vote that was seen as the answer. Contemporary social historians have amply shown this to be the case.[135] His perspicuity was owed to the fact that, again unlike many of his propertied fellows, his political education was in large part conducted by working men at his father's mill, and in the town of Rochdale.

As we have noted, Bright would have witnessed great political gatherings at first hand, on Cronkeyshaw Common in Rochdale.[136] One of his first political expressions was held to be chalking 'Hunt For Ever' on the wall of Greenbank Mill: the epic Preston election of 1830, in which Hunt deposed the ancient rule of the aristocratic Derbys over the town, seems to have been significant for the nineteen-year old, as was the tutelage of several working men radicals in the mill, with whom he did not necessarily agree.[137] One such was Isaac Sladen, who came to get the mill keys off him every morning,[138] another Charles Howarth, a hot radical, a founder of the Rochdale Pioneers, and a man Bright was said to have used as the whetstone for his views.[139] Bright was in a sense an 'insider' then, knowing workers at first hand, and being exposed directly to men who were ultra-radicals.

Yet he was an outsider too, a man of property and authority. At the same time as his political education was being conducted at the mill, he pursued the education of a 'gentleman'. The Rochdale Literary and Philosophical Society contained 'most of the gentlemen of the town'. This was in part concerned with the necessity of 'the universal education of the lower classes'. The gentlemen were rigidly distinguished from the lower classes. Edwin Waugh was not a member of this Society. The Working Men's Educational Institute, patronised by Bright, was the institution appropriate to his station.[140] Such marks of social distinction were legion at the time. The Britain of that time was almost caste-like in its observance of social differences,[141] and the vocabulary of class, of 'working man', 'working class', 'middle class', gave one kind of expression to this. There

[135] For example, G. Stedman Jones, 'Rethinking Chartism', in *Languages of Class: Studies in English Working-Class History 1832–1982* (Cambridge 1983).
[136] W. Robertson, *Life*, pp. 47, 49.   [137] G. M. Trevelyan, *Life*, p. 18.
[138] J. Bright, 'Memoir', p. 10.
[139] W. Robertson, *Life*, pp. 64–5.   [140] *Ibid.*, pp. 76–78.   [141] See above, p. 6.

is no doubt that its terms sometimes represented a clear sense of economic and political difference, as well as conflict. But it is the fluidity, the de-centredness, of social vocabularies, and identities, that is striking, something represented, for instance, in the way the terms 'class' and 'people' were often used interchangeably at the time. The 'working class' might be subsumed in 'the people' or 'the millions', 'the multitude', 'the nation'. Or, conversely, 'the people' might be construed to mean working people, those who were manual workers or got their hands dirty. At the same time, 'working class' could express conflict, but could also – as in Gladstone's case[142] – be framed in terms of different classes coexisting within 'organic' wholes, for example, that of the nation.

Which interpretation dominated depended on the precise historical conjuncture. It can be said that the contrast between the early, and the mid- and late-nineteenth century, sees a shift from a relatively conflictual set of meanings accruing around all these terms to a relatively consensual one. The consensual elements in Bright's deployment of the social were to achieve a quite major success. But this was only because earlier on these consensual elements were present too, and therefore capable of being worked upon. The self that Bright deployed socially was always framed in terms of these underlying commonalities drawing rich and poor together – under God, as a 'common people', under the banner of humanity, and so on. And these feelings and aspirations were echoed just as much among working people, however great the feelings of conflict and betrayal experienced early on (betrayal by the state, and by a 'middle class', the latter especially after 1832).

Rochdale is the best place to examine something of this. After the Church Rates controversy of 1840, Bright took surprisingly little active role in local politics, and local affairs more widely. In the 1840s and 50s, we do not find him as the tribune of the Rochdale people. This honour fell to Thomas Livesey, the hugely popular leader of Chartism in the 1840s, who up to the late-1850s led a popular movement perhaps better ensconced in local administrative authority than any in Lancashire. 'Tom' Livesey, or 'Alderman Livesey' as he was also called, was a much more popular figure in the town until Bright's national emergence as a hero of political reform in the late 1850s. Livesey's funeral in 1864 was a huge affair.[143] There is no disguising the disagreements between Bright and these popular radical leaders. This was expressed in 1856 in the bitter quarrel over Incorporation, the popular party fearing that the proposed five-ward solution would throw undue influence into the hands of the

---

[142] For a full discussion of 'class language' see P. Joyce, *Visions of the People*, chaps. 2 and 3, also chap. 1.
[143] *Rochdale Observer*, 6 February 1864.

millowners.[144] Bright lined up with the five-ward party, though his brother Jacob and some of the biggest millowners of the town supported the popular side (Jacob was the first mayor of the incorporated borough).[145] The great majority of the wealthy were said to be for the five-ward cause, and the mouthpiece of the radicals, the *Rochdale Observer*, explicitly mentioned how it had been 'their duty' to 'differ from him [Bright] on almost every point on which he has expressed definite opinions'.[146] They were mainly concerned with his opposition to the Factory Movement's cause of legislative interference in the conditions of labour. Bright's extreme libertarianism opposed state interference, just as it had led to his opposition to trade unions. 'Outside' bodies were regarded as an unwarranted intrusion on the right of masters and workers to make their own bargains. The other great difference, in 1856, was over the Crimean War, the popular radicals, as so often, being the party of war, not peace.

These differences were considerable, and were to be a gift for Tory propaganda later on.[147] They were, however, differences over issues and measures far more than differences over principle. Similarly, for Bright, but also for many working men, the choice between the Charter and Repeal in the 1840s was over tactics. Both measures were enthusiastically supported. As regards principles, in 1851, for example, we find Livesey and the popular radicals enunciating views of the social order just the same as Bright's. 'The people' were now increasingly benefiting from the new dawn of progress and popular education. '"Who were the people" it was asked.' The answer was 'all those who by the sweat of their brow or their brains contributed to the comfort of society'.[148] These were good Brightean sentiments, good ones for Edwin Waugh as well, who was a prominent figure at this particular meeting. Eminently Brightean, and Cobdenite too, was the stress on municipal institutions as the great barrier to the despotism of state 'centralisation'.[149] For all their differences on issues, the radicals could conclude a meeting with a toast to John Bright. By the time of Livesey's funeral, eight years later, the Liberals and the radicals had cemented their similarities of view into a political alliance:

[144] *Ibid.*, 5 July 1856.   [145] *Ibid.*, 12 July 1856.
[146] *Ibid.*, 13 December 1856 (Editorial).
[147] J. Cole, 'Betrayal of a People's Hero', and 'The Making of John Bright', in *Rochdale Revisited: A Town and its People* (1990), II.
[148] *Public Dinner and Testimonial to Mr. Thomas Livesey, Chief Constable of Rochdale* (1851), copy in Rochdale Public Library. See also the very similar accounts of another notable radical leader, William Aitken (from the Ashton neighbourhood), in *Rochdale Observer*, 12 July 1856, report of tea-party.
[149] *Ibid.*, see comments of Mr. J. W. Harris. On Livesey see also Miss M. R. Lahee, *Life and Times of the Late Alderman Livesey* (1865). Miss Lahee was one of the very few successful women dialect writers of her time.

Bright praised the 'rough diamond' Tom Livesey after his death, and the *Observer* had become almost a Brightean broadsheet.

Bright had become a power in the land once again, in the process deploying a self the universalist aspects of which eclipsed the particularities of class. The struggle was now that of the many against the few, the people against privilege. The people, the democracy, were defined against the rulers and the dependent. The created self of the common man achieved its greatest triumph. The outlines of this change, in particular Bright's sense of betrayal by the 'middle class' during the Crimean War, have been traced by a number of historians.[150] If the 'middle class' would not do, the nation must be tried.[151] This involved the 'working class' adopting the mantle of 'the people' earlier discarded by an unworthy middle class.[152] In this change, Cobden as well as Bright played a central role, Gladstone ultimately benefiting as the legatee of a language which enabled political democracy to be consolidated in Britain.[153]

This language was given much of its force by being attached to 'humanity', not to a class. In turn, the purchase the cause of humanity had on contemporary feeling was owed to the identification of humanity with the very course of history itself. Gladstone confided to his diary in 1860, 'I feel within me the rebellious, unspoken word . . . I will not be old . . . It is an age of shocks.'[154] Bright, as much as Gladstone, felt this sense of the tumult of the present issuing forth within him. The rebellious word within in Bright's case was no less a religious one than in Gladstone's, but, perhaps even more than Gladstone, Bright himself symbolised the fall of the *ancien régime* and the sweeping away of 'feudalism'. Bright not only symbolised the seemingly inevitable course of history – as progress destroyed 'feudalism' – but he embodied history directly as the resurgent plebeian 'Commonwealthsman' of the seventeenth century come again, the man who suffered like the martyrs of old so that the historical wheel might turn. As Vincent has remarked, Bright profited greatly as a politician from the fear and loathing of his enemies, a fear based on the perception that he symbolised the fall of the old order.[155] As the slayer of 'feudalism' (a term frequently used at the time) Bright, no less than Marx and Engels, created the tenacious myth of the world-historical mission of the bourgeoisie.

Bright functioned effectively as a principle of history precisely because he had no sense of history himself, or at least of the past as different from

---

[150] J. Vincent, *Formation of the Liberal Party*, pp. 133–5.
[151] P. Joyce, *Visions of the People*, p. 54.
[152] *Ibid.*, pp. 27–31, and the working out of this in the rest of chap. 1.
[153] See below, pp. 162–3, 199–204.
[154] Cited in A. Briggs, 'John Bright and the Creed of Reform', p. 234.
[155] J. Vincent, *Formation of the Liberal Party*, pp. 197, 211.

the present. In this he differed little from the dominant Whig historiography of his day. The notes he made for his speeches, for example, see him plundering thirteenth-century records in order to show that the Commons, when properly functioning, was always on the side of the people.[156] The liberties of England were immanent in the institutions of England. One merely reached back to the past so as to find in it a reassuring replica of the present, or of how the present should and could be. This literal mindedness about the past is best exemplified in his view of the English constitution: it was the foremost embodiment of English liberties, and English values more generally, and therefore history was the rock upon which the present dispensation would be built. We begin to see how political movements, and the social identities they helped create, depend very greatly on conceiving of subjects as located within a narrative sequence, in this case a story about liberty in English history.[157]

The other great exemplification of liberty in the present was the United States. America was one culmination of the narratives of liberty, and hence of the cause of humanity for which Bright spoke. His vision of America was of one vast democratic confederation, one people with one language, one law, and one faith, the home of freedom and the refuge of the oppressed.[158] This concept of a grand uniformity to society was in many respects decidedly illiberal. Not all could enter the promised land.[159] Being on the side of history was being on the side of the light. Liberty took as its 'other' all that represented the darkness of history, the slavery, ignorance, and delusion of the *ancien régime*, whether the aristocratic state or what Bright termed 'the bog priestcraft'.[160] Evil could be conquered and was not endemic to human nature, as the old order had it. One looked within, in Bright's case assuredly not to 'conscience' or 'reason', but to the Inner Light. None the less, Bright's view of history, of salvation, and therefore of the progress within men's grasp, fitted very closely with other currents within popular radicalism, particularly the legacy of eighteenth-century rationalism and its social optimism, even though his Quakerism should not be confused with this. Those who sinned against the light were therefore those who sinned against history in denying their own humanity. The 'not-human' defined the 'human', those who were enlightened, free and independent, unlike the 'materialistic', the ignorant, and the dependent classes (women, labourers, the demoralised poor, and also those races not yet exposed to reason and

---

[156] British Museum Additional Manuscripts, 43392, ff. 120, 124.
[157] See below, pp. 154–7.
[158] A. Briggs, 'John Bright ... Reform', pp. 231–3.
[159] K. Robbins, *John Bright*, p. 168 on Bright's American dream.
[160] *Ibid.*, p. 24.

Christianity). The embodiment of the 'not-human' was of course the Tory, and, as will be seen, the creation of the nineteenth-century Liberal is literally inconceivable without the creation of the Tory. Bright's demonisation of the Tory was not the least of his gifts to political Liberalism.

History was also sanctioned by providence. One looked to history not only for the secular design of feudalism's destruction, but also for religious corroboration of this design. One looked, in short, for the moral legibility of providence. Bright believed that in repealing the Corn Laws he had 'put Holy Writ into an Act of Parliament'. Just as often, in his private as well as public life, he sought to find the reassurance of providence rather than presuming to aid it, for its workings were not always welcome or reassuring. Providence took his first wife, and towards the end of his life we find him seeking knowledge of her beyond the grave. Similarly, in old age his 'Memoir' dwelt on the, for him, extraordinary events surrounding the drowning of his father's partner (the body was borne by the currents from Anglesey to Blackpool, where it was washed up on the shore in front of the hotel his father was staying at; watches were mysteriously stopped at the time of the original shipwreck, and so on).[161] The quietist tradition in Quakerism sanctioned the practice of divining the workings of providence by gifted ministers.[162] There was an almost daily concern with the manifestations of providence, a quotidian equivalent of the grand design sought for, and found, in history. The legibility of Holy Writ, of quite literally the hand of God, was all the more urgently sought because of the influence of Evangelicalism. The Evangelical emphasis on the doctrine of the Atonement meant that providence needed to be punctually seen in the workings of the world in order that reassurance of salvation might be found.[163] Gladstone, as much as Bright, looked to read the signs. As will be seen in the next study on narratives, politics was about legible moralities, and the melodramatic theatre was one of the most vital means by which simple moralities were made available for political narrativisation. Even where religious faith was not so deeply felt, as in Bright's case, the religious categories of thought and feeling that characterised the age meant that the moral legibility of providence was sought by all. History, providence, and politics were intimately linked, not least in the figure of John Bright. In deploying himself as a sign Bright showed how important for a mass democracy was a reading of the signs.

[161] J. Bright. 'Memoir', pp. 14–15.   [162] E. Isichei, *Victorian Quakers*, p. 24.
[163] See the discussion in B. Hilton, *The Age of Atonement*, chap. 1.

11   Creating the democratic imaginary

Bright and Gladstone were the two greatest popular political leaders of their day. The most recent study of Gladstone's leadership, that of Biagini,[164] presents a figure similar to Bright in many respects. Their 'charismatic' leadership expressed the same mixture of familiarity and veneration, the description the 'Grand Old Man' summing this up for Gladstone. For Bright the combination of the figures of the plain man and the white-haired prophet of the moral law represented the same combination. The demotic implications of the persona of the plain man provided the shape of the future in the creation of the democratic imaginary, the reassurance of venerability delineated its past, the necessary counter-balance to hope. The wider significance of the cult of Bright as the plain man can therefore be appreciated: this dual nature of charismatic leadership was one of the central means by which a nascent mass democracy was both mobilised and managed.

For Biagini, in the sentimental vein of an ever-new Whig interpretation of British history, this new politics is without shadows and depths. It is about democracy, not demagogy. Gladstone is its hero, the man who equips Victorian Britain for democracy by fusing charismatic leadership and 'rationalistic' Liberalism in such a manner as to prevent authoritarianism and a bureaucratic party system.[165] Now, demagogy is certainly not the character of this new politics and its leadership. If nothing else, the study of Edwin Waugh's struggles would make plain enough the shared moral and political understandings of 'working-class' and 'middle-class' people, a mutuality of cultural formation which simply disallows the description 'demagogy', just as it disallows the Marxian terms of class domination. The implications of the term simply do not fit. There is no manipulative leadership and no pliant, combustible led. But the liberal–romantic view of democratic aspirations from below finding wise leadership from above will not do either. Gladstone, like Bright, attempted to balance liberty with authority. Both men's views of 'the democracy' were hedged around by many qualifications, and, as we have seen, many exclusions from the ranks of the democratic elect. For both men 'democracy' was always to be weighed alongside other components of a 'balanced constitution'.

Both men's style of leadership was about creating the democratic fantasy, projecting a demotic social imaginary. This may have been a response to 'democratic' aspirations from 'below' (themselves based on an

---

[164] E. F. Biagini, *Liberty, Retrenchment and Reform*, chap. 7, esp. 'The Cult of the Leader', pp. 395–405.
[165] *Ibid.*, p. 425.

elaborate series of exclusions), but that response was measured and deliberate, concerned with implementing its own view of democracy. It is also the case that the democratic imaginary in which these leaders dealt itself became an actor in the political game, defining, and hence limiting, how democracy might be thought. As such it was not the creation of the leadership alone, but of leaders and led together. There was no single centre of power within the resulting social imaginary, no centre of gravity from which emanated either the domination of the mass or the leadership, let alone the dominations of class rule.

Much of the deployment of Bright by others is evident in the foregoing account of his popular biographies. These were concerned to emphasise the figure of the plain or common man as the hero of the democracy, the democratic subject as protagonist. Sometimes these works had a clearly party-political use. The role of the political party in creating the cult of Bright was, however, more direct than this. 'Charismatic leadership' was always accompanied by party organisation, which was by no means an insignificant adjunct to the role of charisma. This was especially marked in the 1870s and 80s, as the role of party organisation was extended. If there were limits to the power of party organisation, its role in the theatrical production of the leadership was increasingly important. An especially revealing instance of this is the massive, week-long celebration put on in Birmingham for Bright's birthday in 1883.[166]

The highlight was a two-mile long procession walking five miles through Birmingham and its suburbs. Bright was met at Small Heath station by the mayor and municipal dignitaries. The event was presented as to some degree a 'municipal' one, the town's long-standing MP being celebrated by the town. There were three sections to the procession, the first comprising the police, the fire brigade, and other municipal bodies, followed by trade societies and temperance associations. But the two following sections were packed with Liberal associations coming in from every party of the country. The day was essentially a Liberal one, not a Birmingham one (though the association of the town with Liberalism was then very close, through Bright but especially through Chamberlain). The 'Official Programme' for the event shows how carefully stage-managed it was.[167] Minute details of the sequence and mode of processing were given, the many associations being carefully drilled. This drilling extended to songs for 'the March', as it was called, which were themselves surrogate military marches. These were also sung at vast indoor meetings,

[166] Account taken from *The Pall Mall Gazette*, 'Extra', 'The Birthday Celebrations at Birmingham', 18 June 1883.
[167] 'Official Programme of the John Bright Celebrations', 1883.

of fifteen and twenty thousand people, on two evenings in this week of democratic junketing.

'The Liberal March', sung to the tune of 'Men of Harlech', invited the foot-soldiers of Liberalism to 'Shoulder Press to Shoulder', in order to secure 'Peace, Reform and Liberation ... Till we win them for the nation,/and our land be free.' It went on, 'Honest principles inspire us/Calls of noble leaders fire us.' The Liberal venture was conceived of in terms of struggle, the struggle for equal rights, and against Tory guile and 'glory false'. And the terms in which it was conceived were unashamedly military, a nice irony for the party of peace. These warriors for peace became in the end themselves the object of their own veneration: the people were themselves deified, as is evident in the grand finale which closed several of these Liberal performances. 'The People's Anthem', sung to the tune of 'God Save the Queen' ended with the words, 'And may the nation's see/That men should brothers be/And form one family/ The wide world o'er ...' Although the aspiration was a universal one it was clear from the remainder of the anthem that glory true was to come from the people of England's Isle, the real home of the brave and the free. At the great procession, which marched in military fashion four-abreast led by brass bands, Bright took the stand to review the proceedings and was saluted by the members as they passed by. Thousands of medals were also issued for the day's event.

The rest of the week's proceedings included a mass indoor meeting of twenty-thousand, at which Bright and Chamberlain expounded on the great benefits of free-trade. This and other events were staged as expressions of Liberal strength, a strength held to be a direct representation of the identity of the great, populous, industrial centres of Britain (now waiting and ready to come to the rescue of an awakening rural Britain).[168] The strength of the Liberal cause was further demonstrated by the ritual presentation of addresses. Again the military overtones in this theatre of the democratic imaginary are evident. At one meeting over a hundred-and-sixty addresses were presented, one after the other, by the different party associations, something strikingly akin to the presentation of flags to a military commander, in Bright's case a general for liberty. The actual presentation of Bright at these meetings echoed strongly the themes of the popular hagiography – simplicity, honesty, 'true nobility of soul', and so on.[169]

We are in a world not only of political theatre but also of political advertisement, rather than simply of demagogy or democracy. Bright was

---

[168] *Pall Mall Gazette*, 'Extra', 18 June 1883, Chairman's remarks at Wednesday and Friday mass indoor meetings.
[169] See remarks of Rev. R. W. Dale of Birmingham at the Wednesday meeting.

manufactured through these great meetings: the week ended, for instance, with a 'Grand Fête and Garden Party', which included a massive 'fire pageant' in which Bright, Gladstone, the free traders' Wheatsheaf, 'The Saxon Cross', and numerous other Liberal and Bright-enhancing verbal and visual slogans were picked out in fireworks. But he was also manufactured in more direct ways too, ones that included becoming a commodity in this new world of political advertisement.[170] The Liberal press throughout the country reported these and all Brightean events in great detail.[171] The *Pall Mall Gazette* from which some of the present account is taken is of particular interest. This was run by W. T. Stead, the great Liberal publicist of his day, and one of the greatest of all pioneers of the 'popular press'. The *Gazette* ran a long series of 'Extras' over the years, of which the birthday account of Bright was one. They catered for the great contemporary interest in parliament and parliamentary figures, an interest akin to contemporary fascination with the 'celebrity'.[172] These sometimes indulged in a mild satire to emphasise the humanity underlying the adulation felt for these great celebrity-heroes of the day, whether Bright, 'the Grand Old Man', or 'Joe' Chamberlain.[173] They were accompanied by 'Extras' of unrelievedly serious intent on various Liberal issues.[174]

The advertisement columns of the *Pall Mall Gazette* show something of this world of political advertisement. The production of political memorabilia has been written about by several historians of this time, for instance kitchen crockery – fine and everyday – cheap engravings, photographs, and printed souvenir ephemera. The *Gazette* 'Extra' for June 1883 ran advertisements for a commodified Bright in the form of prints of Millais' portrait of him, cheap editions of his *Life*, and J. Alfred Langford's *The Bright Birthday Book*, a Birmingham souvenir which was promoted as a 'Text Book' for Liberals, and took the form of a calendar with sayings of Bright for each day of the year. This was in the vein of a more widely circulating genre than political literature alone, the genre of the Sayings of the particular notability in question.[175] The party imaginary was filled out in many other directions through the advertising pages of the *Gazette*. The respectable, independent party faithful were invited to heighten their demotic ardour by empathising with the dependent poor (at a suitable

[170] See above, pp. 93–7.
[171] H. C. G. Matthew, 'Rhetoric and Politics in Great Britain 1860–1930'.
[172] For example, 'The Electors' Picture Book ... 1882–1892', *Pall Mall Gazette*, 'Extra' (1/- for 96 pages).
[173] *PMG*, 'Extra', 'Not For Joe: A Political Medley', 5 November 1888; 'The Grand Old Man', 5 November 1888.
[174] For example, *PMG*, 'Extra', no. 11, 'The Peers and the People: An Appeal to History', 1d.; 'No Reduction: No Rent', no. 30, on Ireland.
[175] Cecil Wedmore, *The Sayings of John Bright* (1911?).

distance): 'How the Poor Live' by George R. Sims, running weekly in the *Pictorial World*, was the outcome of a journey by the author and an artist through the most poverty-stricken districts of the metropolis. Sims, suitably enough, was one of the foremost writers and producers of the populist melodrama of his time.[176] Through the 'National Press Agency' one could indulge one's appetite for the rationalism of the leader's printed speeches, contemplated in tranquillity after paying one's penny. Bright's *Birthday Book* was akin to the cheap lives of other Liberal heroes on sale (Cromwell, say, or *President Garfield, from Log Cabin to the White House*, a fine example of the democratic fantastic). Nearer home, the poems of Janet Hamilton could be bought cheaply. Hamilton was an old Scots woman of the people, deeply revered by Bright, and held to be the equal of the great Robert Burns, the 'ploughman poet'. Burns and Hamilton exemplified the fantasy of the British plebeity, Garfield and above all Lincoln the equivalent for America.

This world of political theatre and advertisement, this manufacturing of the democratic, and of the wider demotic that went with it, was all the more necessary given what seems to have been a strong counter-current at the time. This might be termed that of the anti-Bright, just as that of the anti-Gladstone and the anti-Disraeli. Again we are aware how 'the Liberal' was produced out of the differences existing between him (not her) and 'the Tory'. Each was essential to the other's being. As suggested, Bright can be understood as inventing the Liberal party by inventing the Tory party. The considerable appetite for 'hard', not 'soft', political satire at the time was fed by the desire political opponents had of thinking badly of one another.

It was also fed by a somewhat paradoxical distrust of the sound and the fury, the evident opportunism and insincerity, of a good deal of party politics. Political activists and the laity wanted their politicians to be at once marshals in a political war, paragons of party principle, and men of disinterested and independent views.[177] A desire for primal innocence on the one hand, and primal evil on the other, fed the party's cultivation of the charismatic leader. So too did a pervasive unease about the sincerity of politicians. The enemy-as-evil of the other side constituted the leader-as-good of one's own. The pressure of the anti-Bright made it all the more necessary for the true Brighteans to assuage a lingering suspicion of politics by making John in the image of honour bright.

Anti-Brights aplenty, sufficiently hard-edged, might be found in the party political propaganda of the day, but more interesting for present

[176] Judith R. Walkowitz, *City of Dreadful Delights: Narratives of Sexual Danger in Late Victorian London* (1993), esp. chaps. 3 and 4.
[177] See below, pp. 216–17.

purposes is the existence of cheap publications with titles like *Brummagen Bright: A Life's Epitome* (1889),[178] *New Gleanings from Gladstone*,[179] *Bits of Beaconsfield*,[180] or *Beaconsfield the Immaculate*.[181] Somewhat in the vein of *Punch*, though more critical and cynical in tone, these depended for their effect on cartoon representation, and a mock-learned array of references to English literature and learning, especially to Shakespeare. They were published from locations throughout Britain, by reputable publishers. There was much plagiarism by the authors concerned, the similarities of the productions being marked. They seem to have fed the scepticism, and cynicism, described. *New Gleanings from Gladstone* is a good example: Gladstone is caste as the epitome of sanctimonious hypocrisy, a man of too many parts, the would-be saviour of his nation. The attack is less on Gladstone *per se*, as on the pretensions of politicians and politics in general. *More Gleanings from Gladstone* dwells on the greasy pole of power and what politicians will do to climb it.[182] The works on Disraeli present him as a liar, a man without principle, given up to the morality of the showground. He is the picture of falsity, of the 'flash', the glib, a political 'quack' to the core. In all this there is a strong anti-Semitic emphasis.

Bright is presented in a similar way to Gladstone, but the emphasis on the supposed inconsistency of the politician is even more marked.[183] The title page cites 'Lydgate; 1460': 'All is not Golde that outward sheweth Bright', and the book proceeds to lambast Bright for disclaiming war in general, while supporting the bellicosity of the North in the American Civil War, also for opposing factory legislation (the white-haired saint, in Quaker garb, stands at the factory gates, 'free-trade' whip in hand, enjoining weeping children to 'work, work, work'). Carlyle is quoted at the beginning of the work: 'Most amiable-looking, but most baseless, and, in the end, baleful and all-bewildering jargon.' Some were immune to the force of Bright's oratory. Again, the emphasis throughout is on the falsity and pretensions of leaders and politics, and upon Bright the supposed demagogue. Dryden is quoted as follows:

> He preaches to the crowd that power is lent,
> But not conveyed to kingly government;
> That claims successive bear no binding force,

[178] Published by Simpkin and Marshall, London and Manchester, and John Menzies, Glasgow and Edinburgh, where it was said to be in its tenth thousand.

[179] Published William Blackwood, Edinburgh and London, n.d., 1880s?

[180] Published Abel Heywood, Manchester and London.

[181] Published F. F. Langley, London.

[182] Same publishing details as in note 179 above.

[183] In the same genre see *The Liberal Leaders* (publishing details as for note 179); n.d., 1880s?, 30th thousand.

> That coronation oaths are things of course.
> Maintains the multitude can never err
> And sets the people in the papal chair.[184]

However, by 1880, Bright the demagogue had in large degree been domesticated, in fact and fantasy. The conservative elements in his politics were evident once political reform and free trade had been consolidated.[185] His opposition to Home Rule was later to make this more fully present to contemporaries. But already by 1880 he was caste in the role not of the demagogue, but of the 'tribune' of the people. This was the great theme of the popular biography, or hagiography, that amassed around his figure from the 1870s onwards. As we have seen, the cult of Bright emphasised the plain man, the homely and simple Bright who was indelibly a part of a large Englishness, and an even larger providence. A closer consideration of popular representations of Bright shows how the figure of the common man, the son of the people, was intimately related to that of the tribune of the people, the demotic vesture of the man finding its culminating expression in the figure of the demotic statesman, the tribune. And here, as is clear from the party political representations of Bright, it is difficult to see where party appropriations of Bright stopped and a more general representation in the wider culture began: the party organs that promoted the figure of the leader tapped into a much wider vein of interest in the lives of the great, especially the humble made great. Bright's subsumption into the figure of the tribune of the people was part of his institutionalisation as a kind of cultural icon of the new democracy. Bright was tamed and made safe for England and British democracy.

This institutionalisation of Bright was one aspect of the creation of the late Victorian democratic imaginary, itself perhaps the major contemporary form of what I have called the social imaginary. It was parallel to the party political productions of Bright we have already viewed, but was of wider effect than party alone. We therefore come full circle from Bright's creation of himself to history's creation of Bright, the process of creation being in truth circular, as one form of creative activity constantly fed into the other. In the 'biographies' the figure of the tribune completed the cult of the common man. The titles of the biographies reflect the tribune theme: *John Bright the Tribune of the English People*,[186] *John Bright the Man of the People*,[187] *John Bright the Tribune of the People*,[188] *John Bright the*

---

[184] *Brummagen Bright*, p. 14.
[185] D. Read, *Cobden and Bright*, 234–5, 236–7; K. Robbins, *John Bright*, pp. 262–3.
[186] N.d., printed as a newspaper format, but in reduced size; no place of publication, but published probably in 1870s, or 80s before Bright's death.
[187] Jesse Page, n.d., probably published shortly after Bright's death.
[188] Rochdale (1911).

People's Champion,[189] and so on.[190]

In the *Tribune of the English People* the connection to classical times is explicitly made. The 'tribunes' of 'olden times' were identified as those in ancient Rome chosen from among themselves by a people made angry by tyranny. The tribune therefore possessed legal immunities and powers. The Middle Ages and modern times have, however, seen little of these tribunes. But their time has now come again, 'warranted by the suffrage' and the new democracy. The equation is between tribune and citizen: Bright's speeches on the Crimean War are cited to show him disclaiming the title of statesman ('that character is tainted and equivocal in our day') in favour of that of citizen. The plain and simple citizen is, therefore, as in ancient Rome, once more the tribune-delegatee of the populace. In Jesse Page's *The Man of the People*, Bright is presented in the usual way, as a simple, plain man immune to earthly honours, but here the term 'patriot' is used as an analogue for 'tribune', the term drawing on its older, eighteenth-century associations of opposition to governmental tyranny rather than the new meanings accruing at the time around the idea of nation. One was a patriot in the people's cause. Though Bright was one of the principal architects of the Liberal party, and a hater of Tories, he constantly presented himself as a man of independence, above party spite and faction. The biographies collude in this, and the tribune figure is now released into general circulation, beyond Liberalism alone. A slightly later biography cites Shakespeare: 'neither to care whether they love or hate him, manifests the true knowledge he had of their disposition, and out of his noble carelessness lets them plainly see it'.[191]

In *Living Lives: Work and Workers* (which includes Carlyle and Gladstone)[192] Bright is cited as the great example of the tribune's 'noble carelessness' in the people's cause: 'He has justified human nature to those who doubt it.' He has also, in a sense, rescued England from herself (always England never Britain). This is because he is profoundly in touch with England, its truest friend because he is so truly English. The earliest account of the hagiography dwelt on this sense of Bright as somehow quintessentially English in his honesty, his Saxon virtue and his Saxon tongue. He is the man, in *Living Lives*, who has saved his country from slavery, revolution, and anarchy by righting the deep wrong done his countrymen. His great achievement is to 'make human beings out of beasts of burden'. One can perceive here the great appeal Bright had for

[189] B. Pickard (1920); in the 'Young Citizen's Series', Rose and Dragon Books.
[190] Revd. P. Hutchinson, *John Bright 'The Tribune of the People'*, London, n.d., 1880s?, Price 1d.
[191] *John Bright The Tribune of the People* (Rochdale 1911), foreword.
[192] London, n.d., 1880s.

working men, men who felt the wrong done by England to them, their England. Their England was now redeemed by their own tribune, John Bright becoming a transformation of John Bull. As we now know,[193] the John Bull figure was far more plastic in its meaning than national chauvinism alone, and one J. B. could at times take the form of the other. In this book Bright is seen to be in touch with yet another version of 'deep England', this time not a Conservative vision of the shires, but a radical one in which Albion has done grave wrong to its children, yet is in its heart the home of right and liberty.

Bright's career is presented as a triumphalist narrative, one in which liberty has at last been gained, or at least is in a position where victory is in sight even if the struggle continues.[194] In these works Bright becomes the acceptable face of democracy, reassuring equally to those who feared, and those who embraced, its consequences. As another such work put it: 'Surely we need not despair of the commonwealth when such men are tribunes of the people.'[195] Bright had become a national institution, from which radiated reassurance on every side, including the radical. He also became the object of non-political moralising, a living guide to moral conduct, for example in the Revd. Charles Bullock's *John Bright. A Non-Political Sketch of a Good Man's Life*.[196] Bright was the subject of a voluminous popular religious literature which it is not possible to discuss here. The Sunday School publication was its chief form. This moral Bright was equally secular and religious. In the former mode, he was the subject of the many biographical series dwelling on the political and moral example of the good and great. One instance is the life by C. A. Vince in the 'Victorian Era' series, published monthly, with Bright, Dickens, and Kingsley in its parts, but also 'The Rise of Democracy' and 'The Free Trade Movement and its Results'.[197] This series represented a peculiarly late Victorian mix of the heroic individual teaching the virtues of a revivified concept of citizenship.[198]

---

[193] Miles Taylor, 'John Bull and the Iconography of Public Opinion in England *c.* 1712–1929', *Past and Present*, 134 (February 1992).

[194] Jesse Page, *John Bright the Man of the People*, foreword. See also Francis W. Hirst, *John Bright as Statesman and Orator* (1911).

[195] F. Watts, *The Life and Opinions of the Rt. Hon. John Bright, An Illustrated Edition* (1880s), p. 312.

[196] 'Home Words', Publishing Office (1889).   [197] C. A. Vince (1898).

[198] Among the many biographies consulted, but not discussed here are: Lewis Apjohn, *The Life of John Bright* (n.d.); J. McGilchrist *The Life of John Bright M.P..* (n.d. 1870s, 80s?); John Waugh, *The Rt Hon John Bright* (1889), in *Living Celebrities* series, a series akin to *Living Lives* and the *Victorian Era* series; G. B. Smith, *The Life of John Bright* (1881); Anon., *A Memoir of the Rt Hon John Bright* (Abel Heywood, Manchester and London), 2d; Joseph Forster, *The Rt Hon John Bright . . . a Sketch* (1883); Mary B. Curry, *A Book of Thoughts in Memory of John Bright* (1907); Jesse Page, *John Bright the Apostle of Free Trade* (1904); R. Barry O'Brien, *John Bright A Monograph* (1911).

By his death Bright had become the respectable democrat, his figure and his career a reassurance to all that democracy was now an English institution, benign and beneficent to all. He had become 'Father Bright', as Marx called him. Bright the institution made democracy an institution. So much is plain from *Punch's* depiction of him during his last illness:[199]

> We are glad you're on the mend,
> For you're everybody's friend,
>   And the troops of your admirers still increase, JOHN BRIGHT!
>
> You've a fashion of your own,
> Which the English race has grown
>   To bear with even when it does not please, JOHN BRIGHT!
>
> So when you're well once more,
> A congratulatory roar
>   Will sound from every section of the State, JOHN BRIGHT!
>
> And each will brim his glass
> To a patriot first-class
>   Who's as sturdy in his love as in his hate, JOHN BRIGHT!

'Everybody's friend' had before his death been given an honorary degree by Oxford University. His colleagues deferred to him as an elder statesman. Newspapers, even where they disagreed, treated his opinions with respect.[200] On his death, Tories vied with Liberals in their eulogies of him, and the nation, including the queen, mourned his passing loud and long.[201] That time had caught up with the old radical and made him acceptable is obvious, and unimportant. What matters here is the creation of Bright and of democracy as institutions, as parts of common sense, common decency, a common Englishness. The cult of the common man had done its work. Bright could be, and was still, a source of a radicalism that did not lie easily with this institutionalisation. He remained to be appropriated to the radical cause, though in the surging narrative of liberty regained the mantle had, by his death, passed to Gladstone. Priscilla Bright knew the real radicalism in the young Bright, lurking still in the old, the man who transformed Britain by a real hatred of privilege and of the aristocracy. She observed on his passing, 'Great has been the tribute of praise given my Brother – but alas! how little do those who joined it follow his example. Where is the moral courage and fidelity to principle which was so much lauded – where do we see them? Not in the House of Commons . . .'[202]

[199] Cited in Herman Ausubel, *John Bright Victorian Reformer* (1966), p. 237.
[200] *Ibid.*, p. 238.
[201] Special Edition of the *Rochdale Observer*, 'Death of Mr John Bright', 27 March 1889.
[202] Quoted in H. Ausubel, *John Bright Victorian Reformer*, p. 239.

The multitude were to disagree, affirming that it was to be found there, if only in the form of Gladstone. Yet in Gladstone too can be found a similar naturalisation, and hence taming, of democracy, a democratic imaginary that, for all the still-evident radicalism, was, for the led as well as the leaders, a source of reassurance, and of a complacency bred by familiarity. To be part of the democracy, part of 'the people', was decidedly of greater moment than to be part of a 'working class' or a 'middle class'. It was to be one with the history of humanity, and its singularly successful manifestation in England. The day of the common man had dawned, and with it a social imaginary, the operation of which was often far removed from the rebellious spirit of the young Bright.

III   Democratic romances: narrative as collective identity in nineteenth-century England

III Democratic romances: narrative as collective identity in nineteenth-century England

Who are the *people*? ... the people implies everyone and no one particular group. Michelet was right: no one (*personne*) made the Revolution. So *le peuple* is a metaphor, a metaphor for reference, for the social referent itself. Though a metaphor, it still exists. It circulates in and out of social class, professional and political groups, in and out of official and unofficial power, both the innermost self and the common whole. It gives justification and identity to all the above, itself without a shape or name. But everything in which it circulates, contradictory and warring, gives it back the effect of a most physical shape, something thick and consistent, with adamantine desire and a will.

(Linda Orr, *Headless History*, 1990)

'Is it nothing', said Mr Roscoe, 'that science has opened our eyes to the magnificent works of creation? ... Is it nothing that she has opened to our contemplation the wonderful system of the moral world? Has analyzed and explained to us the qualities of our own intellect? Refined the proper boundaries of human knowledge? Investigated and ascertained the rules of moral conduct, and the duties and obligations of society? Whatever is wise, beneficent, or useful in government, in jurisprudence, in political economy, is the result of her constant and indefatigable exertions ...'

(James Heywood, Manchester Athenaeum, 11 January 1836)

I am concerned that just laws and an enlightened administration of them, would change the face of the country. I believe that ignorance and suffering might be lessened to an incalculable extent, and that many an Eden, beauteous in flowers and rich in fruits, might be raised up in the waste of wilderness which spreads before us. But no class can do this ... Let us try the nation. This it is which has called together these countless numbers of the people to demand a change; and, as I think of it, and of these gatherings sublime in their vastness and in their resolution, I think I see, as it were, above the hill tops of time, the glimmerings of the dawn of a better and a nobler day for the country and for the people that I love so well.

(John Bright, Speech at Glasgow, 16 October 1866)

Our party is just the people, of whatever way of thinking about anything else, who believe in right and wrong.

(E. A. Freeman on the 'Bulgarian Agitation', November 1877)

To make sense of a life is to make it into a story. The very idea of a 'life' involves emplotment, a matter of a beginning, duration, a closure of some kind. Edwin Waugh and John Bright both understood themselves as acting subjects in the world in terms of their place in various stories. Waugh made a self out of the repertoire of roles he found in his reading, but these roles took their force from being part of narratives of which he could feel a part. For instance, he looked back to the seventeenth-century pantheon of liberty's struggle, but the figures he found there were only appropriate as models because they were part of a narrative about Protestant liberty and its struggle against political and religious serfdom. Personal identity was implanted in 'social' identity, personal narrative in social narrative. This study concerns the ways in which social narrative conferred collective identity, the collective identities involved being chiefly, but not solely, political.

Something of the relevance of this idea of 'social narrative' may already be apparent: both Waugh and Bright thought about social relations in terms of a collectivity called humanity, something elaborated in terms of a human nature and a human heart. This collective subject was unthinkable outside a narrative framing. To be human, personally and collectively, was to be emplotted in a story about humanity, the story of humanity's fortune under God's providence, say, or the Enlightenment narrative of human progress. Both men, but especially Edwin Waugh, were made into acting subjects by subscription to this second narrative, the autodidact story of knowledge's self-realisation in the shape of the all-powerful spirit of 'improvement' (I shall use the small case initial letter, though the large was often used at the time). If only an autodidact at one remove, Bright subscribed passionately to this very Victorian actualisation of the narrative of progress.

Both men were committed to the idea of humanity, yet accented it in different ways. As has been suggested, social relations in Victorian England can in large part be understood in terms of the concordances and discordances operating within shared discourses about the social, whether we think of these in terms of collective subjects like humanity, myths of origin such as those clustering around the value of independence, or the 'roles' of gender. We can, if we choose, think of these different appropriations of discourses at some level shared as 'class languages'. And the same applies if we think of these different subjects, myths, and roles in terms of narrative: narrative, in its differentiated uses and meanings, may offer us a powerful means of understanding the concordances and discordances of which I speak.

For instance, there were marked differences, but also striking similarities, in the ways in which Bright and Waugh dealt with a myth or narrative of origin about a golden age of modest competence and independence. Or, the narrative of progress, as it formed around the advance of knowledge, brought both men together on many things, while for Bright at other times Edwin Waugh and his like might be not a shared subject, but an object, the unlettered or half-lettered upon whom needed to be directed the ministrations of those who held true knowledge and hence exemplified best the real spirit of improvement. For the powerful concordances possible in political narrative one need look no further than the shared narrative of liberty's struggle, especially in its seventeenth-century manifestations. Bright and Waugh were adamantine in their subscription to this story.

One may think about social relations by means of the concept of narrative. The bearer of roles, concepts, stereotypes, and so on, it has particular relevance for present purposes as the bearer of major forms of collective identity, such as class, people, nation, 'woman', etc. It is evident that dominant narratives were the bearers of multiple identities. They may offer us a means of enumerating these identities and looking at the relationships between them. But it is also evident that single collective identities can serve as the central element around which a narrative is constructed. 'Class', for instance, in the course of the nineteenth century, accrued its own narrative, which will be considered later.

Linda Orr's description of the category of le peuple in nineteenth-century France helps us to understand how narrative may have worked in relation to the operation of collective identity.[1] She is describing how legitimacy was secured for the Revolution through the institution of le peuple as a new principle of political sovereignty. One could substitute any form of collective identity for le peuple here, 'class' being a circulating metaphor just like 'the people', but it is in fact fitting that the populist category is cited here, in a study of democratic subjectivities.

Who are the people? ... the people implies everyone and no one particular group. Michelet was right: no one (personne) made the Revolution. So le peuple is a metaphor, a metaphor for reference, for the social referent itself. Though a metaphor, it still exists. It circulates in and out of social class, professional and political groups, in and out of official and unofficial power, both the innermost self and the common whole. It gives justification and identity to all the above, itself without a shape or name. But everything in which it circulates, contradictory and warring, gives it back the effect of a most physical shape, something thick and consistent, with adamantine desire and a will.

Narrative can be understood, therefore, as the means by which collective identity-as-metaphor circulates. But it does more than simply bear

[1] Linda Orr, Headless History: Nineteenth-Century French Historiography of the Revolution (1990), pp. 15–16.

le peuple, for that metaphor is shaped differently in and by different narratives, so that identities can be said not only to circulate in the medium of narrative, but also to be constructed by it in relation to its greatly differing emplotments. This claim that narrative both circulates and structures social identities is a big one, and in order to substantiate it I shall turn to narrative theory in the next chapter. By far the bulk of my substantiation will be the historical analysis of what seem to be dominant patterns of narrative in nineteenth-century England. Edwin Waugh and John Bright give me my cue: they suggest not only the relevance of narrative, but also something of the real narratives of the past. Improvement, providence, liberty, all these give names to narratives that circulated in their day, likewise the 'golden age' form of these imaginings, something less itself a narrative, than cutting across different stories.

I take their lead in what follows, and so my choice is governed by what their lives suggest. It is also governed by my particular task of understanding the kinds of social identity extruded in the political culture of later nineteenth-century England, identities, however, that were formed by far more than formal politics. My concern is with what I earlier termed the 'democratic imaginary' of this time, a particular, more politicised, manifestation of the many social imaginaries of its day. Cued in this way, and governed by this interest, my choice of narratives will inevitably be slewed in a particular direction. The approach is episodic, but when it comes to charting social narratives there are few maps to go by.

The present map begins with the narrative of improvement, and the social and intellectual milieu the young John Bright encountered in travelling from his native Rochdale to the growing, pulsating city on his doorstep, Manchester, the 'shock city' of its day, and the perceived home of the modern. The cultural life of the city, the category of 'culture' itself, helps locate and dissect the narrative of improvement. This enables something to be said about a 'middle-class' identity. A 'working-class' one, merging inexorably into demotic ones after mid-century, begins to be traced in the chapter following on the consideration of improvement: the aesthetic framing of perceptions of the social order found in different kinds of popular fiction, both written and performed. Another way of looking at these perceptions is focused by employing the term 'the political unconscious': my aim is to show how social relations and power were conceived of in aesthetic ways, ways which then can be seen reflected in, and exploited by, popular politics. This structuring of the political, seen, for example, in melodrama, is then traced in terms of politics in the last three chapters, which are all variations on the theme of what happened when improvement and melodrama met politics. The narrative of improvement, the narrative framing evident in popular fiction, above all in the melodramatic form, are traced in their relation to the politics of Reform in the 1860s (in which the political master-narrative of the constitution is much in evidence), then in relation to foreign policy in the 1870s (which saw a deepening moralisation of politics in which the narrative of providence made an appearance), and finally in relation to political leadership (when politicians themselves became leading actors in the stories of politics).

12   Narrative and history

It is ironic that historians, so much concerned with the deployment of narrative, have for the most part been so little aware of how the concept of narrative has come to have a central place in the epistemological frameworks of a whole range of disciplines, spanning the natural, as well as the human, sciences. I quote from a recent overview of narrative theory, that of Somers and Gibson, itself an attempt to appropriate this theory for sociology and a sociological history,[2]

The expressions of this narrative reframing are broad and diverse. One aspect of many of the new works in narrative studies, however, is especially relevant to our understanding of how identities are constituted, namely the shift from a focus on *representational* to *ontological* narrativity. Philosophers of history, for example, have previously argued that narrative modes of representing knowledge (telling historical stories) were representational *forms* imposed by historians on the chaos of lived experience. More recently, however, scholars (political philosophers, psychologists, legal theorists, feminist theorists, social workers, organizational theorists, anthropologists, and medical sociologists) are postulating something much more substantive about narrative: namely that social life is itself *storied* and that narrative is an *ontological condition of social life*. Their research is showing us that stories guide action; that people construct identities (however multiple and changing) by locating themselves or being located within a repertoire of emplotted stories; that 'experience' is constituted through narratives ... and that people are guided to act in certain ways, and not others, on the basis of the projections, expectations, and memories derived from a multiple but ultimately limited repertoire of available social, public and cultural narratives.

This gives a good idea of the range of disciplines involved,[3] and helps validate the high claims for narrative made in this introduction. In particular, the shift from representation to ontology in the understanding of narrative indicates the centrality of narrative to the formation of social identity (though, it could be added, those like Hayden White, who see narrative as representation, also conceive of it as co-terminous with the cognitive process, part of the human condition in which knowing occurs through telling, knowledge through narrative). Whatever theoretical understanding we have of narrative it invites us to dissolve the traditional dichotomies of a realist epistemology in which representation and the

---

[2] Margaret R. Somers and Gloria D. Gibson, 'Reclaiming the Epistemological "Other": Narrative and the Social Constitution of Identity' in Craig Calhoun (ed.), *From Persons to Nations: The Social Constitution of Identities* (forthcoming).

[3] *Ibid.*, for a good account of the literature, but see esp. Theodore R. Sarbin (ed.), *Narrative Psychology: The Storied Nature of Human Conduct* (1980); Victor Turner and Edward M. Bruner (eds.), *The Anthropology of Experience* (1986); J. Shoffer and K. J. Green, *Texts of Identity* (1989), esp. part III, 'Drama and Narrative in the Construction of Identities'; and the synoptic Christopher Nash and Martin Warren (eds.), *Narrative in Culture* (1989), covering many disciplines.

'real' are kept at arm's length, the former being understood as representing or reflecting the latter. On the contrary, and to recall the discussion in the introduction of this book,[4] the constitution of the real is seen to
be inseparable from representation, narrative inviting us to think, along
with Hayden White,[5] about the agency of representation, 'the content of
the form', in which the forms of representation, implicated so completely
in the forms and operations of the cognitive process,[6] have their own
agency in history, as will be seen.

The concept of narrative is particularly relevant to the question of class.
Geoff Eley has recently chided historians of class for dealing with identity
as fixed.[7] Versions of class consciousness do not usually, as he says, turn
on the idea that identity is fractured, unstable, mobile. As Eley says, 'We
need an opposing concept of identity which stresses its unfixity and sees it
as an unstable ordering of multiple possibilities whose provisional unity is
managed discursively.' Talking of politics he suggests 'that politics is
usually conducted as if identity is fixed. The issue then becomes, on what
bases, in different places and at different times, does identity's non-fixity
become temporarily fixed in such a way as to enable individuals and
groups to behave as a particular kind of agency, political or otherwise?
How do people become shaped into acting subjects, understanding themselves in particular ways?'

Narrative is a very important answer to the question. But this answer in
turn throws up a range of questions. First, the 'unstable ordering' and
'provisional unity' of Eley's formulation are necessary cautions when
considering narrative, for all narratives can be regarded as carrying within
themselves the possibility of their own dissolution. Narratives aim for
closure, but are invariably open-ended. This is because of the split subject
positions involved in their operation. In the case of an autobiographical
narrative, for instance, there is an inherent paradox. To put one's life
retrospectively in an ordered sequence one has to pretend that the life is
characterised by some kind of closure. Yet, of course, the act of writing the
autobiography is itself an addition to the sequence, potentially changing

---

[4] See above, pp. 6–9.
[5] Hayden White, 'The Value of Narrativity in the Representation of Reality', also 'The
Question of Narrative in Contemporary Historical Theory', in *The Content of the Form:
Narrative Discourse and Historical Representation* (1989).
[6] David Carr, *Time, Narrative and History* (1986), for a valuable argument with theorists like
White, mounted from a phenomenological point of view, and owing much to Ricoeur's
seminal work on narrative. See also, 'Narrative and the Real World: An Argument For
Continuity', *History and Theory*, 1986, esp. pp. 121–2.
[7] G. Eley, 'Is All the World a Text? From Social History to the History of Society Two
Decades Later', in T. McDonald (ed.), *The Historical Turn in the Human Sciences* (Ann
Arbor 1992).

it. A split subject position is demanded of the autobiographer, one both
inside and outside the tale; as it were, both 'dead' and 'alive'.[8]

The same holds true for what can be called social narrative, its open-
endedness also making it prone to instability. This is evident in the
narrative of the nation, where, in drawing the distinction between the
pedagological and the performative in narration, Homi K. Bhaba has
observed, 'the people are the historical "objects" of a nationalist pedagogy
... the people are also the "subjects" of a process of signification that must
erase any prior or originary presence of the nation-people to demonstrate
the prodigious, living principle of the people as that continuous process
by which the national life is redeemed and signified as a repeating and
reproductive process'.[9] This suggests the caution that self and social
narratives must not be taken on their own valuation.

However, far from the open-ended and inclusive nature of master-
narratives invalidating employment of the concept of the master-
narrative, the opposite is the case. It is paradoxically true that only the
most open and unfixed narratives could secure the fixity necessary to
achieve coherent identities and a workable sense of political agency. To
encompass different and sometimes competing narratives, and the insta-
bilities inherent within narrative itself, stories were needed that did not
foreclose options. Only by allowing multi-vocality could a measure of
uni-vocality be achieved. The effect of master-narratives is akin to the
operation of the metaphor of *le peuple* described by Orr: this could
circulate only because of its flexibility and openness, but in circulating it
acquired a massive density and power. So, far from being too vague and
unwieldy for useful analysis, the master-narratives, and grand identities,
discussed here were important because of, not despite, their very open-
endedness.

The second problem concerning narrative is a simple but basic one: in
what way is the material we study illuminated by being called a story when
everything is a 'story'? An immediate reaction to this would be to say that
the storied nature of human existence has been either ignored or taken for
granted, and that it is necessary to examine these stories systematically.
But questions still remain: what is it about stories that make them so
revealing a tool of analysis? And, should we not continue to employ older
terms that are more precise, such as drama, myth (as in the usage here of
'myths of origin'), symbols, logics, and so on. The answer to this is a
simple 'yes', and that not all categories of cognition are usefully seen as

[8] I should like to thank Dr John Dickie of the University of Wales, Cardiff, for discussion of
these points.
[9] Homi K. Bhaba, 'DissemiNation: Time, Narrative and the Margins of the Modern
Nation', in Homi K. Bhaba (ed.), *Nation and Narration* (1990), p.297.

narrative (though there are important insights to be gained by the recognition that so much 'experience', seen on the surface as without a narrative content, does have a marked narrative structure). The answer to the first question can only emerge fully in the actual employment of narratives as a tool of investigation, though some general remarks are in order here.

Questions about the constitution of social and political identities involve the creation of a sense of purpose, agency, empowerment. To have identity, at least in the senses pursued here, was to have a sense of purpose. Narrative in its very nature, conferred purpose, in that it involved a sense of motion and direction. To tell, or be in, a story, involved a sequence, a movement, from inaugural, to transitional, to terminal motifs. The extent to which this sense of motion conferred purpose depended on what story was told: the stories that I am concerned with were of a kind which were exciting, and which therefore transformed motion into purpose. Twentieth-century stories were not always as exciting as their nineteenth-century counterparts: often they did not involve the drive to a limitless future, the optimism of the characteristic Victorian narratives. For instance, around the time of the First World War, irony can, to some extent, be said to have replaced romance as a dominant mode of narrative,[10] an earlier assuredness of purpose being shattered in the process.

The situation I describe in nineteenth-century England can be said to have brought into the most active being the sense of motion involved in all stories. My story is, therefore, about the power of exciting stories to move people. It is also in large part about how politics, in order to function, depended on creating a sense of movement, and so of purpose. It is about political *movements* in fact, particularly popular Liberalism, and its absolute dependence on exciting stories. And it is about a culture grounded in the exciting story itself, the optimistic, utopian narrative. This takes me to my final point, the choice of 'romantic' for the kind of narrative I describe. Following Northrop Frye, Hayden White describes the 'mode of emplotment' of romance as follows,[11] 'The Romance is fundamentally a drama of self-identification symbolized by the hero's transcendence of the world of experience, his victory over it and his final liberation from it. It is a drama of the triumph of good over evil, of virtue over vice, of light over darkness, and of the ultimate transcendence of man over the world in which he was imprisoned by the Fall.' The narratives I have described so far for the nineteenth century can be described under this heading better

[10] Paul Fussell, *The Great War and Modern Memory* (1975).
[11] Hayden White, *Metahistory: the Historical Imagination in Nineteenth Century Europe* (1973), pp 9–10.

than under those of the other major modes of emplotment, comedy, tragedy and satire.

Turning to historians' uses of the idea of narrative and then to something of the narrative structure of historical writing, one may note, first, some recent examples of the deployment of narrative, examples which can be seen to complement other earlier uses, particularly in the area of class. Class has occupied recent attention too: recent fusions of history and sociology in the US have seen narrative put to use here. One approach is to arrive at a definition of class and then to decide whether narratives facilitated or obstructed class thus defined.[12] The second approach, putting the horse before the cart this time, looks to actual narrative patterns in the past, and then to the sorts of identity these carried[13] (which is the approach adopted in this study).

In employing a Freudian interpretation (a very loose one) of the 'family romance' of the French Revolution, Lynn Hunt's recent work can be said to employ the previous of these two approaches.[14] None the less,[15] in putting the symbolic order, in the form of narrative, at the centre of her analysis, and at the centre of politics, the book points the way forward for the sort of work undertaken here. Hunt shows how it was necessary for political forms in the Revolution to be imagined before they could be realised (precisely in the spirit of the treatment of 'democracy' in this study). She suggests how the family romance at work in the Revolution set up its own dynamic, and that a narrative of the Revolution needs in turn to be written around this romance, a narrative allowing narrative its own autonomous role. What is evident may justly be called a case of the content of the form in actual historical operation.

The author's subject is gender and politics, rather than class and politics, and gender is the focus of Judith R. Walkowitz's *City of Dreadful Delights*, along with Hunt's book the most interesting example so far of the use of narrative in historical work.[16] This deals with what are termed the 'narratives of sexual danger' evident in late Victorian London. What both books show is that narratives about political legitimation and the social order are gendered to their core. Following Foucault, Walkowitz sees power as located in the distinction between the personal, and private, on

---

[12] George Steinmetz, 'Reflections on the Role of Social Narratives in Working-Class Formation', *Social Science History* (Winter 1992).

[13] Margaret R. Somers, 'Narrativity, Narrative Identity and Social Action: Rethinking English Working Class Formation', *Social Science History* (Winter 1992). The University of Michigan has been the venue for the particular fusion in question.

[14] Lynn Hunt, *The Family Romance of the French Revolution* (1992).

[15] Much in this book can, however, be criticised. See my review of the book, 'The Fraternity of Patricide', *Times Higher Education Supplement*, 14 January 1994.

[16] Judith R. Walkowitz, *City of Dreadful Delights: Narratives of Sexual Danger in Victorian London* (1993).

the one hand, and the public on the other, sexuality being the major arena in which this distinction was policed. The political culture I describe below was profoundly gendered, as was the public realm in which it operated: this will be evident later, for example in the discussion of the 'Bulgarian Horrors' agitation in the 1870s, where a somewhat different narrative of sexual danger erupted into politics. However, so firmly was the popular politics of the time rooted in the masculine gender that explicit eruptions like this were relatively few: gender was for the most part implicit, though none the less central for that, the masculinisation of politics being taken as the common sense of the age. These recent uses of the concept of narrative can be seen as complementing earlier work, particularly on class, which may usefully be interpreted as working within the conceptual framework of narrative, even if this frame was not always evident to these writers.

William Sewell, for instance, has dwelt on the ways in which a language of individual rights and democratic participation emanating from the French Revolution was inflected with the accents, and hence meanings, of labour.[17] Under the pressures of political exclusion, and a rampant liberal individualism in the state and the economy, workers voiced collectivist and democratic aspirations by redefining the ideology of the Revolution in terms of an evolving, collectivist language of the trade. This was in large part an appropriation of a narrative about the Revolution. In a very similar way Sean Wilentz has looked at the formation of class in America in terms of the artisan's appropriation of the narrative of the Republic and its mission,[18] a narrative closely tied to the religious sense through the identification of providence and the Republic.[19] In nineteenth-century America there developed a particular craft or artisan variation of the central narrative, the idea of an 'artisan Republic' as it were, seen in the fusion of the emblems and political language of the Republic with the social traditions and labour relations of the crafts.[20]

The English, or British, case can be understood in the same way. Stedman Jones' work on early nineteenth-century popular radicalism, particularly Chartism, fits into this category,[21] and, more recently and explicitly, James Epstein has dwelt on popular, oppositional appro-

[17] William H. Sewell Jnr., *Work and Revolution in France: the Language of Labour from the Old Régime to 1848* (Cambridge 1980).
[18] Sean Wilentz, *Chants Democratic: New York City and the Rise of the American Working Class* (1984).
[19] Sacvan Bercovitch, *The American Jeremiad* (Madison, 1978).
[20] Michael Denning, *Mechanic Accents: Dime Novels and Working-Class Culture in America* (1987), chap, 5.
[21] Gareth Stedman Jones, *Languages of Class: Studies in English Working Class History 1832–1982* (Cambridge 1983).

priations of a pervasive constitutionalist rhetoric and ideology as a 'language', or bearer, of class.[22] A narrative about the 'English Constitution' was a vital carrier of collective identities, though not merely, or perhaps mostly, ones of class, at least in the sense of what is commonly understood as 'the working class'. However, as soon as we touch on 'narratives of class' we are alerted to a rather different sense of the narratives historians of class have used. We need to attend to the narratives contemporaries employed, but also to the narratives, often unacknowledged, that have structured historians' work.

The historians of class in Britain, especially the British Marxist historians, are a clear example of this. A good account of this Marxist narrative has been given in terms of the 'Communist populism' which has, in my view rightly, been claimed to mark the British Marxist tradition in historical writing.[23] What emerges in a diverse range of historians is a common emphasis on what they take to be a radical tradition. This concerns the long history of popular anti-capitalism and democracy in England, particularly in the protracted period when small commodity producers were losing control over the means of production and consumption, from the sixteenth to the nineteenth centuries. The subject of, and agent in, this history was the 'common people', as they experienced dispossession and loss of rights, and exerted an intrinsic sense of democracy, a sense powerfully, and often quite consciously, tied to their awareness of national identity and tradition. The ways in which such cultural motifs as 'the Norman Yoke' and 'the Free Born Englishman' weave their way in and out of these historians' accounts of popular susceptibilities from the seventeenth to the nineteenth centuries are evidence of how they see this powerful radical tradition at work.

This whole Marxist project is powerful and suggestive, but not in the ways it is usually interpreted. It gives an account not of a tradition, nor class consciousness or a process of 'class formation',[24] but of a narrative, a narrative oddly enough often marvellously in tune with the narratives of the historical actors it describes. First, 'Communist populism' describes a

---

[22] James Epstein, 'Understanding the Cap of Liberty: Symbolic Practice and Social Conflict in Early Nineteenth-Century England', *Past and Present*, 122 (1989).

[23] R. Johnson, 'Culture and the Historians', in R. Johnson *et al.* (eds.), *Working-Class Culture* (1979); B. Schwarz, '"The People" in history: the Communist Party Historians' Group 1946–1956', in Centre for Contemporary Cultural Studies, *Making Histories: Studies in History Writing and Politics* (1982).

[24] Hayden White has observed how many narratives of 'class formation', so called, are marked by a rhetorical trope fixed by teleological metaphors of growth evident in psychology and biology, among other sources. Predicated on culturally derived models of development, human and otherwise, they are not, as so often happens, to be confused with 'objective reality'. See Hayden White, *Tropics of Discourse: Essays in Cultural Criticism* (1978), pp. 16–19.

narrative form, that of the 'golden age' account of dispossession and struggle, which, I shall suggest, was a very important part of how political and social identities were formed. Secondly, this narrative form in the nineteenth century was chiefly melodramatic in character. The melodrama of Marxist writing on class is seen to be of a piece with the melodramatic imaginations of people in the past. This is particularly the case with E. P. Thompson. As Renato Rosaldo has recently observed,[25] E. P. Thompson fails to separate his own understanding from those of his subjects, treating his own narrative as a neutral medium, rather than one selected from a range of modes, comic, tragic and so on. As Rosaldo suggests, Thompson employs a melodramatic mode of narrative representation. Although Rosaldo does not fully see it, Thompson's melodrama enables him to have both empathy with, and insight into, the lives of those he writes about.

This Marxist narrative was in turn heavily indebted to the earlier radical–liberal critique of capitalist industrialism evident in the Hammonds and the Webbs. Less critique, but still critical, the work of G. M. Trevelyan employed the same narrative patterns as those of the radicals, and later the Marxists. Trevelyan's biography of Bright, dwelt on so much in the last study, is a fascinating document in the history of class discourse, as well as a biography. It shows the same emphasis on the struggle of a dispossessed 'common people', though, more than his successors and rather like Bright himself, this is couched in terms of the Victorian belief in progress. Like his later counterparts, the collective identity the 'golden age' narrative form carried could be that of class, though again, in line with his Victorian mentality, this is interchangeable with 'people' to a degree not so evident later, at least not in the Marxists. What Trevelyan and these later historians of class evince, however, are different chapters in their own story of class, a story that still continues today: contrary to what so many historians then and now have thought, and, contrary to those sociologised notions of the social growing up after the instance of men like Trevelyan, class is the object of its own narrative, and in adding to this narrative historians have not been reporting on what is 'out there' in the real world of the social, but actively elaborating a discursive means of handling an ever-evasive 'real'. It is ironic that the most recent biographer of Trevelyan, David Cannadine, provides yet another chapter in this story: such is his ardour for Trevelyan's liberalism he is unaware of (or disengenuous about?) the narrative structuring not only Trevelyan's work, but also his own, the narrative of class, and also

[25] Renato Rosaldo, 'Celebrating Thompson's Heroes: Social Analysis in History and Anthropology', in Harvey Kay and Keith McClelland (eds.), *E. P. Thompson: Critical Perspectives* (Cambridge 1990).

the narrative of progress to which it is always linked in these liberal manifestations.[26]

13 The romance of improvement

Recent research on the vocabulary of class suggests that this did not emanate chiefly from the new economic conditions and outlook of rapid industrialisation.[27] The political context seems to have been crucial, particularly that of the period of the Napoleonic Wars (for the designation 'middle class') and that of the Reform agitation of the early 1830s, in which 'middle' and 'working' classes became equally prominent. Moderate opposition to war split the ranks of property, the liberal Friends of Peace, for instance, being led from the idea of a political middle to that of an economistic social middle as the putative hinge around which society was articulated. Appropriated by the Liberal opposition in the 1790s, Dror Wahrman argues that the terms of class had by the 1810s become directed against radicalism; the term 'middle class', for instance, becoming politically tamer, and associated less with social critique and more with political stability and conservatism. In the early 1830s all political sides sought to appropriate the notion of the 'middle class' for themselves. Class identities were, therefore, a product of arguments about meanings, arguments which were primarily political in character. Class does not seem to have been the collective cultural experience of new economic classes produced by the Industrial Revolution.

In the 1790s and later, radicals and Tories did not adopt the notion of a middle layer in society, continuing to think in terms of higher and lower classes, the natural way of thought for them given their notions of benevolent paternalism and oppression. After 1832 the radicals turned increasingly to the language of class, this time of a 'working class', to make sense of their feelings of betrayal and exclusion following on 1832. They came to jettison the dualistic notions of oppressor and oppressed. In all this one may see the operation of narrative to be quite crucial: the language of class, and therefore the identity of class, arguably only came

[26] David Cannadine, *G. M. Trevelyan: A Life in History* (1992); G. M. Trevelyan, *The Life of John Bright* (1913).

[27] Dror Wahrman, 'Virtual Representation: Parliamentary Reporting and the Languages of Class in the 1790s', *Past and Present*, 136 (August 1992), esp. pp. 110–13; 'National Society, Provincial Culture: An Argument About the Recent Historiography of Eighteenth-Century Britain', *Social History*, 17: 2 (May 1992); *Imagining the Middle Class: Language and the Politics of Representation in Britain, 1780–1830* (forthcoming, Cambridge). I am grateful for Dr Wahrman's permission to cite this work.

to have real purchase when it was put into narrative form. For instance, the Reform Bill came to be justified by representing the recent origins of this new and powerful middle in society, one generated by unprecedented social change. The 'middle class' increasingly came to be appealed to as an objective social fact (a facticity it has ever since retained, such is the power of this nineteenth-century discourse over us). Very quickly this nascent narrative, and nascent facticity, took firmer form as a lineage was discovered that went further and further back into history, beyond 1832, to the Civil War, the Reformation, and the Middle Ages. In this account it was not the middle class who brought about 1832, but 1832 that brought about the middle class.

This, however, may be to give the context and meanings of class too political a slant. None the less, some of the primary candidates for thinking about class as the expression of economic circumstances do come under intense scrutiny in this reading. The Anti-Corn Law League is a case in point.[28] It has traditionally been taken as the expression of a new middle-class identity which was economic in character and origin. The term 'middle class' was in fact only prominent in the League's activities towards its very end. For the most part it was not used, as it did not represent a clear social constituency, nor clear social and economic interests, around which a successful political agitation could cohere. The debates around Repeal continued within alternative social vocabularies: as the account of Bright has revealed, the idea of 'humanity' was central in the agitation, not that of class.[29] It was only later that a 'middle-class' League came to figure in the lineage or narrative of a middle class. We can, therefore, see that a narrative can grow up which has a single collective identity at its centre, in this case that of class. Formative as this narrative was, however, class was articulated by other narratives, which were arguably of as much, and perhaps more, historical weight. These others, chiefly that of improvement, carried not one, but many, collective identities.

This account of Wahrman's work is corroborated by the recent, unpublished, work of Stedman Jones on the language of class in early nineteenth-century England and France.[30] In these cases, the argument goes, the 'middle class' was a discursive construction of political liberals and radicals concerned to steer a middle course between, on the one hand, legitimism and aristocracy, and on the other, Jacobitism and ultra-radicalism. In England Cobden sought, and failed, to mobilise a social and political middle in this cause. Hence he, with Bright, turned to the

[28] D. Wahrman, *Imagining the Middle Class.*   [29] See above, pp. 128–30.
[30] Gareth Stedman Jones, 'The Rise and Fall of Class Struggle: "Middle Class" and "Bourgeoisie", 1789–1850', unpublished paper.

'working class', and thence to the construction of a political and social vocabulary with 'the nation' and 'the people' at its centre. This shift from class to people has already been seen to be of central significance for Bright's development and for his influence.[31] The political marginalisation of class discourse after the 1840s occurred at all levels: as Stedman Jones suggests, Peelite Conservatism did not identify the state with any interest or class. Social relations, and the state, were to be moralised and purified, and, by definition, as class was equated with faction and interests, this meant the exclusion of class. Gladstone continued Peel's refusal to identify the state with class.

In looking to contexts other than the political, and to narratives other than 'the rise of the middle class', it is fitting to turn first to Manchester, for so many, then and since, the cradle of the English bourgeoisie. When we do so it is apparent that the economic is not the only alternative to the political in understanding the contexts and narratives of the social. It was to Manchester that the young Bright and Cobden came, also the young Engels. No others perhaps, by their own efforts and as symbolic figures, have had as much to do with the elaboration of the class narrative as these three men. In the case of the first two, however, it is apparent that the elite cultural life of the city, the life of the rich manufacturers and merchants, shaped them as much as they it. The city, like all provincial cities in the first half of the century, was producing its own understandings of the social order, ones that, if related to politics and to metropolitan intellectual life, also had their own histories and priorities.

These priorities have for long been seen in terms of the economy. Economic concerns, of course, shaped the way in which capitalists saw the social order, but neither these, nor political concerns, give an adequate account of how capitalists saw things. This account is to be sought, in the much broader concerns evident in what they felt the ends of human life to be, and how they thought social arrangements might bring about these ends. They gave the terms 'culture' and 'civilisation' to these purposes and it is to the social narratives and collective identities present in these capitalists' attempts to manufacture a culture for their manufacturing city that I shall attend in this section.

The general nature of this grand cultural project may be briefly sketched, before its social and narrative content is considered.[32] Recent work on the nineteenth-century middle class has revealed not a distinct

---

[31] See above, p. 133.

[32] This account is based upon research on Liberalism and ideas of culture in Lyon, Manchester, and Hamburg 1830–80, run as a British Academy funded programme by myself, John Breuilly, and Iowerth Prothero, Department of History, University of Manchester. Part of this research is presented in the unpublished, Patrick Joyce, 'Manufacturing Culture: Civilizing the Industrial City, Manchester 1830–1860'.

and class-conscious social entity, but diverse social groupings split along economic, social, political, and religious lines. These elements often held views that seem to have had very little to do with the 'acquisitive individualism' long held to characterise a bourgeoisie (they are Tories in politics, say, stout defenders of the Established Church, and believers in a paternalist, hierarchical social order). This is the picture presented for Leeds by R. J. Morris,[33] where a measure of rather fragile class unity is held to have been achieved through the actions, and the ideology, of the voluntary society. It is also the picture presented in Simon Gunn's important new study of the post-1850 Manchester middle classes,[34] where, it is argued, the unity of purpose achieved was somewhat greater, if still considerably qualified.[35] Morris talks of an 'elite-led' middle class. In what follows the term 'elite-created' is perhaps more to the point, bearing in mind the hegemony of these cultural projectors over the public life of the city in the first half of the century.

These men were the self-described 'wealthy and influential inhabitants' of the city, 'the opulent classes'. Their unity of purpose was provided by religion, particularly Unitarianism,[36] and by liberal politics. Their family and business connections were other sources of cohesion. Such men were far from the stereotype of Dickens' Mr Gradgrind. They were highly educated, not infrequently at Oxbridge, though the Unitarians did not take their degrees there. Translators of Persian and German poetry, founders of their own gentlemen's library in the city, the Portico, they were the very figures of the 'industrious gentleman', which was how one of their sort described his kind in the early part of the century.[37] Other cities saw different groupings, for instance the greater Nonconformist presence in Leeds, or the presence of Anglicans in Bristol. But the composition of these groups matters less than their influence and cohesiveness.

These were achieved through their membership of city institutions, especially those concerned to both define and regulate the cultural life of

---

[33] R. J. Morris, *Class, Sect and Party: the Making of the British Middle Class, Leeds 1820–1850* (Manchester 1990).

[34] Simon Gunn, 'The Manchester Middle Class 1850–1880', Manchester University Ph.D., 1992. On the nineteenth-century 'middle class' in general see Leonore Davidoff and Catherine Hall, *Family Fortunes: Men and Women of the English Middle Class 1780–1850* (1987).

[35] On divisions within a provincial 'middle class' see also Helen Meller, *Leisure and the Changing City, 1870–1914* (1976), on Bristol.

[36] John Seed, 'Unitarianism, Political Economy and the Antinomies of Liberal Culture in Manchester 1830–1850', *Social History*, 7:1 (January 1982).

[37] Thomas Henry, president of the Literary and Philosophical Society from 1807 to 1817, quoted in R. H. Kargon, *Science in Victorian Manchester: Enterprise and Expertise* (Manchester 1977), pp. 8–10.

the city. In Manchester the Unitarian–Liberal alliance was further expressed in local parliamentary seats, and domination of the Town Council, the Chamber of Commerce, and the local press (not to mention the Anti-Corn Law League itself). The Unitarians were the key group in the cultural institutions, the foremost of which were the Mechanics' Institute (founded 1824), the Royal Manchester Institution (1823), the Manchester Athenaeum (1835), and the Literary and Philosophical Society, founded in 1781. From the earliest days of the 'Lit and Phil' there was the desire to create 'the marriage of polite learning and utility', as exemplified in the figure of the 'industrious gentleman'. A new, young, generation of businessmen in the 1820s and 30s were however concerned to broaden the remit of knowledge, looking beyond the gentleman to its wider social 'diffusion' (itself a key word of these decades). Along with this went a new awareness of the social responsibility of the industrious gentleman, and a mightily enlarged ambition for knowledge itself as – in the form of culture or cultivation – the key to society's and the person's ills. One reflection of these developments was the foundation of Statistical Societies, which would provide the information, the 'social facts', upon which their grandiose conception of culture would work. These societies were established in the provincial cities in the 1830s, with Manchester being the first in 1833.

The aim of these cultural projectors was clear – to create a unity of purpose among the influential classes so that education could be utilised successfully to handle the needs and problems of the growing city. Their discourse about knowledge was laden with prescriptions and descriptions concerning the social order. The projectors were constantly concerned to make their proceedings non-religious and non-political. They were acutely aware of the deep division that marked even their own ranks of the wealthy, and the hostility and rank indifference their activities elicited in the city (from Anglicans and Tories for instance). So, in speaking of their hegemony the fragility of this construction must be borne in mind, together with the inherent divisiveness of the city's 'middle classes'. None the less, in terms of their creation of institutions and their influence over the media of public communication (for example the *Manchester Guardian*) they seem to have gone far, at least for a time, in dominating the public sphere. It is, however, what the discourse of this project and its projectors tells us about formative social narratives that is the subject for concern.

This discourse addressed the social subject of 'classes' frequently and directly. Yet the discourse of culture was perhaps most significant when it articulated manifold social identities. It did this most completely in its form as narrative, in this case a particular variant of the narrative of

improvement. It addressed a class subject in its designation of different
sorts of education for different social groupings: the Mechanics' Institute
was to provide 'useful knowledge' for 'artisans' and the 'working classes'.
The Athenaeum, on the other hand, provided an education suitable for
'the younger classes of our commercial fellow townsmen'. Yet this
deployment of a class vocabulary was anything but straightforward. At
times these men of the 'wealthy and influential classes' thought of themselves as 'middle class', but at others deployed that term in a very different
way, one in which they were forging others' 'middle-class' identity, not
their own, which was that of the 'opulent'. This is plain from the public
concern with providing a 'middle-class education'.

In the 1830s the Athenaeum was seen as catering for the commercial
youth that flooded into the city, and seeing that they were qualified for
'the duties of the station to which wealth will elevate them'.[38] They were
explicitly seen as members of the 'middle classes'. In fact, for the 'opulent'
at this time the 'middle classes' were what we would term the 'lower
middle classes'.[39] This was exactly the same thirty years later. In the
proceedings of the Manchester Statistical Society in the early 1860s, the
'middle classes' to which a 'middle-class education' applied were defined
thus: they were above the level of the 'artisan', but only that of the artisan
unaided by education. They were described in terms in which education,
appearance, and character were more important than occupation alone.[40]
This 'middle-class youth' were those of 'unimpeachable character'
needing to keep up 'the conventional requirements of their position'. As
in the 1820s and 30s, it was felt that the wealthy had a duty to the middle
class, whose position was felt to be difficult.[41] The spokesman for the
Statistical Society hoped that the public spirit of the merchants would lead
them to found what he directly labelled a 'Middle Class College'.

So, the vocabulary of class was itself unstable, and cannot automatically
be given the meanings so often imputed to it. This example shows that the
moral and intellectual criteria which education defined might be as important as the 'economic' ones with which they intertwined. It is this conjunction of the moral and intellectual in education which takes us to the heart
of contemporary narrative understandings of 'the social'. If the collective

[38] *Addresses to the Members of the Manchester Athenaeum at Their First General Meeting*, 11
November 1836, remarks of George Wood, p. 14.
[39] See the remarks of Absalom Watkins, *Report of the Proceedings of the Public Meeting ... for
the Purpose of Establishing an Athenaeum* (Manchester 1835), on the 'opulent' and the
artisans having their institutions, but not the middle classes.
[40] T. Browning, 'Middle Class Education', *Transactions of the Manchester Statistical Society*,
1861–2.
[41] For a rather similar definition of the 'middle class' see the report of James Bryce on
Manchester education, *Parliamentary Papers*, 1867–8, Schools Enquiry Commission
(1866–VIII), XXVIII, Pt. VIII, pp. 712–32.

subject culture addressed could be socially particularised in terms of classes (ambiguous as these were), culture told its narratives most eloquently when it spoke to those universalised subjects which we have seen to be so important at the time: 'mankind' or 'humanity'. And, again, the universal is at the same time a category of exclusion, defining the cultured in terms of an 'other' which is not, or not yet, or fully, of 'man' or of 'humanity'.

In this discourse, if certainly part of humanity, women were not fully a part of 'man', in the sense that this public provision of culture was for men, not, or not yet, for women. Education was part of a public sphere, and this was a male sphere. As Cobden said, one did not come together thousandfold, in the Athenaeum, for the purpose of infidel or obscene studies. Men secluded themselves for such debased studies. It was in the public domain that 'intellectual and refined recreation' took place. But the private sphere buttressed the public: there was much talk among these cultural projectors about the temptations awaiting young men in the city. Women's role was found not in the public, educational sphere, but in bringing restraint to bear, through their femininity, upon these young men, especially in the Athenaeum, with its enormous annual soirées. At these 'the ladies' were fêted and their role in creating 'amicable and respectable members of families' was celebrated. At the same time, functioning as male 'clubs', these institutions represented a subtle distancing from home and family life, however 'amicable'. None the less, after mid-century women began to take up this educational provision in increasing numbers, though these institutions chiefly remained male bastions.

When these cultural projectors talked of education it was in the grand terms of 'humanity', and of education's ends and ultimate purposes. These were felt to lie in the full development of the potential of the person. 'Culture', most often in their terms 'self-culture', was a term that denoted this process of growth and ultimate formation. The narrative was clearly the Enlightenment one of *Bildung*, the word 'culture', according to Raymond Williams, having by then firmly taken on its sense as 'the independent and abstract noun which describes a general process of intellectual, spiritual and aesthetic development'.[42] Yet at this time the word would have retained more of its sense of tending, of bringing on, a noun of process redolent of the agricultural and biological, and close to the sense of 'cultivation' (itself a true cognate of 'culture' at this time). While both terms had by then acquired associations of superior social status, the aim of these Mancunians was to contest this, and to

---

[42] Raymond Williams, *Keywords: A Vocabulary of Culture and Society* (1981 edn.), p. 90, also pp. 87–93.

democratise culture. They constantly invoked the idea of the 'Three Sisters' of Science, Literature and Philosophy. They also spoke of the 'Two Fountains' of the Athenaeum and the Mechanics' Institute. In speaking to a collective human subject, however, all mankind was to sit at the feet of the Three Sisters, and, if there were different fountains, all would drink of the same waters of knowledge.

James Heywood was the single most active and influential of these promoters of 'culture': of a rich Victorian merchant and banking background he was fresh from Cambridge in 1836 when he set out to fashion the city's projected Athenaeum. He did this first by describing what he took to be a desirable education.[43] This comprised the classics, together with contemporary European language and thought, and the scriptures. The emphasis on utility was, however, integral to this: one drew moral lessons from the classics, 'brief and sententious precepts ... descriptions of high action and high passion affording solace and support in busy life'. For the 'middle class', and for himself, education had to be of relevance to a busy and practical life.

There were two central aspects of this concern with culture, one the understanding of modernity, the other the romance of 'science'. Both can be regarded as particular manifestations of the narrative of improvement. Heywood's understanding of education involved the attempt to reconcile tradition and modernity: of particular importance in this was the English vernacular as one fusion of the two. Its living forms, particularly in dialect, connected past and present, for instance the blunt and honest Lancashire man of today, in all his late-Saxon love of liberty, with a past Protestantism to which the English vernacular was central (the Protestant heritage of Wyclif and the English Bible for instance). Language was one dramatisation of the relation between past and present, which was to be of vital importance for all social groups in the industrial north and elsewhere.[44]

The accent on language merged with the idea that Manchester and its industry were the bearers of the new. However rooted in the soil of the old it was modernity that was glorified. In Manchester, Heywood averred, inventive genius and creative industry were greater than anywhere else on earth. Invention and industry in this account were centred on the great individual, above all – for Heywood – the inventor of the steam engine, James Watt. For it was Watt who was 'the first to give to senseless matter an almost instinctive power of self-adjustment'. We begin to see that a narrative of modernity is here also a romance of industry, a romance that involves the very transformation of matter itself. Some ten years before

---

[43] James Heywood, *Addresses to the ... Manchester Athenaeum* (1836).
[44] Patrick Joyce, *Visions of the People: Industrial England and the Question of Class 1840–1914* (Cambridge 1991), chaps. 8, 11–12.

Heywood's address, his cousin Benjamin Heywood spoke to the Mechanics' Institute in a similar vein.[45] For him 'there cannot be a more beautiful and striking exemplification of the union of art and science than is exhibited in the steam engine'. He dwelt on the primitive technology of Indian cotton production. Adherence to the same technology for generations meant that 'these poor Indians' were bound firmly by superstition. Stasis was the result, and India the home of an inert, sluggard form of tradition, unlike the English conception of a flexible tradition, evident for example, in language. The principle of a beneficent 'tradition' was movement, and the principle of movement was the invention apparent in industry. This changed the nature of man as well as of matter, for 'mere imitation', as in the Indian case, 'precludes all advancement: it reduces man to the condition of a machine. Skill thus acquired is little better than an instrument.' The first step out of this prison of instinct is observation, in doing which, he told his artisan audience, 'you are already on the threshold of improvement'. The next step was to learn the reasons behind observation, which was the purpose of the Mechanics' Institute.[46]

It needs to be remembered that these men witnessed at first hand the transformation of the natural world they spoke of in such grandiose public terms. The patrons of the institutions had close links with the seminal scientists and inventors of the Industrial Revolution, men like John Dalton, George Stephenson, and Boulton and Watt, the engine makers. Sometimes, like William Fairbairn, the engineer, and Richard Roberts, the inventor of the self-acting spinning mule, they were major inventors themselves. And they had seen invention transform the city and region in which they lived. With justice we may call this a romance, 'a drama of . . . the ultimate transcendence of man over the world in which he was imprisoned by the Fall', a drama about man's victory over the world of experience and his final liberation from it. In this regard Cobden was only one of many, though he is sometimes taken as a lone architect of these views. None the less, he extended the romance of industry and invention into the realms of the romance of trade. We may say that free trade was far more than an economic and political doctrine. It was one of the fantasies of progress, an exemplification, and justification, of the narrative of improvement. This is how Cobden addressed the Athenaeum in 1835,

It had indeed been said by an aristocratic poet that 'while commerce fills the purse she clogs the brain' – but he thought that the history of commerce proved the reverse of this – that wherever commerce alighted and made her abode, the

[45] *Addresses Delivered at the Manchester Mechanics' Institute by Sir Benjamin Heywood* (Manchester 1843), 1825 Address.

[46] *Addresses* (1843), p. 5. On the Mechanics' Institutes see D. S. L. Cardwell (ed.), *Artisan to Graduate* (Manchester 1974); M. Tylecote, *The Mechanics' Institutes of Lancashire and Cheshire Before 1851* (Manchester 1957).

decencies, comforts and refinements of life, the science and the arts, sprang up in her train; and spread from these spots to enlighten and bless the whole earth – (Cheers).[47]

Speaking again in 1839 he defended commerce once more, this time against 'the great and imaginative mind' of Lamartine. Lamartine's *Voyages in the East* represented a homage and pilgrimage to the great cities of the East, but these cities had in truth been made by commerce. He spoke of 'the stream of commerce' in its Mediterranean manifestations, from which sprang the stream of science, learning, and art, the stream that deposited Galileo and Michelangelo on the shores of history. That stream was now rising in England, and it was a 'low and degrading fallacy' that there was anything in the pursuit of science and literature that was inimical to the pursuit of commerce. Commerce was something like the spirit of history, infusing 'culture' with purpose and direction in the great utopian project of improving mankind.[48]

The 'science' to which industry, invention, and commerce gave rise became the subject of a romance, or, perhaps better, the instrument of a romance, the means by which man transcended the world in which he was imprisoned by the Fall. Audiences at the Athenaeum and the Mechanics' Institute may have been occupationally different but, as we have seen, the patrons of both institutions held out the same heady vision of knowledge as the key to transforming the world, the world of matter and of man's prison house of instinct. The stream of commerce gave man 'science', and science promised in turn to complete the work of commerce and liberate man. It is difficult today to appreciate the majesty with which 'science' was invested, and the audacity of the claims made for it. It embraced all of 'learning' and 'art'. Though these and other terms were employed, they were ultimately seen as part of a unified field of knowledge, 'science', which subsumed all variants.

This is evident in James Heywood's Athenaeum address of 1836. Here science reveals the wonder of the world, 'the magnificent works of creation', and is 'an infinite source of the most exalted pleasure and truest knowledge'. But this seemingly natural world is at once the moral world. Science opens to our contemplation 'The wonderful system of the moral world'. It explains our intellect to us, investigates the role of moral conduct, together with 'the duties and obligations of society'. To science, says Heywood, we therefore owe our understanding of the economic and political as well as the moral world. 'Literature', chiefly history, 'reveals the lights and landmarks by which we steer', but it is science that sees into

[47] *Report of the Proceedings* (1835).
[48] *Report of the Proceedings ... on the Fourth Anniversary of the Manchester Athenaeum* (1839).

the heart of how things work. It is at once material, moral, and social in character and contemplation of it releases us from the domination of the purely utilitarian, material world of the senses. We contemplate Watt, says Heywood, and when we do we withdraw from the present and the power of the senses.[49]

To understand the wider remit of this grandiose vision of science it is necessary to turn to the contemporary 'science' of phrenology, in which it was claimed that investigation of the exterior of the human person, the cranium, would reveal the interior workings of the mind. George Combe was the leading populariser of phrenology, and popular the science assuredly was in the second third of the nineteenth century: Combe's *Constitution of Man* ranked in sales with Smiles' *Self-Help* and *The Rights of Man* of Paine. By 1860 it had sold 100,000 copies in Britain, and 200,000 in the USA.[50] Earlier in the century phrenology had been immensely popular in the Literary and Philosophical Societies of England, in which the Manchester cultural projectors learned their conception of knowledge. Codben was a close friend of Combe, and an adherent of phrenology.

The point, however, is not so much the direct influence of phrenology, but the conjunction in time of different threads of the great and consuming romance that all knowledge was one, and so at once the means and the proof of mankind's improvement. Phrenology was one of several keys to realising this dizzying ambition at the time. They all had in common the belief that the many were one, the moral, the social, the religious, the economical, and so on, forming a unity with the material world and the laws of nature. The laws of political economy were of a piece with the laws of the human mind and the natural world. But, as will be evident, because laws might be found in nature, this did not mean the abrogation of the moral and religious responsibilities of the self. Quite the opposite.

Phrenology was symptomatic of this belief, in holding that there was a material basis, rooted in nature, for moral behaviour and social relations. It promised a 'science of morality', a science of the social. True knowledge of the organisation and function of the brain permitted actual scientific laws of human nature to be derived. Nature was the court of appeal, the element in which 'laws' were felt to be inherent. Phrenology, like science in general, both revealed progress in action in the world, and, in its actual

---

[49] *Address* (1836), p. 11. On Science in Manchester see also A. W. Thackray, 'Natural Science in Cultural Context: the Manchester Model', *American Historical Review*, 79 (1974); J. V. Pickstone, 'The Social History of Science in Manchester', *Memoirs and Proceedings of the Manchester Literary and Philosophical Society*, 120, 1977–8.

[50] Roger Cooter, *The Cultural Meaning of Popular Science: Phrenology and the Organization of Consent in Nineteenth Century Britain* (Cambridge 1984).

practice, exemplified this progress in action. As a historian of phrenology has put it,[51]

Had not the philosophers of the Enlightenment optimistically predicted that once nature was properly understood society would arrange itself harmoniously. Combe, it seemed, through phrenology, had supplied the necessary key to that understanding. Henceforth humankind would be free from the false secular and religious restrictions of the past and be free from 'the conditions of savage and barbarian life in the present day'. Humankind, located (at long last) in a *natural* evolutionary process, could now be propelled into a future of unbounded progress, perfection and harmony.

Important here is the sense of social agency provided by narrative, and how, in this particular context, its deployment can be seen as a major means by which social relations were lived at the time. 'Culture' had a double force, inherent in the term itself, and expressed in the allure of the particular manifestations it took. The concept 'culture' was intrinsically narrative in character: it signified a story sequence of inaugural, sequential, and terminal elements organised around metaphors drawn chiefly from nature. To be engaged in providing and receiving culture and cultivation, including 'self-culture', was already to be set in movement as a subject by a story. To be part of the particular story of 'culture' I describe was to be drawn into subjectivity in a particularly compelling way, as an agent of history and not as its object.

The intoxication of this view of industry and knowledge will be apparent: to be a true seeker after knowledge was to stand almost on the brink of paradise. The narrative element present provided just that sense of movement and purpose that I have identified as of interest in considering narrative, in differentiating it from other analytics. It was not only a story, but a story that was irresistible, one in which to involve oneself was to be, quite literally, transported. Because it was so compelling it attached personal and social identities to it, in ways that were also compelling.

These identities were diverse. The exaltation of industry and commerce, alongside that of science, was a narrative in which what we often term 'bourgeois' identities were emplotted and hence given shape. The terms of class are obviously relevant in this case, though 'middle class' is by no means always appropriate, and when we look closer the collectivities involved could be 'industrialist', 'employer', 'businessman', or 'capitalist'. At the same time the universalistic character of the collective identities constituted by this narrative understanding of knowledge meant that they were very often de-coupled from their 'bourgeois' meanings.[52] Much of the intoxication provided by the one science of man is akin to the

---

[51] *Ibid.*, p. 124.   [52] See above, pp. 41, 51–2.

intoxication of the young Edwin Waugh as he practised his religion of
humanity and his cult of improvement. And Waugh was of a piece with
the countless 'artisan' autodidacts who played such a powerful role in the
culture of the labouring poor in the nineteenth century. Phrenology is a
good example of this: far from being the expression of some 'bourgeois
hegemony' of ideas at the time, it was central to the vision of progress and
emancipation that inspired so many working-men radicals and Liberals
in mid- and late-Victorian England[53] (and for whom, it might be added,
free trade had a distinctly romantic, as well as practical, attraction).

I shall dwell briefly on the public face of one of the key 'improving'
institutions of Manchester at this time, the Athenaeum. This will reveal in
more detail the collective identities carried by the discourse on culture and
its narratives. Through the 1830s and 40s addresses were given at the
Athenaeum on the subject of culture and its improving potential by the
likes of Dickens, Disraeli, Chambers, Emerson, Rowland Hill, Lord John
Manners, Bright, and Cobden. Up to 5,000 people attended to dance and
to listen on these occasions. The public pronouncements of the famous of
their day were fully reported in the newspapers.[54]

The political and social range of the speakers suggests how improvement can not be seen simply as a class narrative. Spanning romantic
Toryism and radical Liberalism, aristocrats and cotton manufacturers, the
discourse of culture here is evidently being released into the mainstream
of English life, as the means of securing not only the unity of the rich and
propertied in Manchester, but also the unity of all social groups and
parties across the nation.[55] Disraeli was especially concerned with how the
Athenaeum's efforts would transcend the sectarianism that had until
recently threatened to tear the country apart. These very diverse men said
precisely the same things about the purposes of culture.

They said, first, that the object of culture was the self. Dickens intoned,
in 1843,

> Though house and land be never got
> Learning can give what they can not.

Culture gave self-respect, irrespective of economic circumstances. This
'inward dignity of character' was a 'property of soul', upholding men of all
degrees. Once got, it was never vanquished, especially among the 'self-
made' and the poor – 'it walked the streets in mean attire with Crabbe',
and followed the plough with Burns. It was very like the independence

---

[53] R. Cooter provides ample evidence for this, the intrusive Gramscian analytic of 'hegemony' notwithstanding. See R. Cooter, *Cultural Meaning, passim.*
[54] They are collected in *Manchester Athenaeum: Addresses by Charles Dickens, Benjamin
Disraeli ...* (Manchester 1885).
[55] Dickens, President of the first Athenaeum soirée, spoke on 5 October 1843.

struggled for by Waugh, in his particular realisation of 'the workers' dream'.

The agent of culture was therefore the self, and the self and its discipline can be seen as a key to social discipline. The self, following Foucault, may rightly be seen as an instrument of governmentality, governance of the soul enforcing the government of society.[56] But this view of self was neither divorced from the categories of the social nor severed from social responsibility. Both Cobden and Bright emphasised the role of self-culture in these addresses. By 'cultivation', as Bright put it, it was our 'divine' faculties that were developed.[57] Cobden talked similarly of tending our 'divine allotment', making it flower or leaving it waste.[58] For all the speakers in Manchester culture was the secular enemy of 'materialism', of what they termed 'Mammon'. Again the 'workers' dream' comes to mind, and its concern to destroy materialism.

The self that self-culture confronted was not at ease with itself, divided as it was between Mammon, and the base, and the spirit that expressed what was divine within it. It had to struggle to overcome passion and bestial emotion (the sorrows of Edwin Waugh are about this struggle). The categories of religion were central here, though not only the religion of Christ. To achieve self-culture the good had to be actively exercised. The struggle of the self may be said to have united the worlds of Bright and Waugh, those of the *laissez faire* advocate and the poor, radical autodidact. This did not mean isolation from the social in the cult of the individual. On the contrary, the conditions needed to be created in which all might with equality struggle for, and exercise, the good, the good being realised in a human nature under God, of which all individual selves were indissolubly a part. One consequence might be the intervention of the state. It certainly meant the unstinting provision of cultural opportunities that equalised the search for self-culture among the rich and poor. The soul of liberalism can be said to lie in this egalitarian narrative about the self-cultivation of the good, the moral and spiritual fruits in the Manchester instance of the 'Three Sisters', the enjoyment of which was for Cobden 'the greatest pleasure I have known'. It is apparent therefore that an intense moralism co-existed in many with the view that nature and 'Science' were the source of laws covering all human activity. Not until later did the two outlooks conflict, when 'the social' took on its own autonomy, threatening the moral and religious responsibility of the self. The religious and moral framework was still dominant, at least for those

---

[56] Nikolas Rose, *Governing the Soul: the Shaping of the Private Self* (1988).
[57] John Bright, *Manchester Athenaeum Addresses* (1885), speaking on 23 October 1845.
[58] *Ibid.*, pp. 24–30 for 1844 Speech, 23 October; also November 18, 1847 speech in this collection.

described here, for whom the message of improvement was that personal moral choice was more, not less, necessary.

For Cobden, as for the other speakers, the pleasures of which he spoke should be accessible to all, because they depended on bringing to the fore what was common to all men. Therefore, starting from the self, culture led back to the 'property of soul' all had in common. Cultivating the self meant affirming one's solidarity with a common humanity. As well as defining the object of culture as the self in its guise as the human, these spokesmen fixed the social identity of humanity by giving it first the form of 'public opinion', and then that of 'democracy' or 'the masses'. These identities, as expressions of the narrative of improvement, in turn acquired their own narrative momentum.

John Bright spoke of education and intelligence spreading across the globe, and expressing themselves as 'public opinion' irrespective of governments. Disraeli spoke of 'that great educational movement which is the noble and ennobling characteristic of the age in which we live'.[59] For Disraeli the 'strong head' and not the 'strong arm' is now 'the moving principle of society'. As civilisation has progressed it has equalised the physical qualities of man, so that force is dethroned, and intelligence put on a pedestal. Knowledge also equalises the social condition of mankind, giving us all the same needs and passions irrespective of our political views. Knowledge had now reached 'the market place', becoming the possession of 'the mass'. Typically, Bright made the direct link between knowledge, power, and democracy: in proportion as nations became more educated so was power diffused among them.[60] The onward march of knowledge became one of the narrative principles around which 'democracy' and 'the people' were constituted. As we shall see, Bright, Gladstone, and others were to shape Victorian popular Liberalism around this narrative, in the process further elaborating the collective identities involved.

The cultural project lost some of its momentum after mid-century (and it was from the beginning of limited success as an institutional initiative, though not in the wider promulgation of the values it espoused). Improvement for the higher classes seems to have been softened, its earlier austerity being qualified by the development of a broader 'polite culture' for the 'respectable' and propertied in the city. The provision of clubs, societies, and concerts for the 'middle classes' saw improvement linked to sociability as a new cultural ideal. These developments are explored by other historians, and seem to have been marked by a re-Christianisation of improvement as well as the accommodation to sociability and a new

[59] *Ibid.*, p.17.
[60] See also the speeches of Sidney Smythe and Lord Morpeth in *Addresses* (1885).

pattern of higher-class social life.[61] New narratives were in turn created in those settings, around which 'middle class' identities were further elaborated, not least that developing around the cult of the civic, and civic pride, the city itself, in such liberal manifestations as Birmingham and Manchester, giving a new shape to the onward march of improvement and the rise of the middle class.[62] Outside the ranks of the propertied, improvement continued to be greatly significant. Like its higher-class manifestations it coalesced with more hedonistic currents, though this had long marked its reception at a popular level.

14   The aesthetic framing of the social

The thinking and framing of the social shape of power is valuably approached through an understanding of the 'structures of imagination' apparent in the aesthetic realm. Frederic Jameson and others have argued the significance of this realm and shown some of its effect.[63] If narrative is as powerful a principle of ontology as theorists of narrative tell us then it follows that it may be a productive means of reconstituting the imaginative structures in question. It is in this hope that the aesthetic is explored here. The emphasis on framing and structure recalls the earlier emphasis on the agency, or efficacy, of the form, though not in any formalistic sense. The social world is categorised in certain ways, and can only be present to us as some kind of configuration of categories. These configurations are always changing, yet there are decided limits to how we see our worlds. One example, drawn from Walkowitz's recent work on sexual narratives in Victorian London, is that of melodrama. The melodramatic constructions of feminist propaganda in the 1880s were only capable of imagining women in a certain way, as a victim, exhibiting modesty, and so on.[64] And this way was extraordinarily important over a long period. Yet it too, in the end, lost effectiveness as other aesthetic frames displaced the melodramatic, chiefly that of realism.

Walkowitz's emphasis on melodrama is apposite, for, as cultural his-

[61] See S. Gunn, 'The Manchester Middle Class 1850–1880', esp. pp. 126–35; P. Bailey, *Leisure and Class in Victorian England* (1978).
[62] P. Joyce, *Visions of the People*, pp. 182–3; S. Gunn, 'Manchester Middle Class', esp. chaps. 6, 7; Charles Dellheim, *The Face of the Past: the Preservation of the Medieval Inheritance in Victorian England* (Cambridge 1982).
[63] A work of particular interest in respect to the kinds of material studied here is that of a student of Jameson's, Michael Denning, *Mechanic Accents: Dime Novels and Working-Class Culture in America* (1987).
[64] Judith M. Walkowitz, *City of Dreadful Delights*, p. 92.

torians are now beginning to realise, melodrama was one of the central aesthetics of the nineteenth century, particularly at a 'popular' level. So, it may be that melodrama offers us a singularly revealing way of getting at the configuration or framing of the social that we seek to understand. In concentrating on melodrama I shall be leaving other aesthetic frameworks out of the account, above all those of romantic literature, which was clearly of such importance in facilitating the narrative of improvement considered in the previous section.

Peter Brooks' account of melodrama has been singularly influential.[65] It is a study of the 'melodramatic imagination', which extends to fiction as well as to theatre: as will be apparent large areas of nineteenth-century popular fiction are decidedly melodramatic in character. Brooks argues that this form of imagination represented the attempt to resacrilise the world after the dissolution of traditional forms of the sacred at the end of the eighteenth century, particularly in the French Revolution, where melodramatic theatre was born. With the invalidation of earlier certainties about religious and socio-political cohesion, the literary forms that depended on them went too. Melodrama was, in important measure, a response to this loss of the tragic vision. It inhabited a world in which truths were violently questioned, yet one in which moral imperatives were still felt to be of overwhelming concern. As Brooks puts it,[66] melodrama sought to expose these imperatives by making the moral accessible and legible to all. Its appeal lay in the reassurance that there was a moral purpose and order to the world.

What light can this aesthetic throw on the framing of the social and political in Victorian England? The shape of melodrama's aesthetic frame has been described by Brooks and others, and can be given summary form here. First, in making the moral legible it dealt in clearly delineated moral contours, expressed in unambiguous modes of presentation (emphatic, for us exaggerated diction, gesture, and so on). Secondly, and working from the same need, it dealt in a polarised world of moral absolutes, in which reality was rendered as a Manichaean struggle of good and evil in their countless expressions. These moral categories were invariably personalised, though this imagination had nothing to do with psychological realism. Therefore, thirdly, it was 'pre-psychological' in character, while

[65] Peter Brooks, *The Melodramatic Imagination: Balzac, Henry James, Melodrama, and the Mode of Excess* (1976); also *Reading For the Plot: Design and Intention in Narrative* (Oxford 1984). There has more recently been a move to question this interpretation as too monolithic and, while there is a need to attend to the dialogic nature of melodrama, the outlines of Brooks' work seem to me immensely suggestive; see Jacky Bratton, 'The Contending Discourses of Melodrama', paper presented to the British Film Institute Conference, 'Melodrama: Stage, Picture, Screen', London 1992.
[66] P. Brooks, *The Melodramatic Imagination*, chaps. 1–3, and see pp. 204–6.

moral attributes were none the less individuated (as such it was situated between older forms like allegory, and the later ones of realism). It follows that this mode of imagination can not be judged by the tenets of realism. It frequently is, however, and dismissed as wish-fulfilment and fantasy, which is precisely why it is interesting.

Fourthly, its mode of emplotment gave a singular shape to the aesthetic framing of the social and political. Unlike comedy it did not posit the emergence of a new society, formed around the reconciliations emerging out of the plot. Unlike tragedy, which partook of the sacrificial body of the protagonist, it did not involve participation in a newly sacred order, one higher than man.[67] It was, in fact, very close to romance, in its desire that evil be transcended by the good, but unlike it to the extent that it desired less a transcendence of the world of experience, a new utopia, than an old utopia, a return to a previous state of innocence. It was the drama of restoration, concerned with driving out what threatened primal innocence. As such, it had a close kinship with the 'golden age' motifs so evident in many forms of popular literature, especially ballads, and in popular politics. The plot structure of melodrama concerned virtue extant, virtue eclipsed and expelled, virtue tested (in struggle), virtue apparently fallen, and virtue restored and triumphant. The emplotment of the prelapsarian narrative form concerned a similar process of primal virtue, loss, usually in the form of dispossession, struggle, and restoration. The 'golden age' form was too widespread to be realised in melodrama alone, but melodrama expressed its sentiments with particular force.

Finally, as Brooks and others have argued,[68] the aesthetic–cognitive frame of melodrama carried its own political message, implicit in its form as it were. The message was a democratic one: recent work has suggested that the form was 'falsely democratic', but this is irrelevant to my consideration,[69] for whether 'conservative' or 'progressive' (whatever these terms may mean) what matters is how it made possible the imagining of the social order, in this case in its 'democratic' form. It is not so much the democratic ingredients of presentation that matter here, for example, the tendency to make merit and not privilege the sign of virtue, or the casting of the hero from 'low' society, the villain from 'high' (by no means always

---

[67] *Ibid.*, p. 32.

[68] David Grimsted, 'Vigilante Chronicle: the Politics of Melodrama Brought to Life', paper presented to the British Film Institute Conference, 1992; D. Grimsted, *Melodrama Unveiled: American Theatrical Culture 1800–1850* (Berkeley 1987, first published 1968); for a contemporary condemnation of the 'Jacobinical' tendencies of melodrama, the 'affectation of attributing noble and virtuous sentiments to persons least qualified by habit or education to entertain them', see Sir Walter Scott, 'Essay on the Drama', *Supplement to the Encyclopaedia Britannica*, 1819.

[69] Julia Przybos, *L'Enterprise mélodramatique* (Paris 1987).

the case of course). Rather, and here I elaborate Brooks' argument in my own way, it can be suggested that simply by receiving the conventions of melodrama those who received them were being constituted as political persons.

Melodrama sought to make the good legible to all. Given that the truth was unambiguous, all could have direct access to it. Melodrama appealed to all, irrespective of social condition, because all were held to be equally able to read the signs of moral legibility. Further, because the moral law was absolute, it actively enjoined readers and audiences to partake of this reading. The 'democratic' implications are clear. All were potentially equal in the task of interpretation and there could no longer be an appeal to the court of tradition and the sacred. Rather, the appeal was to the moral law and to a demos that sanctioned it. But, if the idea of the moral absolute was thereby sanctioned, the content of this law always lay in the assumptions and values of the audience. There was no other source of legitimation. The eternal verities of melodrama were the shared, mundane moral conventions of those to whom it spoke. Therefore, simply by partaking of the melodramatic aesthetic, audiences were being spoken to and hence constituted as social subjects, ones varying always by the context of the audience, but at a general level very much akin, in this aesthetic egalitarianism, to the imagined communities that made up a 'democratic' culture, including the political community itself.

Melodrama spoke to a socially mixed audience in England, at least until the late nineteenth century.[70] The virtue in which it dealt was absolute. Its triumph showed that all might be virtuous. The lowly were, however, often closest to virtue – their friendlessness and helplessness represented best the helplessness of virtue expelled and tested. The triumph of the helpless meant the truest of all restitutions of virtue, for only with the low made morally high could the victory of virtue be most fully assured. On the one hand, the melodramatic imagination can be seen as deeply implicated in the construction of categories often cutting across classes, like 'the people', 'the audience', the theatre 'public', and so on, categories closely linked to the democratic imperative. It addressed a socially undifferentiated 'popular' audience, and was important in itself in creating the idea of 'the popular'. But on the other hand, it can be said to have made a particular appeal to the lowly, the excluded, and the powerless.

Melodrama was about symbolic reassurance. In assuring its audience that there was a moral purpose and order to the world, it can be regarded as speaking most eloquently to those whose circumstances exposed them to the fear that there might not be. Historians of the form have noted its

[70] Michael Booth, *English Melodrama* (1965).

special appeal to the powerless, not least, in the nineteenth century, women.[71] The representation of the lowly and powerless became translated into an appeal to that condition. It has been observed how the empowerment brought by melodrama involved the ability to say the truth out loud: the eternal verities could be named without embarrassment, and the crust of convention, fear, and silence broken. The powerless could be given a voice: a poor, persecuted servant girl could confront her rich oppressor with the truth about their moral condition.[72] It is this twin function of speaking to both demos and the powerless, inserting the latter in the former, that to my mind gives melodrama its fascination as a means of understanding the political unconscious, particularly in its Victorian realisations as popular radicalism and popular Liberalism.

Melodrama is equally suggestive in constituting collective *social* identities, sometimes outside, sometimes within political ones. If the eternal verities were simply the shared moral conventions of audiences, then it follows that this aesthetic is a privileged point of access to these conventions. And, as the conventions are so involved in what 'communities' and collectivities felt themselves to be, it follows that melodrama is directly implicated in the very construction of the sense of 'community' and social identity itself. Melodrama was implicated in the moral being of audiences, and the moral being of audiences was implicated in their social being.

Walkowitz's recent work is a good place to begin what of necessity is going to be a brief and selective consideration of an enormous field,[73] that of nineteenth-century popular fiction.[74] Her examination of the 'narratives of sexual danger' evident in W. T. Stead's 1880s agitation over child prostitution shows how these achieved their effect by being linked to the narrative patterns evident in the melodramatic theatre, and literary forms such as the Gothic romance, crime fiction, and Victorian pornography. Her suggestion is interesting, partly drawing on earlier work, that the coalescence of Stead's agitation in the *Pall Mall Gazette* with the popular radical cause was brought about because both functioned by recycling the narratives of these popular literary forms, especially on the radical side, in the mass-selling, radical weekly press, journals like *Reynolds' News*, *Lloyd's Weekly Newspaper*, the *Weekly Times*, and the *News of the World*. One example is the way working men, in the 'Maiden Tribute' agitation, were positioned as grieved, wronged fathers, and the seducers of children as

---

71 Martha Vicinus, 'Helpless and Unbefriended: Nineteenth-Century Domestic Melodrama', in J. L. Fisher, *When They Weren't Doing Shakespeare: Essays on Nineteenth-Century British and American Theatre* (University of Georgia Press, 1989). See also the discussion of melodrama in P. Joyce, *Visions of the People*, chaps. 9, 13.

72 P. Brooks, *The Melodramatic Imagination*, p. 44.

73 Judith K. Walkowitz, *City of Dreadful Delights*, pp. 86ff.

74 P. Joyce, *Visions of the People*, chaps. 9–12 on popular fiction.

depraved aristocrats, through the deployment of the narrative and sym-
bolical resources of the broadside ballad tradition, a tradition in this
regard by then long conscripted to the radical cause. Consideration of the
great Hyde Park demonstration of August 1885 shows this clearly: the
Gazette fulminated against 'Society'; the rich, the well born, and the
powerful, who until recently had smothered 'the new factor in politics',
the English people coming together to 'kindle in the popular heart a new
and deeper reverence for women'.[75] Drawing on the venerable resources
of the ballads, the East End contingents, in their thousands, marched with
banners calling on Englishmen everywhere to protect their daughters
from a rapacious 'Society'.[76] One contingent paraded 'a dozen little maids
in white' to prove the point.[77]

Walkowitz's account also shows how Josephine Butler, the leader of the
anti-Contagious Diseases Act movement, and Stead's co-campaigner,
framed her autobiography around the conventions of melodrama[78] (as we
shall see this prophetess and suffering magdelene presented herself as the
leader of a popular cause in much the same way as the prophet-martyr
John Bright was presented). Walkowitz's work therefore does a great deal
to put narrative on the historical map, particularly in its melodramatic
manifestations. In showing that the *Gazette* was a major player in this
game her account points to how new cultural forms, in this case a new
kind of demotic press, depended for their effect on recycling old forms.
This suggests the importance of tracing the lineage of the old in the new
and is the route I will take here, attending first to the generation of
magazines that preceded the *Gazette*. Stead was concerned to 'democratise' the paper, making it accessible to a wide audience, and hence part of
quotidian life. This involved the use of colloquial language, 'human
interest', and arresting, 'sensational', presentation (as in the 'Maiden
Tribute' instance). What we see in the *Gazette* however, is a restrained,
almost respectable, sensationalism, one in keeping with Stead's Nonconformity, and the greater gentility of his audience, when compared to the
rawer edge of *Reynolds'* or *Lloyd's* sensation. None the less, sensation it
was, and one is aware here of the widening social constituency of the
marriage of respectability and sensation long seen in the less 'gentlemanly'
popular press. From whatever direction it came, it is evident that in imagining a 'democracy' that was then consumed by its readers this press
had a central role in constituting the democratic form of the social
imaginary of its day.

[75] *Pall Mall Gazette*, 21 August 1885, Editorial.   [76] *Ibid.*, 24 August 1885.
[77] See also 20 August 1885, for account of the demonstration. For earlier manifestations of
these themes in the ballads see Anna Clark, 'The Politics of Seduction in English Popular
Culture, 1748–1848' in J. Radford (ed.), *The Progress of Romance: the Politics of Popular
Fiction* (1986).
[78] J. Walkowitz, *City of Dreadful Delights*, pp. 90–9.

The generation of magazines considered here reached, and created, a mass audience between 1845–60, *Reynolds' Miscellany*, *Cassell's Illustrated Family Paper*, and the *London Journal*. Claims vary, but the latter was reputed to be selling between half and three-quarters of a million in the 1850s, *Reynolds* probably half this amount.[79] In these the marriage of improvement and melodramatic fiction was cemented, but it is necessary to go back to the *Penny Magazine* to understand how this marriage began. The audience that read these journals was the audience that made up the cohorts of the popular politics considered later: the link to politics would appear direct, the social imaginary, and the political unconscious, of this first generation of the new democracy being shaped by this experience of reading (just as the journals prospered by speaking to the predilections and fantasies of their audiences, there being little or no advertising in them, profit being solely by sales).

The peculiar synthesis of improvement and sensation has for long been misunderstood by historians. These currents have usually been assigned to different social constituencies in the 'working class', the supposed 'rough' and 'respectable'. The putative bifurcation has often been taken to represent a cultural divide exploited by a bourgeois 'hegemony' over the respectable part of this popular constituency. But the fusion of the two sorts of appeal, and the clear indications they spoke to the same subject are striking. Although unable to throw off the weight of the Gramscian perspective so evident in 'social history' until recently, the first historian of these journals none the less indicates the reality of the case. She is considering Charles Knight, the founder and editor of the most important forerunner of the generation of journals I consider here. After denying that the readership, content, or underlying themes of the *Penny Magazine* were in any sense 'middle class', she goes on,

Knight ... seemed to believe himself to be part of a social and intellectual vanguard, capable of unusual and advanced insights into the relationship of knowledge, morality and society. As he put it, he and other social and educational reformers were not just 'educated and intelligent men'; they were also the representatives of 'high thinking' and dedicated to 'duty not pleasure'. In this he stressed they were different from members of the middle class ... Knight's apparent goal was the ... ambitious one of delimiting an ideal, not necessarily class-specific, system of social, moral and cultural values – a system which he believed would foster the improvement of individuals at all levels of society.[80]

---

[79] Gertrude Himmelfarb, *The Idea of Poverty: England in the Early Industrial Age* (1984), chap. 18; A. Humphreys, 'G. W. M. Reynolds: Popular Literature and Popular Politics', in Joel H. Wiener (ed.), *Innovators and Preachers: the Role of the Editor in Victorian England* (Westport, Conn., 1985).

[80] Patricia Anderson, *The Printed Image and the Transformation of Popular Culture 1790–1860* (Oxford 1991), p. 79, also p. 80.

Knight, therefore, was involved in creating a new sort of 'public', which contributed greatly to the creation of a democratic culture: an informed reading public, including all in society (or at least all who were 'intelligent'). G. W. M. Reynolds and Edward Lloyd were also part of this vanguard, but the great difference was that they fused improvement and entertainment in an entirely new synthesis, one that was much more successful than Knight's (even so, the *Penny Gazette* sold around 200,000 copies monthly in the 1830s). The dedication to pleasure as well as duty in both men was reflected in their literary activities: Reynolds was reported to be the biggest-selling author of the century, and Lloyd similarly wrote rafts of immensely popular 'Penny Dreadfuls' before developing his newspaper (itself probably the biggest selling paper of the nineteenth century). The editors of the *London Journal* and *Cassell's* similarly moved in this nether world of the improvement vanguard and the sensation-monger. We are aware then of another station on the way of improvement, as it passed from Manchester and the provincial England of the 1830s and 40s, to the popular politics of the 1860s and 70s.

This new and potent appetite of demos was not entirely a novel departure: Iain McCalman has brilliantly explored the underworld of radical politics in early nineteenth-century London in which reason and pornography were allies.[81] However, the product of the cultural entrepreneurs of the 1840s and 50s was innovative: a typical number of the *London Journal* in 1848, for instance, mixed together features with a radical edge, the chaste pleasures of improvement, and the titillations of sensation.[82] Articles on contemporary French politics, on the history of 'popular outbreaks' in Britain, and on 'Our National Defences' (nicely combining patriotism and radicalism, these being ours, the people's defences), were combined with sections on 'Gems of Thought', 'The Fine Arts', 'Topographical and Historical Notes', and so on. A typical sentiment was that contained in the article title 'Be Something', a typical maxim – of which many were quoted – 'Reason requires culture to expand it. It resembles the fire concealed in the flint, which only shows itself when struck with the steel.' This assortment of delights was completed by long-running romances, or shorter stories and articles, with titles like 'Visits To A Harem', 'The Child of Retribution, or the Smuggler's Fate', and 'Love Letters of Remarkable Persons'.[83] Eugene Sue's 'The Seven Cardinal Sins' was the leading attraction of the moment.[84]

---

[81] Iain MacCalman, *Radical Underworld. Prophets, Revolutionaries and Pornographers in London 1795–1840* (Cambridge 1988).

[82] *The London Journal*, 11 March 1848.   [83] *Ibid.*, 18 March 1848.

[84] Running through 1848. For typical home-grown products see 'Gideon Giles the Roper', the *Journal*, through November, 1848, or 'Harding the Moneyspinner', through much of 1857.

However, it is best to look at the home-grown variety: John Frederick Smith, in *Cassell's Illustrated Family Paper*, was a characteristic author (the content of all three journals was extremely similar). Smith is interesting because of his immense popularity. In May 1858 *Cassell's* led with a large engraving of him.[85] Smith was 'universally acceptable' because of his insight into 'the human heart and character', and his appeal to 'the intelligent reader'. As a result his tales are 'wide in philanthropy' and 'deep in significance'. Far from being antitheses, fiction is here seen as the instrument of progress. The arresting vision of the public service romance was distilled in the sentence that capped this encomium on Smith: 'He renders essential service to the cause of human progress'. A decade before in the *London Journal* the sentiment was expressed that '... the best of civilization is to make good things cheap'.[86] What civilisation made cheap was fiction as much as fact therefore. The sentiments of the *Journal* were expressed in an advertisement for 'Tracts for the People', selections of fact to cultivate 'the Million' (the advertiser was *The Weekly Times*, another of this stable, advocating in its case 'the cause of Progress and the People'). Smith's literature was therefore to transform a 'People' ennobled through improving facts by appealing to the fictive truths of the heart (again one sees a cult of the human heart). But there was also a more immediately apparent social purpose than this, one that takes us into the area of Smith's fiction itself.

The melodramatic romances of Smith have the same combination of 'social realism' and a pre-psychological rendering of 'character' evident in melodrama, the hold of social realism strengthening in the second half of the century. Smith's characters are 'realities', we are told, the result of 'extensive experience and close observation'. The 'reality' Smith is close to is that of the helpless and the poor, the quintessential protagonists of melodrama. Smith's fiction serves progress because, above all, he has stood forth as 'the unflinching advocate of the poor, the wretched and the ignorant', while never failing to denounce vice, whether it be clothed in 'rags or purple'. The writer upholds the reign of virtue, speaking out for the lowly as the embodiments of the moral law. This is the polarised and absolute moral world of melodrama, of rich and poor, purple and rags, vice and virtue. Innocence may be dethroned but in Smith's hands its lost kingdom, its golden age, will be restored in the end.

This is Eugene Sue's world: Umberto Eco has written of the endless movement of this fictional tide, the fearful series of climaxes followed by

[85] *Cassell's Illustrated Family Paper*, 22 May 1858.
[86] *The London Journal*, 11 March 1848.

the inevitable return to the familiar, the known, the consolatory.[87] Smith's own fiction is the best place to show this melodramatic framing of the social, of the political unconscious: 'Smiles and Tears: A Tale of Our Times' ran throughout much of 1858.[88] The story addresses a morally sensitive, respectable, almost fastidious reader, one who is already redeemed by improvement. It is full of authorial asides buttressing the moral pretensions of those whom it addresses. The story deals in the personalised moral attributes of melodrama: characters have 'deep, thoughtful eyes', an 'intelligent open brow' and even the internal organs testify to identity in this literature of the 'humours'. The 'strong heart' of the good almost bursts in its attempt to get out, and to testify to the truth. Characters are surrogates for moral attributes, with the 'cunning of a serpent', the 'gentleness of a dove', the 'courage of a lion', and so on.[89]

This is fiction, but the debt to the melodramatic stage is overwhelming. David Vincent, in writing on literacy and popular culture at the time, has spoken of cheap fiction as 'writing by numbers' produced for people either with limited or no literacy, or those relatively new to reading (melodrama in its early French origins was self-confessedly a theatre for the illiterate).[90] The contours of plot, action, and character were sketched in, and readers left to fill in the details from their own cultural resources. One sees here, therefore, precisely that function of melodrama as the vehicle for the collective moral sensibilities of its audience, its dramatic condensation of particular manifestations of what was none the less held to be the eternal moral law. As a kind of 'writing by numbers' it was the fixed form of the protean moral law. One could put almost anything in to it, so long as it fitted the very generous shape.

However, 'writing by numbers' may also be a slur on this particular audience, many of whom were adepts at improvement and therefore well versed in its very taxing texts. None the less, as sometimes new readers they may have luxuriated in these less demanding 'tracts for the people' (which as we have seen in Smith's case were anyway presented as unmediated expressions of the spirit of improvement). At the same time, the open-ended nature of these fictions probably did include those with limited literacy, which suggests the force of the earlier claim that this mix of improvement and sensation appealed to a broad swathe of the contemporary poor. Whatever the precise nature of the readership, the melodramatic was, quite simply, one of the chief modes in which 'the Million' apprehended the real.

[87] Umberto Eco, 'Rhetoric and ideology in Sue's Les Mystères de Paris', International Social Science Journal, 19 (1967).
[88] See the opening, Cassell's, 5 December 1857.
[89] See also 'Left to Seven, or a Mass of Money', Reynolds' Miscellany, 3 November 1868.
[90] David Vincent, Literary and Popular Culture: England 1750–1914 (1989), p. 219.

So much is suggested by Sue's romances, which were consumed by all social levels in both France and England. Sue's 'Seven Cardinal Sins' ran in the *London Journal* of 1848, and it reads like a piece of melodramatic theatre.[91] Enormous chunks of conversations are interspersed with stage directions to characters, who 'Soliloquize thus ...', and are despatched from, and summoned to, the action by the stage-manager Sue. A knowledge of the stage was probably called on by these writers, and it is clear that a high degree of intertextual reference obtained between these forms; plots, characters, and themes being imported wholesale from the stage to fiction, and back again. Smith's 'Smiles and Tears' exemplifies the plots of melodramatic fiction, and hence the most direct exemplification of its social and political meanings.[92]

The social drama of this 'unflinching advocate of the poor', and scourge of vice, unfolds thus: a poor clerk marries a 'lady' of higher birth. Her father discovers this and disowns and disinherits her. The poor clerk is led into temptation and numerous adventures, set in low life local settings and exotic foreign ones. He is pursued remorselessly by the villain, who threatens to take away his lady. The villain dies a horrible death. The hero triumphs. The two lovers live happily thereafter, and are reconciled to the father. The essential moral drama of melodrama is self-evident, the social attributes of the rich and the poor being mapped upon the moral ones of evil and good.

In interpreting similar kinds of popular fiction I have previously dwelt on the usefulness of Michael Denning's work on cheap, 'dime' fiction in the USA.[93] Contrary to the private, individualised reader of realistic literary convention, 'pre-naturalistic' modes of presentation and reception suggest a more collective or at least 'social' reader. Unlike the hermeneutic code of the narrative in 'high' fiction, Denning emphasises how at the levels in question narrative should not be read as a developmental sequence (with truth lying at the end of expectation in a framework of psychological realism) but as metaphor or allegory. Sensational stories such as Smith's should not be read as escapist fantasy.[94] The hero in question in 'Smiles and Tears' is both a clerk/poor man *and* a gentleman/rich man, a unity represented in the form of metaphor. The fiction involved exploring the relations of the rich and the poor, at the same time as affirming the virtues of the latter. Denning suggests how 'cheap fiction'

[91] See for example, March 1848 instalments.
[92] Chapter one begins in *Cassell's Illustrated Family Paper*, 5 December 1857.
[93] M. Denning, *Mechanic Accents*, chap. 5 and pp. 146–8. The following are also very revealing, John G. Cawelti, *Adventure, Mystery and Romance: Formula Stories as Art and Popular Culture* (1967); Jean Radford (ed.), *The Progress of Romance: the Politics of Popular Fiction* (1986).
[94] P. Joyce, *Visions of the People*, pp. 225, 227.

of this sort comprised allegories of social redistribution, but also, I would add, of social reconciliation. Smith's stories are strikingly similar to the 'romances' circulating thirty years later in the *Cotton Factory Times*: these were allegories about how the world should be – imaginative projections into ordinary utopias – but they were also judgments about how the world was.[95] They concerned romances about labour and capital, Smith's romances the more capacious categories of rich and poor, but the end result was the same.

In the *Cotton Factory Times*, as in these illustrated magazines, it is clear that women were readers as well as men (*Cassell's* was after all a 'family' journal). It is evident that the imaginative framing of the social and political described here would have applied to women as well as men. In this account I have described the melodramatic in such a way as to emphasise the similarities, or else bring out the male subject, more than the female, as the object of aesthetic address. A more adequate account would undoubtedly bring out the feminine gendering of the aesthetic more, and attend in a more systematic way to the process of gendering going on, so that the 'masculinisation' and, as it were, the cross-gendering evident in it would be seen as inseparable from its 'feminisation'. None the less, as my interest is in a political culture that was overwhelmingly masculine, and in social and political categories that worked because of their very neutrality and openness, there is some justification in the approach taken (for my purposes, for instance, it is as interesting that melodrama seems to have appealed to a condition of powerlessness that cut across gender, and other, distinctions, as that it appealed to men and women differently in respect of this condition).

In considering the aesthetic framing of the social, certain contents are evident as well as the structuring spoken of here. In an absolutely central way it can be seen that this fiction saw the world in 'class' terms, in the general sense that it dichotomised the social world, between high and low, rich and poor, and so on. However, the rich were not automatically evil. If less frequently than the poor, they could enact the eternal moral verities. Social reconciliation was often the fictional theme. In this dichotomous understanding many collective identities were circulated. 'The poor', just as 'the rich', covered a considerable range of possibilities. One of the identities carried in this narrative code was certainly that of the labouring man. For instance, at the same time as 'Smiles and Tears' *Cassell's* carried 'The Triumph and Defeat of Want: A Legend for Every Fireside'. This was allegory, in a much more explicit sense than the melodramatic romance. The figure of Want (so-named) was the central 'character' of

---

[95] *Ibid.*, pp. 123–4.

the tale. The poor here were decidedly 'the laborious poor'. Never tired of banging on the door of 'the resolute and laborious' poor, Want is repulsed by the sound of the hammer and the cheerful song of labour. Want then decides to preside at the feast of the foolish, idle, rich man. In the end justice and reconciliation are both achieved, when – aided by the 'cheerful working man' – the rich man manages to banish Want (Want is represented in an accompanying engraving as a skeleton). It is evident that this is a link from melodramatic romance to earlier forms of 'popular' cultural representation, ones to which the new were closely related.

Other instances of 'the poor' as the 'artisan' and 'working man' could be given, but there is no doubt that the central dualism was between rich and poor, and the essential drama one about the understanding of want (as in the case of Edwin Waugh, we are aware how want, not work, is fundamental).[96] This is amply evident in the 'Penny Dreadfuls', cousins to the journal fictions, despite the aspirations of the latter to respectability.[97] Only the most cursory attention can be given these:[98] the relations of rich and poor were mapped on the terrain of the city in one particularly successful variant of these (one closely linked to Eugene Sue's *Mystères de Paris*).[99] The most compelling city for this readership was London, the seat of the most self-indulgent wealth and the direst poverty and depravity. Again, one is sometimes aware of an implied reader, one of a 'working class' sort: the 'other' that is defined against these Gothic stories of London (and nineteenth-century Gothic fiction grew up in the closest relation with melodrama) is the reader who can work and will work, the 'industrious' as opposed to the 'dangerous' poor of 'outcast London'.[100] As has been seen, the 'industrious classes' was itself a very capacious designation.

The essential social drama, however, was about the moral relations of an unequal society, about the rich and the poor. It concerned want, and how the good life might be lived in its shadow. This is an antique theme in the cultural representations of the powerless: therefore, by way of conclu-

---

[96] See above, pp. 63–72.
[97] The Dreadfuls had their own claims to improvement in turn. *Life in London: A Romance* (1846), ends 'May everyone who peruses *Life in London* have some good and useful sentiment thereby awakened in his breast. The End.' See also *The Mendicants of London. A Romance of Real Life (by One Who Carried a Wallet)* (1849).
[98] I have consulted the voluminous Barry Ono Collection of these stories, in the British Museum.
[99] Henry Thornley, *Life in London*; See also G. Smeeton, *Doings in London, or Day and Night Scenes of the Frauds, Frolics, Manners and Depravities of the Metropolis* (7th edn., 1850). This wonderful work was in turn indebted to the 'Tom and Jerry' genre of Regency London.
[100] On gothic representations of the poor, particularly those of G. W. M. Reynolds, see G. Himmelfarb, *The Idea of Poverty*.

sion, I shall very briefly look beyond the sort of fiction so far considered to much older forms of representation. The chapbooks of the eighteenth and early nineteenth century show the antiquity of the primal categorisation of the social as a mapping of rich and poor upon the moral absolutes of good and evil. Secondly, the broadside ballads, continuing to be immensely popular up to the 1870s, and beyond,[101] will serve to complete this consideration of the social codes of the melodramatic imagination, by showing how rooted the drama of moral restoration was in older forms, particularly in the shape of the 'golden age' theme of the ballads. The chapbooks, as the name implies, were stories peddled by chapmen, crudely put together, and produced by specialist printers. They and the ballads gave way to the much more commercial forms considered here.[102]

The chapbooks have been written about as if they were subversive of established authority.[103] Some may have been, but a closer inspection reveals a quieter, and more subtle, probing of the moral drama of an unequal society.[104] Like later forms, but in a stark and immediate way, they typically concern the poor woman who inherits riches and does not have her head turned,[105] or the poor man/beggar who amasses a fortune, but does not forget his origins and the fact he has fought for his country.[106] These are small dramas which test the moral order, in ways that melodrama was later to do in a new fashion: in *Cat-Skins or The Wandering Young Lady's Garland* a father banishes his daughter and then adopts a disguise to see how she manages the test on her human nature imposed by her reduction in circumstances.[107] She passes the test, and goes on to marry the squire. The moral lay in the retention of dignity and humanity through the trials of poverty. Criticism of the rich may be made,[108] but the basic function of the tales seems to have been as a vehicle in which the moral order of the day was rehearsed. Not overtly anti-

---

[101] P. Joyce, *Visions of the People*, chap. 10 on the broadside ballads.

[102] See Phil Eva, 'Popular Song and Social Identity in Victorian Manchester' (University of Manchester Ph.D., forthcoming).

[103] S. Pedersen, 'Hannah More Meets Simple Simon: Tracts, Chapbooks and Popular Culture in Late 18th Century England', *Journal of British Studies*, 25:21, Jan. 1986.

[104] These remarks are based on a reading of chapbook collections in the British Museum, esp. *Chapbooks* (1820), 11601 aaa 47; *Chapbooks* (Otley, 1850?), 11622 df 40; *Chapbooks* (1820?), 11601 aa 55; *Dicey Chapbooks*, 1.A-F, 1079 i 13. See also J. Ashton, *Chapbooks of the Eighteenth Century* (1882, reprinted 1969); Victor Neuberg, *Chapbooks: A Bibliography* (1964); Margaret Spufford, *Small Books and Pleasant Histories: Popular Fiction and its Readership in Seventeenth Century England* (1981). I have consulted chapbook collections of as late a vintage as possible, but it is extremely difficult to know the date of their actual circulation.

[105] 'Berkshire Lady's Garland', in 11601 aaa 47.

[106] 'The History of the Blind Beggar of Bethnal Green', in *Dicey Chapbooks*.

[107] In 11601 aaa 47, *Chapbooks* (1820).

[108] E.g., 'A Description of the Assembly Held at Appleby ...', in 11601 aa 55, *Chapbooks* (1820?).

authoritarian they were no less 'political' in their quiet way. Like the melodrama they were a framework, a grid, capable of containing a multiplicity of meanings, and identities, yet giving the social order a determinate shape.

The notion of a lost golden age, linked to the restoration of the lost reign of virtue, simply permeates the broadside ballads and the culture of the poor more widely. In previous work I have explored this theme in great detail, dwelling not only on the ballads, but also on the ways in which in the industrial regions of northern England the transition from domestic to factory production was accompanied by a mythologising of the 'good old days' of yore.[109] This was not necessarily nostalgic or conservative. It could, as in the dialect writers that gave it expression, be fused with a belief in improvement and progress. In the case of Edwin Waugh we have seen this meeting of historical perspectives. The extraordinary force and longevity of the myth of the golden age of the handloom weaver is a case in point. The influence of such golden age notions was felt far beyond dialect literature, and the ballads (with their talk of the 'good old days', 'the good old town', 'old England', the 'fine old English gentleman', the 'old-fashioned farmer', and so on).

And, of course, it was felt throughout the whole of society. Keith Thomas has dwelt on a dominant form of the golden age narrative, that of 'Merrie England'.[110] He has shown how, progressively up to the mid-Victorian period, this 'old England' was positioned increasingly nearer the present, until by that time it was almost too vague to be placed at all. As the container of all sorts of concerns about the present, the content of this imagined past varied enormously. Thomas indicates how it was diffused in all sorts of cultural artefacts. The same can be said of the 'Norman Yoke' story, though its political cast was none the less clear. Christopher Hill has explored this motif, though, contrary to his Marxist teleology, which sees these 'historicist' notions giving way to more 'modern' natural-right theories, and to class, it was widely prevalent in the later nineteenth century.[111]

But, if apparent throughout society, it can be suggested that the 'golden age' form had a special salience for the poor and powerless. Its drama of dispossession, lost virtue, struggle, and eventual triumph spoke most urgently to those who had felt loss and dispossession. To those engaged in struggle it gave hope, precisely that sense of agency spoken of earlier.

[109] P. Joyce, *Visions of the People*, chaps, 9, 11–14, and 6, 8, but esp. 7 on 'The sense of the past'.
[110] Keith Thomas, 'The Power of the Past in Early Modern England', *Creighton Trust Lecture*, 1983.
[111] Christopher Hill, 'The Norman Yoke', in *Puritans and Revolutionaries: Studies in Interpretation of the English Revolution of the Seventeenth Century* (1965).

Early nineteenth-century popular radical politics fed on this narrative directly, or by linking itself to other social movements themselves imbued with the prelapsarian narrative form. The Factory Reform movement is a good example of the latter,[112] the idea of the labourer's 'cottage economy' symbolising opposition to aspects of the factory system through its emphasis on a supposedly 'natural' rhythm of labour and family life which obtained in the past; a time (not so long distant in the mythology of the handloom weavers) when the independence of the labourer was assured, an independence closely linked to conceptions of manhood.[113] Chartism drew directly on such ideas (one thinks of O'Connor on the 'artificiality' of modern society), but also on the language of the Bible, especially the story of the exiled Israelites, Moses and the promised land.[114] The golden age form had its most extensive and perhaps most profound formulations in this religious character: for instance, Keith Snell has recently shown how, for agricultural workers throughout the entire nineteenth century, images of society were articulated primarily through biblical exegesis.[115] The promised land had a very immediate meaning in the nineteenth century, and not for agricultural workers alone: if religion was perhaps the chief instance of the golden age narrative form,[116] then the land itself was of great significance too, a matter of practical interest and reform, but at the same time one which carried an enormous emotional charge, as historians are now beginning to discern more clearly.

That charge was in large part delivered through the conductive element of the golden age narrative form. This form was in turn closely linked to the general cultural characteristics of the society in which it was imbedded. It can be understood as speaking to a 'popular' culture that still retained, up to the late nineteenth century, pronounced customary characteristics. Custom looked to precedent to regulate present social

---

[112] For some interesting observations on this see R. Gray, 'The Languages of Factory Reform in Britain, c. 1830–1860' in P. Joyce (ed.), *The Historical Meanings of Work* (Cambridge 1987).

[113] Sally Alexander, 'Women, Class and Sexual Differences in the 1830s and 1840s: Some Reflections on the Writing of Feminist History', *History Workshop* (Spring 1984).

[114] James Epstein, *The Lion of Freedom: Feargus O'Connor and the Chartist Movement 1832–1842* (1982) and P. Joyce, *Visions of the People*, pp. 31–4, 95–102, and ff.

[115] Keith Snell, 'Deferential Bitterness: the Social Outlook of the Rural Proletariat in Eighteenth- and Nineteenth-Century England', in M. L. Bush (ed.), *Social Orders and Social Classes in Europe since 1500: Studies in Social Stratification* (1992), esp. pp. 173–4, on the theme of deliverance and the Promised Land. See also J. F. C. Harrison, *The Second Coming: Popular Millennarianism 1780–1850* (1979), p. 24.

[116] In forthcoming work Iain MacCalman dwells on the great importance of Hebraicism in early nineteenth-century popular radical politics. Painite rationalism, constitutionalism and 'radical restorationism' were often happily combined in a utopian politics unified by the narrative pattern of a lost golden age. See I. MacCalman, 'New Jerusalems: Radicalism and Prophecy in Britain 1786–1832', paper given at Manchester University, May 1992.

practices and social relations. In so doing the affinity with the golden age form is clear. The fate of the two, of custom and the golden age form, seems to have been connected: the desuetude of one seems to have been accompanied by the desuetude of the other.

15 The constitution as an English Eden

The second half of the nineteenth century saw the emergence and consolidation of mass, party-political democracy in Britain.[117] The Second and Third Reform Acts, of 1867 and 1884, still left sizeable proportions of the male electorate unenfranchised, and women were not enfranchised until after 1918. None the less, mass democracy was real enough, albeit mass male democracy. Handling the problems posed by this new democracy involved handling narrative, for narrative conferred what the new democracy needed, namely political subjectivities which created agency and legitimacy. This was so for the politicians and the people alike: the latter acquired a sense of political identity, a sense that enabled politics to go forward in the hands of the former. Out of the imaginative projections of leaders and led, in their interaction, was produced the democratic imaginary of the time. Parties, leaders, issues, and ideas certainly produced this, but these were only effective within particular patterns of narrative.

Consideration of these narratives suggests that the legitimation of mass democracy involved existing political narratives drawing on the resource of narratives lying beyond the purely political sphere, in particular those narrative elements so far considered, the narrative of improvement and the narrative patterns or framing evident in popular fiction. In this process what was usable in existing political narratives was refurbished, and adapted to new circumstances. The most evident, pre-existing political narrative was that of the constitution (usually the 'English constitution') the nearest thing to a political master-narrative of its day.

Until recently, historians had tended to argue that the constitutionalist narrative restricted the radical potential of popular movements in England. A supposedly backward-looking ideology of historical rights was contrasted with Painite notions of natural rights, for instance. Or, the 'old' constitutionalist analysis was superseded by the 'new', supposedly class-based radical analysis of the 1830s, one informed by a popular political economy in which the political analysis of wrong was superseded by the

[117] M. Pugh, *The Making of Modern British Politics 1867–1939* (1982, new edn. 1993), for a useful overview.

creation of meta narrative
zeitgeist - into which
ind. + collective narratives were
positioned.

economical, the corrupt and tax-eating aristocrat and placeman, say, by the capitalist. This was all part of a teleology closely linked to class: a more forward-looking popular radicalism presaged the emergence of class in the second quarter of the century. However, as Belchem and Epstein in particular have shown,[118] early nineteenth-century radicalism and Chartism were suffused in the language of the ancient constitution, and Painite radicalism and constitutionalism were often perfectly compatible. At the same time, the non-socialist character of the so-called 'new' radical analysis has for long been understood, particularly its identification of a manipulative ruling class controlling the political system as the source of wrong, rather than a new system of industrial production.[119]

Long-ago Christopher Hill, in his essay on the 'Norman Yoke', and more recently historians such as H. T. Dickinson, John Brewer, and Kathleen Wilson have identified how the constitution acted as the focus of political conflict in high and popular politics from the early eighteenth century onwards.[120] The work of younger scholars, more directly informed by the 'linguistic turn', has taken up these approaches and expanded them in novel and very productive ways, especially the brilliant contributions of James Vernon.[121] What has become evident, right into the twentieth century, is just how central a role the constitution played in the generation of political identity and conflict. The narrative through which the meaning of the constitution was made evident might commence with the Glorious Revolution of 1688, but most often this was but one event in a much longer history begun in 1066, if not before.[122] And Toryism was every bit as adept as radicalism and the Whigs at appropriating the constitutional cause. The emphasis here might be on duties rather than rights, 1688 often representing the constitution attained, and

[118] J. Epstein, *The Lion of Freedom*; 'Understanding the Cap of Liberty: Radical Reasoning, Rhetoric and Action in Early Nineteenth-Century England', *Past and Present*, 122 (1989); John Belchem, *'Orator' Hunt: Henry Hunt and English Working Class Radicalism* (Oxford 1985); 'Republicanism, Constitutionalism and the Radical Platform', *Social History*, 6:1 (1981).

[119] Gareth Stedman Jones, 'Rethinking Chartism' in *Languages of Class*.

[120] C. Hill. 'The Norman Yoke'; H. T. Dickinson 'The Eighteenth Century Debate on the Glorious Constitution', *History*, 61 (1976); John Brewer, *Party Ideology and Popular Politics* (Cambridge 1976), esp. chap. 12; Kathleen Wilson, 'Inventing Revolution: 1688 and Eighteenth Century Popular Politics', *Journal of British Studies*, 28 (Oct 1989).

[121] James Vernon, *Politics and the People: a Study in English Political Culture 1815–1867* (Cambridge 1993); J. Vernon (ed.), *Re-reading the Constitution: New Narratives in the History of English Politics* (Cambridge, forthcoming); Jonathan Fulcher, 'Contests Over Constitutionalism: the Faltering of Reform in England 1819–20'; unpublished paper, Cambridge, 1990. My treatment of the constitution owes much to Vernon's work.

[122] For nineteenth-century historians operating on the narrative of the constitution, in an unashamedly political fashion, see J. Vernon, 'Narrating the Constitution: Macaulay, Stubbs, Maitland and the Invention of Nineteenth-Century Constitutional History', in J. Vernon (ed.), *Re-reading the Constitution*.

Toryism appealing to its popular following on the basis of its supposed inclusion in the established constitutional order (even when that inclusion was not registered in the possession of a vote). At the same time, Tory versions of the constitution could serve to focus conflict and the sense of exclusion and of the excluded's rights: Tory 'country party' ideology is one instance, and in the Victorian period perhaps the most striking example of the longevity of the constitutionalist master-narrative was the popular Toryism of the mid- and late- nineteenth century.[123] In this, working men were encouraged to rally to the constitution against the depredations of the Fenians, papists, Jews, Nonconformists, *laissez-faire* Liberal employers, infidels, and others. The central element was probably the Protestant religion and its history, and if Protestant Englishness could speak to people's sense of inclusion in the social order, it could also do the opposite, speaking for the poor, the exploited, and the excluded.[124]

If we look to the agitation preceding the Second Reform Act it is evident that justifications for action drawn from the narrative of the constitution were just as evident across the political divide. One quotation from Bright must suffice here, a good one none the less in conveying how strongly contemporary narrative was historicised, and how the resulting certainty assumed an almost mystical clarity when it came to politics,

I am in accord with our ancient Constitution. I would stand by it, wherever it afforded support for freedom, I would march in its tracks. That track is so plain that the way-faring man, though a fool, need not err therein. I would be guided by its lights. They have been kept burning by great men among our forefathers for many generations. Our only safety in this warfare is in adhering to the ancient and noble Constitution of our country.[125]

In the warfare of which Bright spoke, that of the 1860s Reform struggle, it becomes apparent that, while the old narrative of the constitution continued powerfully, it is its changed meanings and functions that are apparent. Bright inaugurated, and Gladstone followed, a process whereby, on the one hand, the constitution became increasingly moralised and linked to notions of 'respectable' behaviour, and on the other, it became associated with the cause of progress, itself increasingly emblematised in moral conduct. It is this process, intimately connected with the emergence of party politics and especially of popular Liberalism, that will be described here. Before doing this, two more general points need to be raised, the function of political narrative and its gendering. The function

---

[123] Patrick Joyce, *Work, Society and Politics: the Culture of the Factory in Later Victorian England* (1980), *passim*, on popular Toryism.

[124] Especially in its ultra-Evangelical forms, see *ibid.*, pp. 250–61 on 'popular Protestantism'.

[125] Speech cited in J. Page Hopps, *John Bright: A Study of Character and Characteristics* (1880s?), p. 11.

of the constitutionalist narrative will be evident: it conferred legitimacy on the political subject. But it did so in a particular way, one which told against class identities, at least in the political sphere. To share in the constitution was to share in the nation. Just as earlier on the embrace of deism, republicanism or Painite radicalism could represent a retreat from a shared code, that of the constitution, so later the appeal to class could abrogate the right to speak and think as one of the nation, an entity which in its contemporary political form of 'the people' conferred legitimacy precisely by its openness and permeability. To achieve political agency was to acquire membership in a moral majority that all, especially the excluded, might have access to. Only the constitution could confer membership of this majority.

The function of the constitution in the individual's imagining of themselves as acting political subjects has recently been raised by Hunt's book on the family romance narratives of the French Revolution.[126] Hunt's argument is that the Revolution dispersed charisma into symbols, language, and the new ceremonial of power. The contrast she draws is with the US, where a stable and sacred constitutional text made it possible for parties to organise their popular constituences: it was possible for parties to cohere around differing understandings of a text's meanings. In France, Liberal party democracy was more difficult because of the unstable and dispersed nature of political legitimacy. The British case can be seen as coming between the two forms of narrative. A historicised constitutionalist narrative, and one also embedded in interpretation of law, gave sufficient purchase for a party system to cohere. None the less, the unwritten, and thus inscrutable, nature of the political metanarrative created a situation in which there was intense scrutiny, and therefore intense conflict, about the true meaning of the constitution.

In all three cases, constitutionalist narratives can be understood as having a central role in the formation of political and social identities: 'the people', 'classes', parties, voters, and so on, were defined as subjects in relation to a dominant narrative. There are many other aspects of comparison that arise from Hunt's work, chiefly the marked difference in the ways narratives of the constitution were gendered in the French and English cases. The notion of 'the band of brothers' was the means by which fraternity was played out in the family romance of the French Revolution. In England, or Britain, the arguably greater emphasis on liberty, rather than fraternity, produced a different ordering of masculine gendering. There liberty seems to have been secured through an emphasis on the independence of the male head of household. The notion of

[126] L. Hunt, *The Family Romance of the French Revolution*, 'Epilogue'.

independence seems to have been a key one in the English case, embracing religion in the form of Protestant liberty, politics in the form of the independent political actor (elector or non-elector), as well as familial relations (not to mention generalised, pervasive notions of the moral worth of independence).

The pervasiveness of the idea of independence was distilled in a particularly clear form in the 1860s agitation for the vote (and the agitation that led up to the Third Reform Act).[127] This agitation was based on the notion of manhood suffrage. The concept of *manhood* was not co-extensive with all adult males, including adult labouring males. The key term in defining 'manhood' was 'independence' by which was meant the full control of one's self, one's property, and one's labour.[128] Those who were not independent were to be excluded – the mentally unfit, the poor and dependent workers, the morally unfit, and – according to majority opinion among the reformers, plebeian and higher class – women.[129] For the Reform League, for instance, the plebeian wing of the Reform cause, the vote hinged on paying taxes and rates, obeying the laws, the capacity to demonstrate moral independence by means of the capacity for organisation (in self-help bodies for instance), and the ability to defend the nation. This all represented what was for women a pretty impossible test of independence.

Women were thus amongst the dependent classes, 'virtually represented' by a husband if married, and in general seen as unfitted to exercise independence and the vote by virtue of their lack of education, and therefore of political awareness. Among radical opinion the manliness that symbolised independence was given political momentum by means of narrative: as Biagini has shown, these gender assumptions were enveloped in the rhetoric of the 'constitutionalist tradition'. This is how one radical spokesman justified demands for the vote,

The plain and simple plan – which the good sense of Simon de Montfort imported into this country, and which the manly vigour of the Gothic nations settled in Spain first invented of the entire manhood selecting their best men to assemble and make laws for all, is just as good now as it was six-hundred years ago ... what we want is an Act which will enable *the common sense and the common honesty of the nation to express itself.*[130]

The 'common honesty' of the nation was unabashedly that of its menfolk.

The identification of manhood, independence, and the vote had a long history before the 1860s. This history included a time when women had sought and failed to make a breach in the unity of the three: in the 1830s

---

[127] For a very illuminating discussion see E. F. Biagini, *Liberty, Retrenchment and Reform*, chap. 3, 'The search for "independence": the ways of solidarity', and chap. 5.
[128] *Ibid.*, p. 272.   [129] *Ibid.*, pp. 306–12.   [130] *Ibid.*, p. 269.

and 40s the rhetoric of Chartist domesticity had created for a time the possibility of a sphere in which women might exercise their own kind of independence.[131] Later on, in the study of Bright it was evident how Cobden and others fixed the 'yeoman' overtones of independence, first on their own origins and the 'shopocracy', and then on the 'working' or 'industrious' classes, especially the 'honourable' and 'independent' artisan. This figure achieved increasing significance in the 1850s and 60s. Bright's stigmatisation of the 'residuum', for instance, the depraved criminal or dangerous classes, was one means of inventing the independent working man as a fit object for the vote. In Gladstone too, but particularly among the popular classes themselves, the same appeal to independence was heard. Keith McClelland has shown how deeply rooted in the culture of certain sorts of industrial workers was this ethic of independence: between 1850 and 1880 a particular view of the 'working man' and 'working class' grew up which was defined by a series of exclusions and oppositions.[132] Based on the view of the adult, male, skilled, and respectable trade unionist, particularly the head of a household, this understanding was to prove extremely durable.[133]

Political narratives therefore drew strength from these notions of independence and masculine identity, and in turn helped further shape them. As will be evident, these notions did not come to the surface of the narratives, at least until the 1870s, when they can be said to have exploded on the scene. None the less, in the fusion of the narratives of the constitution and improvement that will now be considered, such gender assumptions were powerful if largely silent, especially in the meanings apparent in the growing moralisation of narrative accompanying the fusion. The assumptions were silent precisely because they were so powerful, so much of the unspoken, implicit common sense of politics. The fusion of narratives spoken of gathered force in the agitation preceding the Second Reform Act. Gladstone's was one major voice: his Reform Speech of 1866 dwelt on the 'pre-eminently rich and fruitful' institutions and traditions of England.[134] These 'institutions' were a shorthand for the constitution in the political discourse of the day, the plasticity of the constitution being its defining characteristic, so that in some readings one might include the ancient universities besides

---

[131] Anna Clark, 'The Rhetoric of Chartist Domesticity: Gender, Language and Class in the 1830s and 40s', *Journal of British Studies*, 3:1 (1992).

[132] Keith McClelland, 'Time to Work, Time to Live: Some Aspects of Work and the Re-formation of Class in Britain, 1850–1880', in P. Joyce (ed.), *The Historical Meanings of Work*.

[133] On 'independence' see also P. Joyce, *Visions of the People*, pp. 32–4, 78–9, 80, 83, 99, 107, 156–7, 315.

[134] Rt. Hon. W. E. Gladstone, *Speeches on Reform in 1866* (2nd edn. 1866), p. 85.

parliament, which none the less remained the jewel in the crown. For Gladstone, England had inherited more of what was 'august and venerable than any other European nation', but it was uniquely modern too.[135] Its modernity was above all apparent in the advance of 'progress', and progress received its most characteristic expression in the 'improvement' of the people. In his Liverpool speech, designed to reach a wide public, but also to win over his propertied audience in the city, he contrasted 1832 with the present day. Now industry was advanced, institutions – like the church – were reformed, and the people were restrained and educated.[136] The people increasingly figured as the leading character in the story of improvement, and the need was to connect this people, and hence the improvement narrative, to the story of all that was good in English institutions. One link, in this speech, was the story of 1832 itself, and this was broadened out to the splendid array of the constitutional past, and its valuable legacy in the present. In Gladstone's speeches the overwhelming theme was that by virtue of their improvement the people should now have a right to share in the institutions of the nation.

This was all given an increasingly moralistic slant. The language of duty is one instance, the people needing to be brought to a level where they could exercise public duty, but – even more urgently – the institutions of this country if they were to survive needed to pay their debt of honour to the people, whose moral worth (but also economic contribution) had made them a proper part of this institutional realm. One sees in this an instance of a general phenomenon, the shift in popular politics from historical and natural to moral rights. Accompanying this, in Gladstone's 1860s speeches, there is the beginning of what will later be overmastering, the embodiment of the people as the moral law, as well as the law of improvement. The two became synonymous, the narrative of providence coming in turn to the aid of the politicised narrative of improvement.

In 1866 Gladstone dwelt on how the truths of improvement were manifest around one every day, and how these bore an irresistible political witness: the idea that 'the signs of the times' must be seized in order to make political progress was evident in all Gladstone's public pronouncements at the time, for instance in the 1868 speeches that preceded the first general election under the new democratic dispensation.[137] Also evident was the by then familiar refrain that the Liberals were the true guardians of the constitution in both its venerable and progressive aspects.[138] Bright's

[135] Ibid., pp. 89–90.
[136] 'Speech at a Public Meeting in the Amphitheatre, Liverpool, 6 August 1866,' Speeches (1866).
[137] Speeches of the Rt. Hon. William Ewart Gladstone, M.P., in South West Lancashire, October 1868 (Liverpool 1868).
[138] Ibid., speech at Liverpool, 14 October 1868.

view of the constitution was more concrete and historicised, but he too spoke of it as mystically dispersed in a wide range of English institutions and codes. The attempt to bring the 'working class' and 'people' within the role of the constitution by appealing to the spirit of improvement was not evident in Disraeli, even though it was the Tories that passed Reform. Gladstone connected political reform to improvement as much within as outside the House of Commons.[139] By contrast Disraeli, inside and outside the House,[140] could not rise to the occasion of the 'signs of the times', so forfeiting the chance of capitalising on the sense of forward motion imputed to politics by this powerful narrative thrust.

In the Reform agitation it was Bright and not Gladstone who did most to narrativise politics in these ways. At his October 1866 speech in Leeds Town Hall Bright dwelt at length on how 'you', 'the working class', have built up the country to what it is. The cities, industries and railways that were the material signs of progress were all due to the contribution of the people.[141] A fortnight before, in Manchester, he dwelt at similar length on all the usual signs of intellectual and moral progress; schools built, ignorance banished, and cultivation triumphant (1867 and the passing of Reform was for Bright the culmination of his youthful efforts in the Manchester Athenaeum). He spoke in the evening of the day following to a reputed gathering of over 100,000 people on the Knott Mill fairgrounds, in the city: the fact that so vast a throng had gathered without trouble was the most eloquent testimony of all to the people's advancement he said.[142]

Bright, unlike Gladstone, was happy to reveal the iron fist within the velvet glove of improvement. As he put it in Manchester,[143] 'It is not more immoral for the people to use force in the last resort, for the obtaining and securing of freedom than it is for the Government to use force to suppress and deny that freedom.' The people's role in the advancement of the nation had given them such an incontrovertible moral case for the vote that even force might be threatened. This force was all the more justified given that the institutions of England were prone to 'every form of corruption and evil'. In particular, they were corrupted by materialism, by 'Mr Money Bags M.P.' in the House of Commons.[144] The accent on material progress was always accompanied by this deep distrust of materialism.

---

[139] W. E. Gladstone, *Speeches on Great Questions of the Day* (1870), e.g. 'The Representation of the People', House of Commons, 12 April 1866.

[140] John F. Bulley (ed.), *Speeches on Conservative Policy of the Last Thirty Years* (1869), 'Representation of the People', February and March 1867 speeches.

[141] John Bright, *Speeches on Parliamentary Reform, by John Bright, Edited by Himself* (1866), 8th October speech in Leeds.

[142] *Ibid.*, 25th September meeting.   [143] *Speeches*, (1866), p. 20.

[144] Leeds speech.

The notion of a moral right sanctioned by progress received its most telling expression in the idea that the constitution might at last be restored to the people, who were its rightful custodians. Life might be restored to a corrupt constitution by the people. At the Free Trade Hall in September 1866, we again find him speaking in the afterglow of the 'transcendentally great' open-air meeting at Knott Mill, this time on the same day.[145] The House of Commons was to be again what its name implied, the house of the common people. It was to be restored to them, their struggle in the present being part of the great struggle for liberty begun by their forefathers in the Civil War, two hundred years ago. Because the constitution was so indelibly the English constitution, it followed that their nation was being restored to them along with their constitution. The ideal that a lost golden age was being restored was also central.

In his famous Glasgow speech of October,[146] extolling the unity of the people above the divisiveness of 'class rule',[147] justice would not be got from a class, only from the nation, the whole people. The reign of justice would restore properly functioning institutions to the country, and these would bring about the profound changes he sought. These changes were imaged in the explicit terms of a restored Eden,

I am convinced that just laws and an enlightened administration of them, would change the face of the country. I believe that ignorance and suffering might be lessened to an incalculable extent, and that many an Eden, beauteous in flowers and rich in fruits, might be raised up in the waste of wilderness which spreads before us. But no class can do this ... Let us try the nation. This it is which has called together these countless numbers of the people to demand a change; and, as I think of it, and of these gatherings sublime in their vastness and in their resolution, I think I see, as it were, above the hill tops of time, the glimmerings of the dawn of a better and a nobler day for the country and for the people that I love so well.[148]

We see here far more than the confluence of the narratives of improvement and the constitution. The whole aesthetic edifice by which the social and the political were framed is in full evidence. The melodramatic shape of the political unconscious emerges with great clarity: this is the struggle of moral opposites, and moral absolutes, in which moral attributes are personified (not least in Bright himself). This is the melodrama of moral restoration, the 'golden age' form characteristic of melodrama itself, but of other aspects of popular culture too. The presentation of the Reform agitation as a drama of lost rights (the constitution, the nation itself), of the struggle of the dispossessed, and of the restoration of a vanished Eden mirrors exactly the narrative forms so apparent in popular fiction and

[145] *Speeches* (1866), 24 September 1866.   [146] City Hall speech, 16 October 1866.
[147] P. Joyce, *Visions of the People*, pp. 54–5.   [148] *Speeches* (1866), p. 35.

popular drama. It does this, further, by the demonisation of the Tory, and the aristocrat, as the principle of evil.[149] The personification of this form of the daemonic in 1866 was Robert Lowe, the reactionary Tory opponent of Reform, who had referred to the people as 'the great unwashed', so denying their moral right as the great improved to enter upon their lost constitution. Men like Lowe had stolen England from the people.[150]

Even more in the political audience's response to Bright, and Gladstone, are we aware of this depiction of politics as a massive drama of struggle, movement, and hope. The hope invested in Bright is conveyed by this description of his speech at the Free Trade Hall in September 1866. The Hall was under siege from early in the day. It filled up with 5,000 people, only a quarter of the throng trying to get in, the streets outside swarming with people. Admission was by ticket, first come, first served, and tickets were changing hands on the black market for up to two guineas:

When Mr Bright stepped forward the scene was such as to baffle all attempts at description. The whole audience rose in his honour. The shouts were deafening and long continuing. When the honourable gentleman rose to receive the address, the same enthusiasm was manifested, and when the time came for him to speak the whole audience listened with rapt attention.[151]

Vast as these indoor meetings were, it is the great outdoor gatherings of these years which are even more striking. Bright did not speak at these, though he often attended. Even though not speaking he was the object of an undimmed popular veneration, and here we became aware of Bright as an icon. Although working men, and women, may never have heard him speak, and may only have read his words, or had his words read to them, he was still a cult object. The relationship of narrative and leadership will be considered later, but the operation of the 'political unconscious' is amply apparent here in the sense of the 'visceral thrill' of politics, the emotional, 'pre-cognitive' delights of being in a narrative oneself, and in a sense being that narrative, enacting it and being its subject at the same time.

The great Woodhouse Moor demonstration in 1866 is a good case: 200,000 were supposed to have gathered, walking from all over the region because the railway authorities refused to put on excursions (the authorities and employers in other British cities were, by contrast, actively co-operative).[152] Each cab and conveyance bore the Liberal colours.

---

[149] *Speeches* (1866), Free Trade Hall, 20 November 1866.
[150] For Lord Derby, the Tory Leader, as the man responsible for class conflict, and for separating the Commons from the people, see Free Trade Hall Speech, 24 September 1866.
[151] *Reynolds' News*, 30 September 1866.   [152] *Ibid.*, 14 October 1866.

Every man and woman was also reported as carrying cards and rosettes, many of these in Chartist colours. The procession was divided between friendly society, reform organisation, and trade society contingents, also 'non-electors' groups. There were also some individual colliery contingents. As was common at these meetings the trade societies marched in their trade attire and bore the regalia of their craft. The other contingents had their own identities conferred by banners and bands.[153] 'Rule Britannia' was sung repeatedly in the vast, two-hour long procession. There were five platforms in a great 'amphitheatrical' area on the moors, from which speeches were delivered by radical leaders and local Liberal potentates.

Gladstone, Bright, and J. S. Mill, were the objects of this enthusiasm, but in homaging these the people were homaging themselves. Bright had revealed the iron fist of numbers within the glove of improvement, so calling into discourse the felt strength of the multitude. Occasions like Woodhouse Moor were in large part about feeling the intoxication of numbers, feeling the leashed power of the people and the working class. This felt strength was expressed in narrative form: it was strength in movement, coming from a past of struggle and heading for the many Edens promised by Bright. The banners of the crowd, like Bright's oratory, reached back to a glorious heritage, telling the tale of liberty. The Great Halton Reformers' banner ran thus: 'Freedom's battle once begun/ Bequeath'd from bleeding sire to son/Tho battled oft, will still be won.' The essential narrative properties lay in this sense of being part of an unfolding story, but strength also lay in the day itself, which was a matter of joining this tidal movement of people, united in one cause and moving inexorably towards it.

That inexorability was further conveyed by the figure of the Tory: just as in Bright's oratory, the banners on the day defined the narrative of liberty in terms of its vicious opponents, an 'other' that was all the more effective in defining the radical self because of the knowledge that it would imminently be destroyed.[154] The resources of comedy here supplemented those of the romance and melodrama of politics: Lowe was frequently derided for insulting the working class (showing and not showing respect was a frequently elaborated theme at these meetings),[155] one banner depicting the Tory cabinet as the Christy Minstrels, with Disraeli ('Ass-man'), Derby, and Lowe, and on the obverse a John Bright earnestly engaged in disturbing the peace of the 'cave of Addullum', the name

---

[153] See also account of Birmingham Reform demonstration, *Ibid.*, 2 September 1866.
[154] For the radical press equating the Tory and the aristocrat, *Reynolds' News*, leader, 2 September.
[155] On 'respect' see leader in *Reynolds' News*, 9 February 1866.

given the anti-Reform Tory conclave. At another meeting a banner read 'Bright Cabinet Makers Wanted. No Addullumite Need Apply', with on the other side, 'No more oligarchic rule. The people are determined to be their own cabinet makers.' Fittingly, the banner was carried by a contingent of cabinet makers.

In the operation of social narrative at this time we are aware also of some of the more theoretical points made earlier, for instance the operation of narratives which carried several identities. Again, one does not do justice to all of these, but the two principal ones of class and people emerge, both highly gendered. The Woodhouse Moor resolutions and banners spoke interchangeably of 'working class' and 'people', though there is no doubt that the latter was in the ascendancy. When 'working class' and 'middle class' were spoken of, however, a moral dimension was, as usual, most often inferred.[156] Rather than a source in production, it was categories like 'treachery' and 'toadyism' that characterised the 'middle class', a political frame of reference shaped by the aftermath of class 'betrayal' in 1832 (and just as deeply shaped by ideas of manliness).[157] At Woodhouse a working class gathered to assert themselves against the interference of 'the influential classes', the men of 1832 who were afraid of 'the people'. At times the 'influential', 'the servile and tuft-hunting' who curried favour with the 'Court and aristocracy', were defined as the middle class, but at other times this moral reading of class was decidedly looser, and left without any clear spatial location. The real enemies of Reform were more often 'the old proud, privileged and stupid class'. At the 100,000-strong Manchester meeting the ascending rhetoric of people was completely in evidence.[158] There an erstwhile champion of the people, Ernest Jones, inveighed against 'class' government and the spirit of class. He spoke of the rights of the people as against 'the oligarchy', the 'people of England' struggling for the right.

The tendency to emphasise people over class was very important. Men like Gladstone and Bright, whilst they spoke of classes and appealed to their better natures, also sought to negate their divisive implications, exalting the principles of unity – 'the people' – over the political divisiveness of different categories. None the less, the frequent use of class and people, in the same sentence often, suggests how unstable, and often ambiguous, collective social identities were. So, while the actual forms of social description, and the uses of these forms, were both important, it is also true that equally, or perhaps more significant, were the narratives in

[156] *Reynolds' News*, 14 October 1866.
[157] On the 'British disease' of 'flunkeyism' see *Reynolds' News*, leaders, 11 August, 16 October 1867.
[158] *Reynolds' News*, 30 September 1866.

which these unstable identities circulated. The narratives provided the sense of purpose, movement, and belonging which defined what it in practice meant to be 'working class' or one of the people. Studying the narratives is often the best way of knowing what contemporary experience of the social actually was. This was especially so for the political narratives of the 1870s.

16   The story of the cruel Turk

When the Reform Act was passed in 1867 the politics of the excluded began to become the politics of the included. The countryside remained to be enfranchised, in 1884, so that the old narratives, which had taken their bearings from the experience of political exclusion, still remained important. None the less, for large parts of the electorate the problem became what to do with power once it was acquired. What happened when the stake in the country asked for in 1866 was given, when England was given back to the people? The politics of democratic representation became the politics of democratic accountability and action. What should the people do to justify themselves? What also should the political parties do to be saved? For their task now became that of allying the old, pre-1867, electorate with the new as the viable basis for the re-invention of party on the basis of a new demos. This alliance also depended on putting demos into action, on a politics of forward movement and accountability.

Here other of the theoretical aspects of narrative discussed earlier become evident. Although we can see in the politics so far described – in the relation of Bright and his audiences for instance – that unity of the tale, the teller, and the told seen to be characteristic of the successful operation of narrative, it is also necessary to bear in mind the fragility of narrative, its tendency to consume itself. As has been seen, to take a role in a narrative is in some sense to anticipate its future closure, and to pretend it has now, or will have, an ending. But immediately on taking this role a new futurity is opened up. The split subject positions created by narratives mean that the sense of an ending is subverted, and that a new chapter in the story is inevitably inaugurated. A distance can then supervene between the old tale, its teller, and those to whom it was told. In the attempt to be relevant and ever-new the old narrative feeds unsuccessfully off itself, and a new or reworked narrative is needed. This was so in the 1870s, when it was necessary that the old narratives be reworked if demos was to renew itself as the potent source of politics. The instability and limitations of the old narrative of progress and liberty become apparent in the new circumstances of politics described here. How might the narratives that drove politics be renewed?

The conjuncture that helps us explore this is that of Gladstone's return to politics after 1876, and his attempt to shape the Liberal party in the image of his moral populism. The famous Midlothian speeches of 1879 were one of the vehicles by which the party's identity as the party of the moral crusade and of *vox populi* was deepened. They were also a vehicle for Gladstone's own return to power in 1880.[159] The roots of 1879 were themselves in the 'Bulgarian Horrors' agitation of 1876, but the Midlothian campaign is the best place to begin considering that renewal of narrative necessary if Liberalism was to prosper.[160] Both 'agitations' electrified the country, helping to launch the politics of democratic justification. With Reform secured, there was a shift to external affairs as the ground on which a moral purpose might be exercised ('external affairs' included Ireland, for Gladstonian Liberalism perhaps the ultimate test of justice).

As in the previous decade the concern of Gladstone was to attach the constitution/institutions of the nation to the narrative of progress. In the first Midlothian speech Gladstone attacked the new-fangled changes proposed by the Tories: these would abrogate the constitution, going too far towards novelty. The constitution should be treated as adaptable, but 'hallowed'.[161] None the less, and again 1866 is echoed, there is the concern that parliament and party may fail the nation by falling into 'faction'. If 'hallowed', the constitution must renew itself. However, since the 1860s an ever-deepening moralisation of the narrative of improvement and of its primary collective subject, 'the people', had occurred. In Midlothian parliament and party had now to comprehend what Gladstone called 'the great human heart of this country': this heart beat outside parliament and parliament ignored it at its peril. Its beat reflected consternation at the 'Bulgarian Horrors', the massacre of thousands of Christian Bulgarians by Moslem Turks. The 'great human heart of this country', in all its moral certitude, was now to dominate politics; 'the country' and 'the people' becoming moral principle incarnate.

In the first Midlothian speech the fate of an enormous Empire is in the hands of 'you', 'a great and free people'. It is not in the hands of an administration, parliament, or a party. Britain is a self-governing country and 'man' is a citizen by nature, beyond considerations of property rights. Man is more than the English or British, and we must not, like the Tories, think we are better than the rest of the world. Gladstone spoke, therefore,

---

[159] R. T. Shannon, *Gladstone and the Bulgarian Agitation 1876* (1963), chap. 8.
[160] W. E. Gladstone, *Midlothian Speeches* (ed.) M. R. D. Foot (Leicester 1971).
[161] *Ibid.*, 25 November 1879.

of the 'sisterhood and equality of nations', 'the absolute equality of public
right among them'. What seems to be happening here was both dramatic
and novel: 'the people' was slowly expanding until it became all people.
The people could speak for all people, the British for the world, but also
women for mankind.

'Woman' moved back to the spoken centre of politics. Earlier she is the
absent trace, the implied presence in politics which defines in its absence,
and by its silence, the all-pervasive 'masculinity' of politics. Gladstone had
always addressed his audience as 'gentlemen', this was one of his characteristic rhetorical ploys, evincing an equality between him and his
invariably male audience, his peers in rational thinking and social worth
(no matter how horny-handed they were). Because 'the people' had now
been expanded to all people, this now required talk of an essential human
nature which would describe, and hence embrace, all people. This nature
could not be described without including women's special place in the
encompassing unity that was humanity. The need was all the more
pressing because those who had been murdered, tortured and raped in
their thousands by the Turks were women and children.

On Gladstone's second Midlothian day woman and the family came to
the centre of attention.[162] On the 26th November he went on from the
Corn Exchange, Dalkeith to the Foresters' Hall. Here he addressed
'women', not 'ladies'. 'Ladies' betokened rank, he said, whereas 'women'
represented the essential principle of the human nature he wished to
enunciate. Women were not 'abstract'. They were not interested in the
'harder, sterner, drier lessons of politics'. Their warmth and softness gave
them access to what Gladstone termed the burden of sin, sorrow, and
suffering in the world, an access men did not have. He meditated publicly,
communing with his female audience, on how the real meaning of 'Peace,
Retrenchment and Reform' was to promote human happiness, and above
all peace. Women touched the deepest chord of the truly human, and in
speaking to them Gladstone went on to develop an account of 'the horrors
of war' that still reads with great force and must have been greatly moving
to hear. His theme was 'Remember the rights of the savage, as we call him,
remember the happiness of his home' (in Afghanistan, in South Africa).
The sanctity of all human flesh must never be forgotten, in Europe no less
than the Empire. The peroration ended with the affirmation that God had
bound us in the law of mutual love and that this law governed all the earth.
The vision was one of a suffering, bleeding humanity, joined by a love
women had a peculiar knowledge of, and overseen by God in his providential wisdom.[163] The motive force in history, however, was perhaps not

[162] *Ibid.*, delivered Dalkeith, 26 November 1879.   [163] *Ibid.*, see first Dalkeith speech.

so much God as man-in-God, the narrative of improvement becoming
the narrative of humanity at large, of all 'people'. A more religious and
providential reading than hitherto is evident, but this is still demotic in its
insistence on a Godhead realised in a law of human love, the aim of which
was to secure and exercise 'freedom'.[164] The message of 'freedom', as has
been seen, spoke loudest to men. Women might testify to this freedom, by
their human, unabstract warmth. But men exercised it. Women were
brought into the discourse of politics, but without power.

The roots of 1879 lay in 1876 and the 'Bulgarian Horrors' agitation.
Shannon has described this agitation:[165] horrific accounts of the Turkish
massacres first appeared in the *Daily News* in late June, and were then
circulated more widely in the press. W. T. Stead took these up and in his
Darlington Echo began the systematic ignition of the public on the issue. In
less than six weeks in August and September five-hundred demonstrations were held throughout the country, with a concentration in the
north and in Wales. Stead knew how to organise an agitation. The
politicians and churchmen, who mostly did not, followed his lead. By late
autumn Gladstone saw his chance, biding his time until he became fully
convinced of the spontaneity of the upsurge of 'the masses'.[166] He then
began to ride the tumultuous tide of popular moral passion. The sequence
of this agitation provides a valuable chance of looking at narrative in
action, but it also prompts some remarks on the action in narrative. Just, as
was earlier suggested, a narrative was a kind of agitation, conferring in its
intrinsic nature a sense of motion and direction, so can we think of the
'agitation' as in itself a narrative. The fact of the name, and of the name
'demonstration', which also came into vogue around this time, is a fact of
the emerging democracy. The terms denoted the populace in movement,
as a collective entity. In denoting demos thus, demos was constituted thus,
as the implied subject and agent in this agitation. A subject in movement
in turn implied its own narrative. In this particular example of the
agitation W. T. Stead was perhaps the most important orchestrator of the
people in narrative movement.

The narratives circulating in Stead's promotion of the agitation are
familiar from the accounts of Edwin Waugh and John Bright. The
primary audience Stead worked upon was a northern Nonconformist one.
He spoke first to a religious memory looking back to a past of persecution.
The seventeenth century again figured hugely, in the form of Milton and
his support for the persecuted Vaudois, but also in the form of Cromwell,
who was the object of a cult for Stead, and for many more, in these years.

---

[164] *Ibid.*, see 27 November speeches also.
[165] R. T. Shannon, *Gladstone and the Bulgarian Agitation 1876*.
[166] *Ibid.*, pp. 100–1.

This Nonconformist narrative was accompanied by a similarly familiar one about the north of England as the true home of liberty. Both were centred upon a Liberal partisanship, casting the Tories as the villains of the piece.[167] Stead travelled to London in 1876, on his 'first political pilgrimage' to the Blackheath demonstration which was to bring Gladstone centre stage. He went sustained by visions of Hereward the Wake, the first, Saxon, 'Free Born Englishman', and of Cromwell. He saw Gladstone as the successor of both.[168] Born in Northumberland, his father was a Congregationalist minister. Like Josephine Butler and John Bright he was a crusader for democracy who detested the metropolitan elite.[169] Proud and vocal in his northernness, it is evident that his formation was the formation of many of his readers. The *Darlington Echo* was well named.

Stead stood at the beginnings of the 'popular press'. His attempts to 'democratise' the press have been seen, though what was understood as 'sensation' in some quarters was by Stead and his confrères seen as the 'Journalism of the Ideal': the newspaper had to be true to the facts, fulfilling its mission to educate, inform, and also to reform, the democracy. The alliance of entertainment and instruction earlier noted for the popular illustrated magazines of a generation before was continued in a new fashion, embracing Nonconformity this time. The narratives of an earlier popular fiction were continued in the *Pall Mall Gazette*: 1840s and 50s fiction on the theme of the 'mysteries' of the city was reflected in 'The Bitter Cry of Outcast London', running in 1883. This perpetuated an older melodrama, adding to it a more emphatic emphasis on social realism. There were other continuities with earlier 'popular' forms, and new departures arising from these, but they amounted in total to a widening of the 'popular' itself, in the sense that a culture of the many earlier ostracised by the few was now, suitably scrutinised, brought within the remit of a still larger majority. In this process the populist tendencies of the 'popular' worked among new social constituencies and in new ways. Nonconformity is a good case in point. Brought within the remit of the popular in Stead's journalism, it developed its own populist tendencies, directing its traditional morality along populist lines: the defence of social purity,[170] described by Walkowitz, was democratically directed at all in

---

[167] *Ibid.*, pp. 68–81.   [168] *Ibid.*, p. 116.

[169] Raymond L. Schultz, *Crusader in Babylon: W. T. Stead and the Pall Mall Gazette* (Lincoln, Nebraska, 1972).

[170] For 'purity' as a rallying cry for Nonconformists, and for all sorts of radicals too, see Raphael Samuel, 'The Discovery of Puritanism, 1820–1914: A Preliminary Sketch', in Jane Garnett and H. C. G. Matthew (eds.), *Revival and Religion: essays for John Walsh* (1993).

society, high and low, rich and poor, with the greatest animus being directed at the rich, the well-born and the powerful.[171]

Gladstone picked up the narrative motifs of Stead, the popular agitation, and the *Daily News*, developing these in his own way. This is most of all evident in his *Bulgarian Horrors* pamphlet of 1876, which sold 200,000 shortly after publication.[172] The pamphlet was therefore itself a major element in the mobilisation of narrative. Gladstone's appropriations turned crucially around the central figure of the Turk: if ever there was an 'other' this was it, the Turk in his absolute evil defining the absolute good of an enraged moral populace. For Gladstone the Turk was 'the one great anti-human specimen of humanity'.[173] The Turk shaped that all-pervasive humanity which, as we have seen, came to refashion, in an enlarged form, earlier notions of 'the people'. The Turk made the moral self of an outraged moral democracy.

Gladstone's pamphlet begins by presenting the military Turks in the long historical narrative of Turk–Christian history. While drawing, gratuitously, from the antipathetic associations of this history, he is at pains to say it is not the religion of Mahomet that is his quarry (to do that would be to deny the brotherhood of man, existing under many versions of the Godhead). No, the Turkish variant is what is evil. And what is evil about it offends every sensibility of Christian liberalism. The Turk practices government by force, not by law. Fatalism is his guide in this life, and in the next, the prospect of a 'sensual paradise'. His is 'an elaborate and refined cruelty', 'the only refinement of which Turkey boasts'.[174] This is how the pamphlet ended,

But I return to, and I end with, that which is the Omega as well as the Alpha of this great and most mournful case ... Let the Turks now carry away their abuses in the only possible manner, namely by carrying off themselves. Their Zaptiehs and their Mudirs, their Bimbashis and their Yuzbachis, their Kaimakams and their Pashas, one and all, bag and baggage, shall, I hope, clear out from the province they have desolated and profaned. This thorough riddance, this most blessed deliverance, is the only reparation we can make to the memory of those heaps on heaps of dead; to the violated purity alike of matron, of maiden, and of child; to the civilization which has been affronted and shamed; to the laws of God or, if you like, of Allah; to the moral sense of mankind at large. There is not a criminal in a European gaol, there is not a cannibal in the South Sea Islands, whose indignation would not rise and overboil at the recital of that which has been done, which has too late been examined, but which remains unavenged; which has left behind all the foul and all the fierce passions that produced it, and which may again spring up, in another murderous harvest, from the soil soaked and reeking with blood, and in the air tainted with every imaginable deed of crime and shame. That such things should

---

[171] J. Walkowitz, *City of Dreadful Delights*.
[172] W. E. Gladstone, *The Bulgarian Horrors and the Question of the East* (1876).
[173] *Ibid.*, p. 13.   [174] *Ibid.*, p. 33.

be done once, is a damning disgrace to the portion of our race which did them; that a door should be left open for their ever-so-barely possible repetition would spread that shame over the whole. Better, we may justly tell the Sultan, almost any inconvenience, difficulty, or loss associated with Bulgaria,

> 'Than thou reseated in thy place of light,
> The mockery of thy people, and their bane.'

We may ransack the annals of the world, but I know not what research can furnish us with so portentous an example of the fiendish misuse of the powers established by God 'for the punishment of evil-doers, and for the encouragement of them that do well.' No Government ever has so sinned; none has so proved itself incorrigible in sin, or which is the same, so impotent for reformation. If it be allowable that the Executive power of Turkey should renew at this great crisis, by permission or authority of Europe, the charter of its existence in Bulgaria, then there is not on record, since the beginnings of political society, a protest that man has lodged against intolerable misgovernment, or a stroke he has dealt at loathsome tyranny, that ought not henceforward to be branded as a crime.

But we have not yet fallen to so low a depth of degradation; and it may cheerfully be hoped that, before many weeks have passed, the wise and energetic counsels of the Powers, again united, may have begun to afford relief to the overcharged emotion of a shuddering world.

What a mix of improvement and 'sensation' this is, the improvement of Gladstone's homiletic, reasoned cadences and locutions, the sensation that produces 'the overcharged emotion of a shuddering world'. The profane and the sacred confront one another, in a climactic melodrama. The 'moral sense of mankind' at large is here formed in this image of the sacred, the image of the purity of 'matron, maiden, and child'. The most depraved of mankind, the criminal, the cannibal, recognise their humanity in the counter-figure of a Turk, the profaner of this sacrality. Three years later, before the 'women' of Dalkeith, Gladstone had summoned up a 'woman' who was not abstract to testify to the universal law of love, and the burden of sorrow, binding all humanity. The being of woman here testified to humanity. Three years before, it was the bodies of women that enunciated in their sacred purity the underlying moral sense of mankind, and hence established the people-become-humanity. The moral populism that triumphed in 1880 and thereafter was rooted in this moment of 1876.

The sensual, fatalistic, and cruel Turk had 'sinned', and the soil was reeking in blood. This representation of the Turk and his 'atrocities' recirculated images already widely dispersed in the press. The 'eyewitness' reporting of the *Daily News* had already combined moralism and passionate outrage in its accounts. For instance, the report of the massacre at Panigurishti at which 3,000 were reported slaughtered, personalised the demonic Turk in the form of Hafiz Pasha, the perpetrator of events.[175] The report talks of horrors too awful to describe, and then goes on to describe them – the bayonetting of babies for instance, their little arms and legs hanging grotesquely down as they were carried aloft. The violation of women was very clearly indicated, and on a mass scale, though here prudence forbade the detail permitted in the accounts of children's deaths (in his speeches Gladstone counselled 'prudence' in public presentation of what clearly were mass rapes). None the less, the accounts of rape were all the more telling for what was not said. Little was left in doubt.

The mode of representation in the press was not a *tabula rasa* upon which Stead, Gladstone, and others wrote their narratives. Rather, the pattern was circular, a diffused moral passion surfacing in the press, being recirculated by the politicians, and thence returned again to the media of communication. In this process the bounds of the permissible in Victorian society were redrawn in novel forms. The discourse of the real enabled these bounds to be transgressed with impunity. What could not be said in fiction, except of course in pornography, could be said in the press accounts of the atrocity. The ideology of the real was sanctioned by the idea of the press itself as impartial truth-teller and chronicler of events (in the 'eye-witness' account for example). It was also sanctioned by the weight attaching to the term 'atrocity': the awful reality of the atrocity demanded expression in the press, the new guardian of the real. A democratic press had arrived, and with it the unprecedented force of a fictive real was conscripted to the cause of the people.

Shannon's account of the Bulgarian agitation dwells on these aspects, and on progress: 'Two special aspects of the High Victorian moral sensibility contributed markedly to the atrocities agitation: the vision of progress and the veiling and exaltation of sexuality.'[176] The Turk exemplified everything that opposed progress, therefore he fortified its narrative, though in the newly moralised ways indicated here. Nor can the notion of progress be detached from hatred and fear of Islam, despite Gladstone's disclaimers.[177] 'The Turk' at this time did symbolise in his negation of progress a humanity 'cursed' to 'stagnate in evil'. As Shannon describes the sexual aspects: 'The dishonouring of chastity, the debauching of the conjugal union, and prostitution, undoubtedly touched on the most sensitive of Victorian nerves. And the accounts of the atrocities provided by the newspapers placed before the Victorian public, in unprecedented fullness of detail, thrilling accounts' (as the *Ross Gazette* put it) 'of rapine

---

[175] *Manchester Guardian*, 28 August 1876 for *Daily News* account.
[176] R. T. Shannon, *Gladstone and the Bulgarian Agitation*, p. 30.
[177] *Ibid.*, pp. 30–3.

on a vast scale'.[178] In early 1877 Gladstone condemned the Turks by asserting that one of the first duties of government was the guardianship of the honour and sanctity of the family, especially of women. The Turkish reputation for pederasty appears to have gained widespread currency from the agitation. The place of 'the harems of the dissolute Turks' in the imagination of the time is amply evident in W. T. Stead himself, who was reported as most affected in the agitation by the thought of outrages upon women 'in the form of his own mother'. Just as the roots of 1879 were in 1876, so too were the roots of Stead's sensational success with the demotic melodrama of 'The Maiden Tribute of Modern Babylon'.[179]

Not so far behind the Turk as moral Other was the Tory. The agitation helped further re-establish popular Liberalism in the counter-image of the Tory. At a Nottingham demonstration in September 1876 one speaker referred to a report that Disraeli had joked about the whole affair. For the speaker, 'Like a flash of lightning over an empty grave it suddenly revealed the heathen and hireling character of the man.' He then went into some detail on 'the blood-sucking apparatus of Constantinople', just as in the big Blackheath meeting around the same time speakers had dwelt on the Turk as a 'fiend', capable of 'fiendish barbarities'.[180] The vampire and the 'fiend', the flash of lightning over a grave, all these were directly taken from the melodrama of the time, particularly in its Gothic form, stage, and fiction. The heathen, hireling Disraeli is the very opposite of the good, especially the good Gladstone. Much of the Liberal attack at this time, especially Gladstone's, dwelt on how the Tories had displayed lies, cunning, and secrecy in keeping the true nature of the atrocities from the public gaze. At the Blackheath meeting Gladstone dwelt on the good press, the *Daily News*, and the bad, Tory, press.

The question of a lying press was closely related to the idea of a properly informed, and hence properly functioning, 'public opinion'. Again one is aware of this dimension of the 'democratic imaginary' of the time, the creation of a 'public' in the sphere of the mass circulation of news and knowledge. Particularly interesting is the association of the idea of an informed public opinion with images of a democracy at last awake, and increasingly empowered. At the Blackheath meeting Gladstone talked of driving that morning through the empty streets of London, being inspired by the knowledge that when the people awoke their earliest thoughts would be of the horrors in a far-off land.[181] It was, said Gladstone, useless to deny the unprecedented power of the agitation. It was not party, not Englishness, not the Christian religion even, which inspired the

---

[178] *Ibid.*, p. 33.   [179] *Ibid.*, pp. 33–5.   [180] *The Times*, 11 September 1876.
[181] *Ibid.*

agitation, but the 'greatest and broadest ground of all – the ground of our common humanity'. Here was the true voice of the people as all humanity. And how irresistible was the simplicity of this message; as a leading agitator in the cause put it at the time, 'Our party is just the people, of whatever way of thinking about anything else, who believe in right and wrong.'[182]

17   Some democratic leading men, or Mr Gladstone's dream

The role of political leaders in enunciating narratives, and the fact that such leaders were also characters within narratives, is evident. At this time political leaders were very important in conveying and enacting narratives simply because the role of leadership was more significant than it was later to be. From 1860 into the 1890s political organisation was of growing, but still limited, importance. This, together with the strong tendency to disunity in these early manifestations of party – particularly in Liberalism – meant it was essential that issues, ideas, and activities be personalised, and dramatised, in the figure of the leader.[183]

There was a good array of leadership styles, at both national and local level, each of them playing out different narratives, and enacting different aspects of democracy. There were, for instance, the just, benevolent employer, the representative of local interests, the sporting hero, the man of *bonhomie*, all particularly telling on a local level.[184] On a national level, a very different proposition from the moralism so far considered, Palmerston as the aristocratic roué had a considerable following among working men, in London especially. His brand of 'Lord Cupid' in private affairs, and ultra-patriotic defender of liberty in public ones, offered a metropolitan contrast to the moral style so effective in provincial England and the rest of Britain.[185] For present purposes the most interesting styles of leadership are those which most directly dramatised the social and moral relations of high and low, rich and poor, the powerful and the powerless, and so gave shape to prevailing notions of the social entity that was 'the democracy'. The figures of the man of the people and the gentleman

---

[182] R. T. Shannon, *Bulgarian Agitation*, p. 23.

[183] P. Joyce, *Visions of the People*, p. 45; E. F. Biagini, *Liberty, Retrenchment and Reform*, pp. 370–9.

[184] P. Joyce, *Work, Society and Politics*, chaps. 6, 8.

[185] Anthony Taylor, 'Modes of Political Expression: Working-Class Politics, the Manchester and London Examples, 1850–1880' (University of Manchester Ph.D. 1993), chap 4, esp. pp. 249ff.

leader seem particularly relevant. Just like the melodrama, and popular fiction from the 1880s back to the eighteenth-century chapbooks, such styles involved the probing of social relations. These styles can be understood as political realisations of the political unconscious revealed in fictional forms. Characteristically, they involved the 'gentleman' who behaved with respect to his fellow, humbler man, and the man of the people who never forgot his origin.

In practice, many figures combined elements of both. William Cobbett, the great early century radical leader, is a case in point. His style as the Oldham parliamentary representative is particularly interesting.[186] Man of the people by origin, these humble beginnings were re-formulated in terms of the yeoman farmer and the fine old English gentleman, characters in this manifestation rooted in the soil of the agricultural labourer. Cobbett prefigured a rural utopia where rank and justice went together. The style was much copied in the town, with the radical W. J. Fox presenting himself as the 'Norwich Weaver Boy'. This in turn called forth the unlikely figure of William Duncuft, 'The Oldham Spinner Boy', the town's Tory MP, and a man of the people only by proxy (but no less successful for that). Cobbett played on the national stage, as did many of the gentleman leaders of the time. The figure of the MP as an 'independent' came down powerfully from the eighteenth century to the later nineteenth. Invariably in the form of the gentleman, the independent MP did not go to the wall with the advent of mass party politics. On the contrary, parties were quick to present themselves as above the sin of 'faction', as seen already in Gladstone's case. John Bright habitually presented himself in the antique form of the independent, the representative of his constituents, responsible to them alone. He, like they, exercised free and unfettered judgment.[187]

The figure of the gentleman leader can be seen to span both popular radicalism and popular Liberalism. It enabled the transition from one to the other. Men like Ernest Jones and George Reynolds were, from the 1840s to the '70s, crucial in bringing about this transition. Their formation fitted them perfectly for being mid-Victorian versions of this earlier style of leadership. Both were romantic heroes in a political melodrama of their own scripting. Both were reared on the romantic literature of Liberal–national Europe in its pre-1848 golden age.[188] Feargus O'Connor, of a slightly earlier generation, was suffused in the legendary poetry and mystical spirit of a romantic Ireland.[189] They were not as dissimilar from Tory radical leaders like Joseph Rayner Stephens and

---

[186] J. Vernon, *Politics and the People*, pp. 258–60, 274–6.
[187] A. Taylor, 'Modes of political expression', p. 161.
[188] P. Joyce, *Visions of the People*, pp. 39–40.   [189] James Epstein, *The Lion of Freedom*.

Richard Oastler as is sometimes thought. The latter's version of 'Altar,
Throne and Cottage' focused a very powerful 'golden age' understanding
of industrialisation, characteristic of men like O'Connor and Jones, based
on the redemptive power of the land. These men tended to be raised
outside the social world of urban-industrial society, being of landed or
military origin. From this vantage they evolved a critique of the industrial
present informed by Romanticism, and cast in the golden age narrative
form.[190] They were uniquely well placed to enact the narrative of loss,
struggle, and redemption characteristic of this form, and of melodrama
and popular politics more widely.

These men lived out their political careers as romantic heroes in ways
which embodied the melodrama of the people in struggle. They presented
themselves as exiled and spurned by their own sort, the higher classes,
doing battle in the cause of the similarly exiled and spurned lower classes.
They deliberately took the side of right and joined 'the people'. The
society they forfeited had, to them and their followers, become the
negation of true society. True society was the society of all humanity,
especially those who by poverty and injustice had been debarred from
their birthright. Forsaking one's own sort paradoxically meant embracing
the underlying unity of all people, and knowing, as was said of Ernest
Jones, that 'the coarse of manners are not the coarse of heart'.

In honouring such leaders the people honoured themselves: this was
said of Garibaldi, and his honouring by 'the working class', and of
Gladstone, and his honouring by 'the people'. Garibaldi, and the Union
general Andrew Jackson, represented the common man as military hero
who, like the gentleman leader, never forgot his origin.[191] The people and
the leader imaged one another. The significance of the leader in this new
politics can be understood from Gladstone's own description of the
politician: 'The work of the orator is cast in the mould offered to him by
the mind of his hearers. It is an influence principally received by him from
his audience (so to speak) in vapour, which he returns back upon them in
a flood.'[192]

The development of mass party politics in the 1860s saw new styles of
leadership, which were intimately related to what went before. There was
a new key and an old key, but for some time the tune remained the old one
of the people in struggle, a political melodrama drawing on the age-old

[190] P. Joyce, *Visions of the People*, p. 38.
[191] On Garibaldi see E. F. Biagini, *Liberty, Retrenchment and Reform*, esp. pp. 372–5; and A.
Taylor, 'Modes of political expression', pp. 329ff.
[192] L. Harvie, 'Gladstonianism, the Provinces and Popular Political Culture, 1860–1906', in
R. Bellamy (ed.), *Victorian Liberalism: Nineteenth-Century Political Thought and Practice*
(1990), p. 160.

form of the 'golden age' story. Bright's leadership was in both keys.[193] The figure of the exiled leader taking refuge from his own side in the arms of a just people fused images of struggle and religion in the form of the martyr (Bright was happy to take on something of the mantle of a martyred Abraham Lincoln).[194] Bright as martyr and leader was as much in the old key as the figure of the 'independent' suffering and martyred gentleman leader was.

The new key of leadership linked this aspect of the democratic fantasy increasingly firmly in morality and religion. The collective subjects of Bright's address were cast in the mould of the upholders of the moral law, and political reform was cloaked in sacrality (in much the same way as, in the early 60s, the emancipation of the Southern slave was decked out). In this process the people became for Bright what the working class was for Marx, the class that would abolish all classes.[195] The history of 'high' political discourse had a close connection in this respect to the development of popular forms. At the former level Stefan Collini has recently charted the shift from the political language of 'virtue' to that of 'character'.[196] This involved a move from a view concerned with maintaining an existing order, by speaking the language of governmental 'virtue', to a notion of progress and an open-ended future. The new language of 'character' was in contrast to the backward-looking and cyclical conception of history evident in the older language. The one was haunted by a fear of corruption, the other by the fear of stagnation. As Collini suggests, the passage from Whiggism to Liberalism, in figures like Bright and Gladstone, was one powerful consolidation of the language of character.

The moralisation of politics deepened as time went on, and Gladstone's progress can be seen to be of a piece with the gentleman leader/ man of the people's enactment of the drama of popular struggle. The upper classes had proved unworthy and reneged on their duty to the people. To renew these classes, Gladstone cut himself off from them, turning to the mass, the people, the poor, where true human virtue was to be found. Gladstone's own search was for a principle of moral unity, the source of moral authority, that would justify government. He found it in what, at the time of the Franco-Prussian War, he called 'the general

---

[193] P. Joyce, *Visions of the People*, pp. 47–8.
[194] A. Taylor, 'Modes of political expression', pp. 161–5. On the figure of Cromwell prefiguring politics as the moral theatre of the 'prophet' traduced and misunderstood see R. Samuel 'The Discovery of Puritanism, 1820–1914', pp. 16–17.
[195] E. F. Biagini, *Liberty, Retrenchment and Reform*, p. 377.
[196] Stefan Collini, *Public Moralists: Political Thought and Intellectual Life in Britain 1850–1930* (Oxford 1991), chap 3. On the importance of 'character' see also R. Samuel, 'The Discovery of Puritanism'.

judgment of civilised mankind'.[197] As time went on it was to be located
not in the church or the state, but in the people, and – as has been seen –
ultimately in the people-as-humanity. By 1885 Gladstone was adamant
that 'class preference' was the sign of the 'lower Toryism'.[198] All his
opponents were marked by the spirit of class. By 1886 he was increasingly
isolated, deserted by the intellectuals and many of the politicians over
Home Rule.[199] As Peter Clarke observes, after the Home Rule crisis
Gladstone's asseveration of his populist convictions seems increasingly to
have marked the primacy of a religious over an intellectual sensibility. The
statesman became the prophet, 'The Ayatollah of Victorian Christianity'.[200] The politics of democracy took on a distinctly religious, as well as
a moral, dimension. However, it was the democracy that was the chief
object of what was religious in politics. As another historian of Victorian
Liberalism suggests, after 1886 the Liberals were bound together by a
recognition of the dignity and virtue of the common man,[201] and, I would
add, a devotion to the cult of the common man.

Gladstone was the high priest and more of this cult. For, if the people
enshrined the moral law and the moral law was God's law, then Gladstone, who was the people's priest and champion, had more than a little of
divinity about himself. The narrative of providence came to the aid of the
narrative of progress, Gladstone being seen as the man who, in exemplifying the moral law, worked out God's providence in the world (Gladstone,
in his own reading of scripture, was ever alert to find signs of providence
at its everyday work). This verged on blasphemy, and, for the most part,
the overtly religious overtones of Gladstone's leadership were muted
(except in Nonconformist circles, where he was openly seen as the hand
of God). None the less, this enormously rich religious resource was the
sub-text of much of Gladstone's appeal. A typical example of the cult of
Gladstone and the cult of the common man, fittingly enough, is that of
W. T. Stead's creation in the *Pall Mall Gazette*. Stead was of vital importance not only in producing the narratives upon which popular Liberalism
thrived, but in creating the narrative of Mr Gladstone himself.[202] The
example is taken from the 'Extra' for November 1888. As evident in the
example of Bright,[203] by the 1800s this newspaper, and the party organisation with which it was associated, were taking an ever-increasing role in
stage-managing the leader, and hence the democratic fantasy. The 'Extra'
was a sixty-four page, illustrated 'special' on the 'Grand Old Man'.

[197] Peter Clarke, 'Gladstone: The Politics of Moral Populism', in *A Question of Leadership:
Gladstone to Thatcher* (1991).
[198] *Ibid.*, p. 34.   [199] *Ibid.*, p. 36.   [200] *Ibid.*, p. 32.
[201] J. P. Parry, *Democracy and Religion, Gladstone and the Liberal Party 1867–1875* (Cambridge 1986), p. 446.
[202] *Pall Mall Gazette*, 'Extra' no. 44, November 5 1888.   [203] See above, pp. 137–40.

The first two sections concerned Mr Gladstone's forthcoming and previous visit to Birmingham. This tied in directly with the party's organisation of the visit, in the manner of the 'Extra' on Bright, serving as a souvenir and programme for the event itself. The Gladstone booklet was divided into twenty sections, on 'Gladstone as Statesman', 'Mr Gladstone at Home', 'Mr Gladstone's Bumps' (his phrenology), 'Mrs Gladstone', 'Mr Gladstone as Worker', and so on. Two series of contrasts can be seen to have situated the presentation of Gladstone, that between the homely and the extraordinary, and that between the past and the future.

Section IV was entitled 'Where Mr Gladstone will stay in Birmingham', and became a paen of praise to the plain folk of that city. The early Birmingham magnates are presented as plain, no-nonsense people, unostentatiously of 'the people' themselves. This is in contrast to the present, the attack on Joseph Chamberlain showing the party conflict always at work in these publications. The Chamberlains were soundly abused for introducing 'flunkeys and silk-stockinged calves' into the city for the first time. The provinces are immediately signalled as the sign of virtue, because the sign of the homely and down-to-earth. There are further sections on Mrs Gladstone, with portraits and much information about the family, also on 'The Host of Hawarden Castle and His Guests', depicting Gladstone as the Lord of one Englishman's home that was literally a castle.[204]

Gladstone squared the circle of being a man of the people who lived in a castle with complete conviction and aplomb. The castle was justified as a demotic castle, a castle that enacted a democratic purpose. The Gladstone family seat was at Hawarden, in North Wales, fairly near to Liverpool where Gladstone was born.[205] The estate reproduced the characteristics of the aristocrat's fiefdom exactly (just as did Disraeli's Hughenden residence).[206] Mrs Gladstone ran an estate orphanage, the village was in the same geo-political relation to the big house as in the 'closed', aristocratic village, and Gladstone was scrupulous in fulfilling the duties of the leading man of the village, especially those as a local parishioner. All this served to show that the man of the people, and 'its greatest sire', had every bit as much right to behave like his betters if it was done in the people's cause. As so often in politics, the language of the opponent was appropriated and used against him. The people's cause at Hawarden was exemplified in the endlessly recycled figure of Gladstone the woodman:

[204] See section XI, X.
[205] For further aspects of the use of Hawarden and the cult of Gladstone in general see E. F. Biagini, *Liberty, Retrenchment and Reform*, chap. 7. See also P. Joyce, *Visions of the People*, pp. 49–50.
[206] See section VI, 'Mr Gladstone at Home'.

Gladstone exercised by cutting down trees on his estate, evidence of the lord of the manor as the honest labourer, engaged in practical and physical labour. In Victorian morality physical labour was so often godly, and in his axe-work Gladstone appealed hugely not only to his labouring audience, but to all groups.

Hawarden had another meaning,[207] one closely related to that vaunting of the provincial seen in the case of Birmingham. Again, it is necessary to urge the ever-present significance of another sub-text, one, as in Stead and Bright, frequently the text itself: the depiction of provincial England as the guardian of both liberty and moral right, and the foremost expression of 'the democracy' at work. In other work I have dealt at considerable length on regional and northern identities as vitally important vehicles for democratic sentiment at this time. If Bright spoke to provincial England, Gladstone spoke to a Britain beyond England. Gladstone had contemplated buying a seat 'beyond the Tweed', so serious was his feeling about his Scottish origins. Hawarden doubled as a sort of substitute for the real thing. Historians have dwelt on the importance for Gladstone of his Scottish upbringing and identity, particularly his sense of the 'folk', a sense extending to the Irish, and the Welsh *gwerin*, as well as the Scots.[208] The Midlothian campaigns drew on this very powerful sense of separate national identities coalescing in a vision of a radical, anti-metropolitan Britain. The ideal of Celtic Britain informed Stead's 'Extra' in 1888, but it was not yet adorned by the product of somewhat later years, the figure of Gladstone the Highland chief. This accent on the extra-metropolitan can be seen to have fitted very closely with the depiction of the home and homeliness, the virtue of the 'ordinary' Gladstone, as of the 'ordinary man' himself.

The other side of the picture emerges in an *extraordinary* Gladstone who is first of all a knight for liberty. King Arthur and the Knights of the Round Table were invoked.[209] The account goes on to speak of the real idolatry involved in the cult of Gladstone. He is, first, 'the uncrowned king of the new democracy'. There is something of the veneration of a royal family in the attention given to Hawarden and the Gladstone family (this is a time before the advent of the family saga of the English monarchy). But in an era of democracy talk of kings was a little suspect, and the figure of the knight in armour is more often present. The potential blasphemy of presenting Gladstone as the hand of God did not however notably prevent religious undertones emerging. After calling Gladstone

---

[207] For still further meanings see D. A. Hamer, 'Gladstone: The Making of a Political Myth', *Victorian Studies*, 22:1 (1978).
[208] L. Harvie, 'Gladstonianism, the provinces ...', pp. 167–9.
[209] 'Extra', section V, 'Mr Gladstone as Statesman'.

knight and king he is then termed 'the centre of the political religion of our time'.

In this presentation of the Grand Old Man, the implied spirituality and near-divinity of the man are most often presented obliquely, but power-fully. It is the library at Hawarden that occupies particular attention: Gladstone is presented as at home there, a man of learning as comfortable in this cerebral, ethereal atmosphere (he is a student of theology and literature) as when chopping down trees. The figure of Gladstone here is quite evidently taking form in relation to the still-powerful narrative of improvement, with all its moral resources of anti-materialism. It is, however, when linked to the relationship of past and present that the extraordinary really comes into its own. This second theme can be approached by means of an extraordinary fiction in the 'Extra', with the title 'Mr Gladstone's Dream'. The theme of past and future was broached in terms of Gladstone himself: he was the narrative principle around which time was organised, making sense of the past and the future in terms of his presence in the world now. We see how the political leader was an active presence in narrative, what was so often implicit being made explicit.

In 'Gladstone's Dream' the spirituality of politics is at once suggested when two angels, 'Freedom' and 'Justice', appear to Gladstone in his dream. These lead him to the scenes of his great triumphs. The narrative of improvement is presented in terms of its fruits, the free press, and an informed and rational public opinion. The narrative of liberty is exempli-fied in terms of the free-trade dream, and the contentment of the poor man's parlour, but also Gladstone's relief of the Bulgars and his disesta-blishment of the Irish Church (Gladstone is depicted in one of the many graphic illustrations as chopping down the tree of the Established Church). But the dream is poised between the past and the future, and essentially utopian. 'The end is not yet', says Mr Gladstone. The moral is that much has been done, but that much is still to be done: the real world has been touched by the angels of liberty and justice, but the very form of the dream and its other-worldly angels indicate the millennium that awaits when such dreams are realised. The problem of Ireland, above all, waits at the door of heaven to be solved.

And it is here, next to paradise, that the spirituality of Gladstone most reveals itself. *Vox populi* begins to assume the shape of *Vox dei*, in this case in the form of Mr Gladstone as Saint Patrick:

And as his guides bade Mr Gladstone look, he heard a noise sounding in his ears with a message that he remembered to have heard in some ancient legend. 'It is the voice of the Irish', he said, 'the voice of those who live near the wood of Fochlad, which is near the western sea, and thus they cry: We pray thee old man, to come and henceforward walk amongst us.' And as he repeated the message, Freedom and Justice took him by the hand and led him to a place of vantage, whence he saw a figure with a face that he knew but clad in the garb of a saint and hero of old, driving a herd of evil creatures into the sea. 'It is a call then for a new Saint Patrick', Mr Gladstone cried, and started to his feet.[210]

The figure of Gladstone narrativised the march of freedom and justice. And it did so quite openly, Gladstone summoning up the past, bearing witness in the present, and anticipating the future in a Liberal view of history. The 'Extra', in discussing 'The Verdict of Posterity' on Gladstone, identified him in this way, as the link between the old and the new, 'standing as it were between the living and the dead – the living democracy of the future, and the dying castes and hierarchies of the past'.[211] In narrativising a Liberal view of history the leader also narrativised a demos that was the subject of this history. For all his spirituality the leader only stood proxy for the people, who were the real leading actors in the story. Bright we have already seen to be a principle of history, the embodiment of the fall of the *ancien régime*, the slayer of 'feudalism'. Like Gladstone, there was however another narrative inherent in the figure of the leader as at once the object of familiarity and veneration, the embodiment of the wisdom of the past and the hope of the future. In the figure of its leader demos could represent itself in terms both of a past transcended and a past renewed by the future. Again, as in the case of Bright, so with Gladstone, the past renewed might present the conservative face of the new democracy, especially when it genuflected to its Englishness. This is how the *Gazette* summed up its feelings about the peculiar genius of Gladstone:

A buoyant confidence in the progressive development of the destinies of mankind is rarely combined with a reverent and grateful appreciation of the traditions and institutions of the past. He represents the perfect flower of the culture and training of the old England, with his roots deeply buried in the past, and all his fibres drawing in nourishment from the ancient springs of religion and morality with which successive generations of Englishmen have for centuries past nourished their souls.

Once again we can see democracy being made safe for England, often at the same time as it was made radical for Britain.

In conclusion it can be observed that, while one account of Victorian Liberal politics describes it as the politics of religion, and another as the politics of democracy,[212] both, and neither, are correct, in that this politics is most fully the politics of the religion of democracy. The central place of social narrative in shaping this politics has been argued here. The overall aim has been to indicate the role of what appear to be dominant narratives,

[210] *Ibid.*, section III.   [211] *Ibid.*, p. 62.
[212] J. P. Parry, *Democracy and Religion*; E. F. Biagini, *Liberty, Retrenchment and Reform*.

and narrative patternings, in constructing notions of collective social and political identity. Certain narratives have been selected as dominant ones: the choice made, and the assumption of dominance, still remain open questions, though hopefully an enormous field is a little less open than at the beginning of this study. None the less, much is left out of the account. Little is said about comedy and irony for instance.

In this regard the music hall is a fruitful source of knowledge. Peter Bailey has written superbly of how the comic narratives of the halls might have buttressed the projections of 'democracy' described here, for instance how the halls symbolised the idea of 'the good time', a time held to be available to all, irrespective of social condition.[213] A 'democracy of pleasure', a kind of liberal populism of the halls, can be seen to complement the other imagined forms of democracy, particularly the party political manifestations.[214] The 'public' or 'audience' of pleasure, in the form of the halls, can also be seen to complement the other collective forms in which democracy, and 'the democracy', were envisaged at the time, the polity itself, but beyond that the other imagined formations that made up the sense of living in a democratic society and culture. Pre-eminent here have been 'publics' going under such titles as 'reading', educated', 'purchasing', and so on, and 'audiences' organised around the mass communication media.

Narrative permits a particularly good view of how this democracy imagined itself. But the comic modes not covered here could work against prevailing narratives too, and again the music hall is a good case. Bailey's work is relevant: he has written of the 'discourse of knowingness' that characterised the music hall audiences, the idea that one was ahead of the game and could not be duped.[215] This would certainly have involved a comic and ironic undercutting of the romantic forms considered here, especially when they went into their characteristic moral and epic over-drive. But that is to begin another story, and there are already sufficient stories about narrative in this study that need further telling. The most important one remaining can have only the very briefest of considerations.

This is the story of what happened to the narratives discussed here. The story of their development and change within the Victorian period is evident, or at least part of it is. From the late nineteenth century the Victorian dispensation begins to dissolve. In explaining change a narrative

---

[213] Peter Bailey, 'Introduction', in P. Bailey (ed.), *The Victorian Music Hall: The Business of Pleasure* (Milton Keynes 1987), and 'The Swell Song', in J. Bratton (ed.), *The Victorian Music Hall: Performance and Style* (Milton Keynes 1987).

[214] See the discussion of Bailey in P. Joyce, *Visions of the People*, pp. 306–10.

[215] P. Bailey, 'Did Foucault and Althusser Ever Play the London Palladium? Music Hall and the Knowingness of Popular Culture', unpublished paper kindly shown to me by the author.

of the narratives is essential, for these forms carried their own content, and their own autonomous effect on historical change. Part of the explanation would certainly turn on the displacement of the moral categories seen here to be such an important part of people's narrativation of their self and social identities. Scientific and 'realist' narratives positing the operation of laws outside individual and moral control (and even consciousness) strengthened their hold and tended to replace the old moral certainties and doubts. Psychological notions of the self and of behaviour helped displace the 'language of character'. What were earlier termed 'sociologised' notions of the social likewise helped loosen the moral underpinnings of the political seen here. Notions explaining the social in 'environmental' terms prospered. Socialism was one heir of these, though the partial nature of the change here, as elsewhere, needs emphasis: socialism inherited much of the old, in the shape of the 'movement' politics of struggle, and the crusade of the excluded and downtrodden. The debt of the Labour party to Victorian Liberalism is frequently, and rightly, remarked upon. Even as the autonomy of a newly understood 'social' realm emerged, it was inflected with moral understandings: the 'social' question of the 1890s, for instance, was still viewed in terms of the invented Puritanism characteristic of the earlier decades of the century.[216] None the less, the changes considered in the introduction did in the end mean the redundancy of the narratives described here. The régime of the twentieth-century 'social' was to differ considerably from the moralism that had preceded it.

These new departures also loosened the hold of melodrama on the social imagination and the political aesthetic. Melodrama personalised good and evil, interrogating and corroborating the reign of the moral absolute. The new realist narratives of the time taught the operation of laws of nature and of society which denied this reign.[217] Realism, naturalism, and the ironic mode of narrative so characteristic of literary modernity ate away at the aesthetic foundations of melodrama, and older popular fictional forms. The erstwhile social unity of the melodramatic theatre audience seems to have been broken around this time too, sundering the 'popular' and the 'high'. But again the change was partial: at a popular level, extending into the twentieth century in the form of cinema and television, melodrama has continued to flourish, and to fashion the social imagination and the political unconscious. The narrativisation of democracy in the new century still owed something to the romances of the old.

---

[216] R. Samuel, 'The Discovery of Puritanism', p. 39.
[217] J. Walkowitz, *City of Dreadful Delights*, pp. 93–4.

Appendix 1   Come whoam to thi childer an' me

EDWIN WAUGH

Aw've just mended th' fire wi' a cob;
Owd Swaddle has brought thi new shoon;
There's some nice bacon-collops o' th' hob,
An' a quart o' ale-posset i' th' oon;   *oven*
Aw've brought thi top-cwot, doesta know,
For th' rain's comin' deawn very dree;   *drearily*
An' th' har-stone's as white as new snow; –
Come whoam to thi childer an' me.

When aw put little Sally to bed,
Hoo cried, 'cose her feyther weren't theer,
So aw kiss'd th' little thing, an' aw said
Thae'd bring her a ribbin fro' th' fair;
An' aw gav' her her doll, an' some rags,
An' a nice little white cotton-bo';
An' aw kiss'd her again; but hoo said
'At hoo wanted to kiss *thee* an' o.

An' Dick, too, aw'd sich wark wi' him,
Afore aw could get him upstairs;
Thae towd him thae'd bring him a drum,
He said, when he're sayin' his prayers;
Then he looked i' my face, an' he said,
'Has th' boggarts taen houd o' my dad?'   *ghosts*
An' he cried whol his e'en were quite red; –
He likes thee some weel, does yon lad!

At th' lung-length, aw geet 'em laid still;
An' aw hearken't folks' feet that went by;
So aw iron't o' my clooas reel weel,
An' aw hang'd 'em o' th' maiden to dry;   *clothes horse*
When aw'd mended thi stockin's an' shirts,
Aw sit deawn to knit i' my cheer,
An' aw rayley did feel rayther hurt, –
Mon, aw'm *one-ly* when theaw artn't theer.

'Aw've a drum an' a trumpet for Dick;
Aw've a yard o' blue ribbin for Sal;
Aw've a book full o'babs; an' a stick,   *pictures*
An' some 'bacco an' pipes for mysel;
Aw've brought thee some coffe an' tay, –
Iv thae'll *feel* i' my pocket, thae'll *see*;
An' aw've bought tho a new cap to-day,'
For aw al'ays bring summat for *thee*!

'God bless tho' my lass; aw'll go whoam
An' aw'll kiss thee an' th' childer o' round;
Thae knows that wheerever aw roam,
Aw'm fain to get back to th' owd ground;
Aw can do wi' a crack o'er a glass;   *chat*
Aw can do wi' a bit of a spree;
But aw've no gradely comfort, my lass,
Except wi' yon childer an' thee.'

Appendix 2 God bless these poor folk

EDWIN WAUGH

God bless these poor folk that are strivin'
By means that are honest an' true,
For some'at' to keep 'em alive in
This world that we're scrambling through:
As th' life ov a mon's full o' feightin',
A poor soul that wants to feight fair,
Should never be grudged ov his heytin',   *eating*
For th' hardest o'th battle's his share.
            CHORUS – As th'life ov a mon.

This world's kin to trouble; i'th best on't,
There's mony sad changes come reawnd;
We wander'n abeawt to find rest on't,
An' th' worm yammers' for us i'th greawnd.
May he that'll wortch while he's able,   *work*
Be never long hungry nor dry;
An' th' childer 'at sit at his table, –
God bless 'em wi' plenty, say I.
            CHORUS – As th'life ov a mon.

An' he that can feel it a pleasur'
To leeten misfortin an' pain, –
May his pantry be olez full measur',
To cut at, and come to again;
May God bless his cup and his cupbort,'
An theawsan' for one that he gives;
An' his heart be a bumper o' comfort,
To th' very last minute he lives!
            CHORUS – As th'life ov a mon.

An' he that scorns ale to his victual,
Is welcome to let it alone;
There's some can be wise with a little,
An' some that are foolish wi' noan',
An' some are so square i' their natur',
That nought wi' their stomachs agree;
But, he that would leifer drink wayter,   *rather*
Shall never be stinted by me.
            CHORUS – As th'life ov a mon.

One likes to see hearty folk wortchin',
An' weary folk havin' a rest;
One likes to yer poor women singin'
To th' little things laid o' their breast:
Good cooks are my favourite doctors;
Good livers my parsons shall be;
An' ony poor craytur 'ats clemming,   *starving*
May come have a meawthful wi' me.
            CHORUS – As th'life ov a mon.

Owd Time, – he's a troublesome codger, –
Keeps nudgin' us on to decay,
An' whispers, 'Yo're nobbut a lodger;
Get ready for goin' away;'
Then let's ha' no skulkin' nor sniv'lin',
Whatever misfortins befo';
God bless him that fends for his livin',
An' houds up his yed through it o'!
        CHORUS – As th'life ov a mon.

Appendix 3   Owd Enoch

EDWIN WAUGH

Owd Enoch o' Dan's laid his pipe deawn on' th' hob,
And his thin fingers played i' th' white thatch of his
   nob;
'I'm gettin' done up,' to their Betty he said;
'Dost think thae could doff me, an' dad me to bed?'   *undress* *lead*
Derry Down

Then hoo geet him to bed, an' hoo happed him up
   weel;   *covered* *well*
An' hoo said to him, 'Enoch, lad; heaw doesto feel?'
'These limbs o'mine, Betty, – they're cranky an' sore; *rusty*
It's time to shut up when one's getten four score.'

As hoo potter't abeawt his poor winterly pate,
 Th' owd crayter looked dreawsily up at his mate, –
'There's nought on me laft, lass, – do o 'at tho' con, –
But th' cratchinly frame o' what once wur a mon.'   *feeble*

Then he turn't hissel' o'er, like a chylt tir't wi' play,
An' Betty crept reawnd, while he're dozin' away;
As his e'e-lids sank deawn, th' owd lad mutter't 'Well
   done!
I think there's a bit o'seawnd sleep comin' on.'

Then hoo thought hoo'd sit by till he'd had his nap
   o'er, –
If hoo'd sit theer till then, hoo'd h' risen no more;
For he cool't eawt o'th world, an' his e'en lost their leet,
Like a cinder i' th fire-grate i' th' deeod time o' th' neet.

As Betty sit rockin' bith' side of his bed,
Hoo looked neaw an' then at owd Enoch's white yed;
An' hoo thought to hersel' that hoo'd not lung to stay
Iv ever th' owd prop of her life should give way.

Then, wondrin' to see him so seawnd an' so still,
Hoo touched Enoch's hond, – an' hoo fund it wur chill;
Says Betty, 'He's cowd; I'll put summat moor on!'
But o' wur no use, for Owd Enoch wur gone!

An' when they put Enoch to bed deawn i' th' greawnd,
A rook o' poor neighbours stood bare-yedded reawnd, *crowd*
They dropt sprigs o' rosemary: an' this wur their text: –
'Th' owd crayter's laid by, – we may haply be th' next!'

So, Betty wur left to toar on bi hersel';   *make a hard*
An' heaw hoo poo'd through it no mortal can tell;   *living*
But th' doctor dropt in to look at her one day,
When hoo're rockin' bith' side of an odd cup o' tay.

'Well, Betty,' said th' doctor, 'heaw dun yo get on?
I'm soory to yer 'at yo'n lost yo'r owd mon:
What complaint had he, Betty?' Says hoo, 'I caun't tell,
We ne'er had no doctor; he deed of hissel.'

'Ay, Betty,' said th' doctor; 'there's one thing quite
    sure;
Owd age is a thing that no physic can cure:
Fate will have her way, lass, – do o'that we con, –
When th' time's up, we's ha' to sign o'er, an' be gone.'

'Both winter and summer tho' owd mower's at wark,
Sidin' folk eawt o' seet, both bi dayleet an' dark!   *moving*
He's slavin' away while we're snorin' i' bed;
An' he'd slash at a king, if it coom in his yed.'

'These sodiurs, an' parsons, an' maisters o' lond,
He lays 'em i' th' greawnd, wi' their meawths full o'
    sond,
Rags or riches, an owd greasy cap, or a creawn, –
He sarves o' alike, – for he switches 'em deawn.'

'The mon that's larnt up, an' the mon that's a foo –
It mays little odds, for they both han to goo;
When they com'n within th' swing of his scythe they
    mun fo'
If yo'n root amung th' swathe, yo'n find doctors an' o, *bundle*
Derry Down

Appendix 4   My Gronfaither, Willie

EDWIN WAUGH

My gronfaither, Willie,
Wur born o'th moorside,
In a cosy owd house
Where he lived till he died;
He wur strong-limbed an' hearty,
An' manly, an' kind;
An' as blithe as a lark, for
He'd nought on his mind.
Derry down.

His wife wur th' best craiter
That ever wur made;
An' they'd three bonny lasses
As ever broke brade;
An' five strappin' lads –
They looked grand in a row,
For they'rn six feet apiece –
That makes ten yards in o'!
Derry down.

My gronfaither's house
Wur a cosy owd shop,
An' as sweet as a posy
Fro' bottom to top;
Parlour, loom-house, an' dairy;
Bedrooms, greight an' smo';
An' a shinin' owd kitchen, –
The best nook of o'!
Derry down.

He'd cows in a pastur',
An sheep o'th moorside;
An' a nice bit o' garden
Wur th' owd fellow's pride;
With his looms an' his cattle,
He'd plenty o' wark
For his lads an' his lasses,
Fro' dayleet to dark.
Derry down.

A gray-yedded layrock
O' three-score an' twelve,
He'd weave an' he'd warble,
He'd root an' he'd delve
Fro' daybreak to sunset,
Then creep to his nook,
At the sweet ingle-side,

For a tot an' a smooke.
Derry down.

An' fro' th' big end o' Pendle
To Robin Hood's Bed;
Fro' Skiddaw to Tandle's
Owd grove-tufted yed;
Fro' th' Two Lads to Tooter's,
There's never a pot
That's sin as much glee
As my gronfaither's tot.
Derry down.

Fro' Swarthmoor i' Furness,
Where th' dew upo' th' fells
Keeps twinkle to th' tinkle
Of Ulverston bells;
Fro' Black Coombe to Blacks'nedge,
No cup mon could fill,
Did moore good an' less harm
Than my gronfaither's gill.
Derry down.

As I journey through life
May this fortin be mine,
To be upreet an' downreet
Fro' youth to decline:
An' walk like a mon,
Through whatever betide,
Like my gronfaither, Willie,
That live't o'th moorside.
Derry down.

Appendix 5

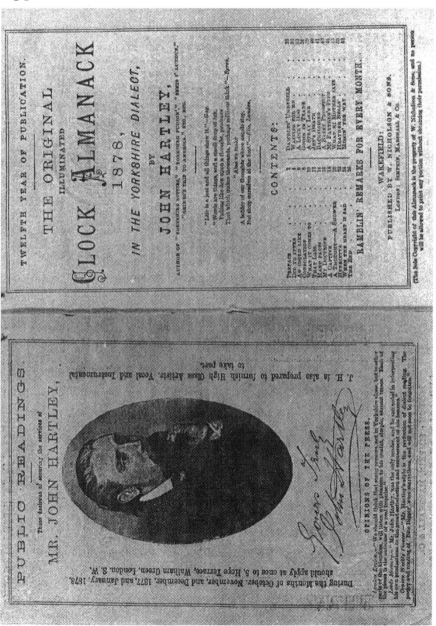

3　Title pages to *The Original Illuminated Clock Almanack*, 1878

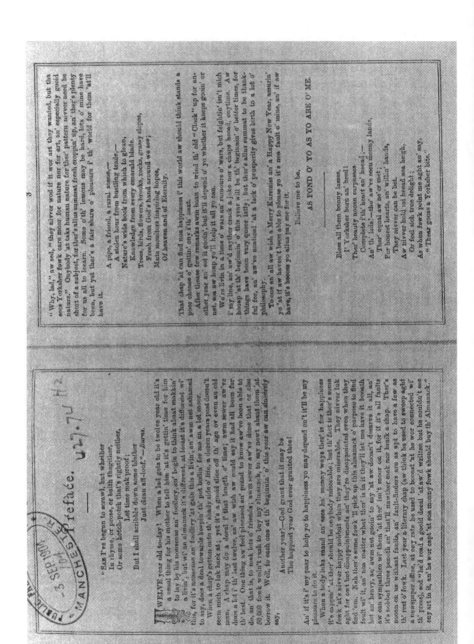

3 (*cont.*)   Preface to *The Original Illuminated Clock Almanack*, 1878

Appendix 6

4   The diary of Edwin Waugh, an entry for August 1847

Index

Printed in the United States
134080LV00005B/163-180/A

9 780521 448024